Exploring Literature in the Classroom:

Content and Methods

Exploring Literature in the Classroom:

Content and Methods

Edited by Karen Wood
with Anita Moss

Christopher-Gordon Publishers, Inc.
Norwood, MA

Permissions and Credits

Chapter 5:

Children's artwork is used with the permission of the illustrators: Lori Leahey, Maxxe E. Collingsworth, Gabriel Guy, Robert A. Oakley, Marcia Hayes, and Melissa Rollins.

Christopher-Gordon Publishers, Inc.
480 Washington Street
Norwood, MA 02062

Printed in the United States of America

10 9 8 7 6 5 4 3 2 1   96 95 94 93 92

ISBN: 0-926842-11-0

This book is dedicated with love to
Eric, Ryan, Lauren
and Kevin

Brief Contents

Contents

Preface

The need to integrate literature across the curriculum continues to receive enormous attention in the field of education. In *Exploring Literature in the Classroom: Content and Methods,* we have taken the notion of integration a step further by merging the current thinking of two closely related, but typically distant fields: English literature and reading education. Our authors have contributed what is the best thinking in each of their respective areas of expertise from multicultural awareness to the role of drama and technology in the classroom. Consequently, what we offer you, the reader, is a book on not only what to teach but how to teach it.

The opening chapter focuses on the personal dimension of reading — that side which concerns the readers' personal reactions, ideas, images, and sensations. In concert with the theoretical basis of this aspect of reading are practical strategies teachers can use for accessing the personal dimension in a classroom setting. This chapter offers some answers to the often posed question: How can I emphasize the skills typically associated with reading and frequently assessed on standardized tests and still imbue my students with a love of literature? It can be done as you will see.

Chapter 2 follows this thinking by posing and answering a similar question: Do basals have a place in state-of-the-art literature programs? The answer from Lapp, Flood and Farnan is an unqualified "yes" as they describe the many changes basals have undergone through the years and the many tasks teachers are expected to undertake in today's classroom while striving to teach students whose needs are more diverse than ever before. A second question addressed in this chapter is how can teachers use basals and whole works of literature together? Here, the authors present concrete approaches for connecting and unifying the language arts processes of reading, writing, listening and speaking by drawing upon a wide array of materials.

Unique to books on using literature in the classroom is a chapter on "Technology in the Teaching of Literature-based Reading Programs." In this chapter, Rickelman and Henk ask: Will the introduction of technology enhance or hinder the literature-based program? Their argument that literature and technology are a compatible duo will convince even the most fervent of skeptics and computer neophytes. A whole new way of exploring and interacting with literature is becoming available to us, including the use of holography to make storybook characters actually come alive — not to mention the use of hypertext through which a reader can request more background information on a topic while in the act of reading. Imagine reading *Beowulf* today and having Grendel appear right before your eyes!

A common concern of teachers throughout the country is "all of this talk about getting students to read good literature is fine, but somebody please tell me how to do it!" Rasinski does just that in his chapter on "Promoting Recreational Reading." Here, he presents a myriad of teacher-tested ways to motivate students to want to read. Everything from providing incentives, to organizing the classroom environment, to engaging parental support is here in one chapter.

While the first half of this book examines methods for teaching, the second half of the book examines what to teach. Therefore, at this point in the text, we explore literature in the classroom from another perspective, that of the English educator, to determine and to analyze the content to be taught. Our authors, representing the field of children's literature, provide more than just a suggested reading list. Instead, they give us new ways of thinking about literature — ways that meet the needs of the children of today and tomorrow.

Because "change is the essence of life," Chapter 6 provides a discussion of transformation stories in which animals, humans, mythical figures, or even inanimate objects change their natural form and develop or grow into something else. Jacoby and Allen believe that studying change in literature prepares readers to deal with changes they may encounter in real life situations. Furthermore, they show how the notion of change can extend across the subject areas and form the basis for integrated unit planning.

In Chapter 7, Harris presents a comprehensive examination of multi-ethnic literature and its importance to the elementary curriculum. The increasing ethnic diversity in our schools has underscored the need for greater understanding and broader knowledge on the part of teachers and peer groups. Harris discusses the multiethnic literature that is available, explores the many issues raised in the literature, and then shows how teachers can use these issues to inform, entertain, and motivate their students.

Chapter 8 follows a similar lead as Stott shows how to interpret the details and patterns of native American myths. He maintains that by coming to know the stories, folktales, and myths of other cultures, we can better understand the people of those cultures. He also shows concrete approaches for presenting these stories that maximize students' cultural awareness and their enjoyment.

Manna and Lawson, in Chapter 9, show other ways to capitalize on the imaginative energies and curiosity which all children from all backgrounds naturally bring to the printed page. The key is to use literature to tap into children's natural inclinations to dramatize and the authors illustrate how books can be used strategically to accomplish that objective.

And lastly, we conclude this volume through the eyes of a writer of children's literature as Natalie Babbitt takes us down "A Writer's Path to Literacy". We will say no more and, instead, just let you enjoy the journey . . .

K. D. W.
A.M.

Foreword

*E*xploring Literature in the Classroom is an excellent resource for those who wish to place literature at the center of literacy instruction. This is by no means a new theme, but it may be more relevant today than ever before. Two unprecedented circumstances make the time right for a literature-based view of the curriculum. First, in recent years, an increasingly strong research base has emerged to support this approach. Second, there has been a dramatic increase in the availability of quality trade books for children, reducing the need to rely on packaged programs as the primary resource for language and literacy instruction.

Throughout *Exploring Literature in the Classroom,* there are abundant illustrations of the many ways in which literature supports the research on how children learn to read and write. For example, we know that background knowledge may be the single most important factor in helping students comprehend and compose. Numerous and varied experiences with literature are critical to building students' background knowledge. Students draw upon the content, wording, and literary structures of literature to add to their repertoire of ideas and information. These concepts link to one another and to experiences outside of literature to help shape the frameworks from which learners operate as they go about exploring their world.

Sharing the language of literature is fundamental to the development of language and thought. The sounds, meanings, and structures of the language are there to enjoy over and over again through stories and informational books to be shared with others. When researchers examine the strong relationship between word knowledge and comprehension it is no wonder that sharing good literature immediately enters the discussion. There is no better way to strengthen vocabulary than to meet the same words over and over again in varied, meaningful contexts. The meanings become deep and real to the learner, unlike superficial definitions memorized and written down in a string of forced, unrelated sentences.

It is the language of literature and the ideas and concepts that language represents, which serves to enhance children's mental development. Literature evokes the child's imagination. Narratives and poetry are filled with metaphor, simile, and other creative uses of language. Writers of nonfiction use the language constructs and vocabulary of their disciplines, thus helping students to think in the ways of the social and physical scientist.

Proficient readers and writers approach text with some degree of predictability. Not only do they have a general idea of what stories are like, they have a sense of how certain kinds of stories differ from others. They immediately "catch on" to the repetitive refrain, or the accumulation of events. They enter the realm of fantasy, biography, or mystery and immediately set up certain expectations. Whether reading or writing, they have a sense of the common understandings within which literate individuals operate. All of this begins very early in the lives of emerging readers and writers as they listen to the written word and scribble their own messages as young authors.

Both the research evidence and the personal experience of our daily lives tell us that comprehending and composing are highly related. The use of literature throughout the curriculum makes a profound statement to students about the ways in which reading and writing are linked. Literature provides models for writing. Students try out what they have learned from favorite books and authors and use it in their own writing. They find added meaning to their reading as they add their personal writer's viewpoint to their literary experiences.

It is not enough to simply teach students to read and write. We must help them to become readers and writers. Throughout *Exploring Literature in the Classroom,* the suggested ideas and activities are meant to empower students to question and think critically. Even more important, they are designed to help students realize the value of literature in their lives. Reading and writing are not treated as ends in themselves. They are critical tools to use as means to explore, learn, and derive pleasure. Literature is integral, not separate from the important learning that takes place in the classroom.

Time for practice is important. Good readers and writers spend more time reading and writing than poor readers and writers. Hardly a new idea! Yet, it is one that is often ignored in planning the literacy program. Students need time to read and write in the classroom. They need to practice with whole texts, responding and creating their own meanings and sharing them with others.

Added to the increasing research base described above, is the growing number of quality books available for use in the classroom. Books of every genre and description, covering a wide range of interest and ability levels, make it possible for teachers to plan entire units of study around works of literature. Theme-based instruction may focus on the literature itself through author studies and genre studies or through the study of some literary elements. Frequently, theme-based instruction will be grounded in the social studies and science topics of interest to students. Here, textbooks and tradebooks are often used in conjunction with one another as resources for instruction.

Today's teachers are in transition. They are operating in the midst of a growing evolution of new ideas about the ways in which students' learn literacy and learn through literacy. Many are moving away from more traditional, commercial programs to construct their own emerging versions of literature-based curricula. They are using the ideas outlined above as a philosophical basis for planning their literacy programs and for incorporating literature across the curriculum throughout the day. Change and transition are not easy. For some, it is particularly hard to adjust to new ways of operating even when the old ways are clearly inadequate. Issues related to classroom organization, assessment, and the acquisition of large numbers of books required to implement literature programs offer challenges that many find difficult to overcome. *Exploring Literature in the Classroom* offers both a philosophical framework and many practical strategies to help teachers and administrators construct and implement a literature-based literacy curriculum that produces learners for whom reading and writing are simply not things they know how to do, they are things they cannot imagine doing without.

Dorothy S. Strickland
State of New Jersey Professor of Reading
Rutgers University

1

The Personal Dimension of Reading: Theory and Practice

Karen D. Wood and William E. Blanton

At the present time, three kinds of reading instruction can be identified in the schools. The first kind, "learning to read," centers on the acquisition of reading skills essential for accomplished reading. Students receive instruction in reading curriculum strands such as decoding skills, vocabulary development, reading comprehension skills, and study skills. In general, students are expected to transfer these skills to the reading of narrative texts.

The second kind of reading instruction, "reading to learn," focuses on using reading as a tool for learning from informational texts. Teachers provide students with instruction on how to apply general and specific reading strategies for the purpose of learning from subject matter material. Pupils are expected to apply these strategies to a wide range of expository texts.

The two kinds of reading instruction described above are usually provided in grades K-6. The major outcome of this kind of instruction is to assist students in comprehending written material. Comprehension is usually determined by having students answer questions, recall what they have read, or retell what they have read. When this is the case, reading becomes a very public behavior. Successful reading ability is determined by convergent agreement on the answers to comprehension questions and the meaning of text.

In contrast, the third kind of reading instruction, "private reading," recognizes that reading is a very personal act (Rosenblatt, 1988). Reading is viewed as an aesthetic activity, done for the activity itself (Iser, 1978; Rosenblatt, 1978). Rather than being concerned with publicly agreed upon correct answers to questions or socially shared interpretations about what was read, this kind of instruction is viewed as providing the reader with a stimulus for experiencing events such as personal sensations, feelings, images, ideas, conflicts, and tensions. Meaning resides in the reader's personal interpretation and response to the text created by the author. From this perspective, then, reading becomes a transaction between the text created by the writer and the reader's reading of the text (Rosenblatt, 1978). The "meaning" to be constructed by the reading event is not found in the text; it is constructed by the reader during the transaction with the text. The meanings constructed by readers may be either convergent or divergent (Purves, 1985). It is also likely that the responses of many readers will be very idiosyncratic.

"Private or personal reading" (we will use the term *personal* reading throughout this chapter) has traditionally been emphasized at the secondary level, usually in the English literature curriculum; however, we believe that it should receive attention during the elementary school years as well. When initial reading instruction stresses that the goal of reading is to obtain correct answers to comprehension questions or interpretations of text, students may internalize the notions that a) the purpose for reading is to answer questions correctly and that b) text has a socially agreed upon meaning. As a result, important ideas related to the personal use and aesthetic appreciation of reading may fail to emerge later.

The purpose of this chapter is to provide teachers with an understanding of the personal dimension of reading. In addition, we will present the concept that reading is the construction of meaning during a transaction between the reader and a text along with the educational outcomes of this kind of reading. We will also offer a number of instructional strategies designed to attain the reading outcomes we discuss.

THE READING TRANSACTION

Figure 1-1 outlines the development of reading as the construction of meaning during a transaction between the reader and the text produced by an author. Beginning at the bottom, the process starts with the author's intention to inform, entertain, convince, express, or create a literary work. In the next step, the writer selects a form in which to present a topic. As can be seen, topics are presented in informational forms such as textbooks or poetic forms such as novels. Next, the writer constructs the text. In this construction, the author uses writer's craft, prior knowledge about the topic, personal experience, and elements of language. At this point the text

READING AS A TRANSACTION	
Reader Responds	
Private	Public
Feelings Ideas Images Tensions Conflicts	Discussion (retelling, collaboration) Enactment (debate, role play, discussions) Oral Presentation Writing (essay, sematic mapping) Extension (further reading, viewing, and (listening) Response to Test

Reader Constructs Meaning Using Purpose and Prior Knowledge				
Purpose	Prior Knowledge			
	General	Social	Text Structure	Writer's Craft
To Update Knowledge	Social	Experience	Exposition Cause- Effect	Word Meaning
To Learn About Text Structure		Topic	Compare/Contrast	Style
To Learn About Writer's Craft			Problems Solution	Point of View
To Interact with Others About What was Read			Listing	Tone
To Relate and Apply Writer's Message to One's Own Life			Process	Metaphor
To Enjoy the Object of Art Created By the Writer			Narrative	Figure of Speech
			Setting Characters Time Place Goal Events Moral	

Writer Constructs Text Using
Prior Knowledge About Topic Prior Knowledge Text Structure Elements of Language

Writer Selects A Topic and Form	
Information	Poetic
Essay Textbook Manual Reasearch Report Autobiography	Story Novel Play Poem Fable

Writer Has an Intention
To Inform To Entertain To Convince To Express To Create

Figure 1-1
Reading as a Transactions

is complete, and the finished text might be viewed as a blueprint or framework to be used by a reader in constructing meaning.

The reader's transaction with the text begins by engaging the text with a purpose for reading. The reader uses prior knowledge to construct meaning, to interpret the text, and to generate a response to the text. As can be seen at the top of the model, the reader may respond either publicly or privately to text. Public responding is concerned with products that are usually measured and evaluated. Private responding, on the other hand, is not measured or evaluated; it is personal and traverses the total spectrum of human feelings.

COGNITIVE ACTIVITY DURING THE READING TRANSACTION

Over the past fifteen years, a major thrust of reading research has been aimed at understanding comprehension. The accumulated evidence seems to support at least four major conclusions. First, readers are motivated to make sense out of reading material. Second, readers make predictions or inferences in constructing meaning. Third, readers' interpretations of what they read and their responses are very personal and idiosyncratic. Last, readers' prior knowledge and purposes undergird the process of constructing meaning, generating interpretations, and responding to literature.

Central to a reader's response to literature are four major cognitive activities: activating, focusing, organizing, and responding. A major goal of reading instruction is to guide these processes so that, during independent reading, the reader can take responsibility for regulating these processes.

Activating

Responding to text begins with the activating process. Here the prior knowledge the reader possesses about the topic to be read is called up and organized. The knowledge activated may be general, social knowledge, specific knowledge about the topic, or knowledge about how the information is organized in the text. Prior knowledge also holds the reader's potential private associations, images, feelings, and ideas about information and events presented in the text. This knowledge is also used by the reader to predict what the text will be about and what will happen as the events in the text unfold. It is also used to construct a personal, inner world to be used as the reader essentially lives through the text.

Focusing

Focusing involves the reader's stance, perspective, or purpose for reading (Blanton, Wood & Moorman, 1990; Rosenblatt, 1988). Purpose enables the reader to attend to and select relevant information in the text. Likewise, purpose is used to coordinate the interplay among the text, the reader's prior knowledge, and the images, sensations, and feelings stimulated by the text during the reading transaction.

Organizing

The cognitive process of organizing enables the reader to construct logical connections among the ideas presented in text. Making these connections is critical to understanding, interpreting, and responding to text. The ability to organize text becomes even more important when the reader's purpose or stance for reading the text differs from the author's intention for writing the text.

Responding

An author may write a text for a single purpose; however, the text created is probably read for more than one purpose. There is, therefore, no single correct interpretation of text. Readers respond to literature in very personal ways. Since readers' responses are personal, responses should only be shared at the discretion of readers. When they are shared, they should not be evaluated. To the contrary, readers' responses must be honored and respected.

OUTCOMES OF PERSONAL READING

Personal reading outcomes are important for a number of reasons. First, as we mentioned earlier, most reading instruction is aimed at acquiring reading skills and reading subject matter texts. As might be expected, most statewide and districtwide testing programs are concerned with similar outcomes. Often, personal reading is not considered a core area of assessment; consequently, most of the time allocated for reading instruction is for areas such as decoding, vocabulary, and comprehension.

Second, the majority of reading instruction is provided with commercial reading programs. Observations of classroom reading instruction reveal

OUTCOME	INSTRUCTIONAL FOCUS	READING OPPORTUNITY	INSTRUCTIONAL STRATEGY
Understanding that reading is part of the communication process	Various language experience activities involving why writer's write and why writers read	Early opportunities to read and write messages Opportunities to write about what one reads	Writing and reading language experience stories
Making and confirming predictions	Prior knowledge and experince is used to predict the meaning of text	Opportunities to make risk free predictions	Exchange Compare Writing Strategy Possible Sentences What If Strategy
Reading to gain a broader view of the world	Reading is a way of experiencing other people, places, things, events and feelings Reading is a way to solve personal problems	Continuous exposure to material convergent and divergent with one's personal background experiences and beliefs about the world Opportunities to discuss changes in one's prior knowledge, perspective or belief	Inquest Procedure Reaction Guide
Understanding literary genre and text structure used by authors in writing reading material	Writers' intentions with story (folk tale, fable, tall tale short story, novel, poetry lyric, ballad, nonsense, and drama (comedy, tragedy) and text structures writers use such as narrative (setting, characters, time, place, problem, events, resolutions, moral, theme, etc.)	Continuous exposure to and opportunities to read different literature	Problem Passages Circle Stories
Using reading as an opportunity for social interaction	Sharing with others what one has read	Continuous opportunities to read in non-threatening settings and discuss with others what one has read	Group Retellings
Developing an appreciation and joy for reading	Reading can be: enjoyable leisure activity, way of relaxing, way of 'getting away from it', way of experiencing human feeling such as sadness, anger, humor	Continuous opportunities to independently select, read, and reflect on material related to one's personal interest	Uninterrupted Sustained Silent Reading

Figure 1–2
Outcomes and Instructional Strategies

that many teachers use basal readers, along with instructional activities such as asking questions and assigning work sheets. Under these conditions, students actually have very little opportunity to read connected text and to develop an appreciation of literature.

Finally, the lock-step following of current basal reader programs does not provide opportunities for reading instruction that are relevant to the outcomes of personal reading. For example, the reading selections in existing basal readers usually do not match the personal experiences and needs of individuals and groups of students. The variety of reading selections included are either contrived to provide vocabulary control or are often abridged versions of good literature. In addition, although plans are under way to reform basal reading programs for the future, the completion of instructional activities such as those presented in existing basal reading programs is inappropriate for personal reading outcomes. Practice activities and discussion questions in manuals are designed for public response to reading. Personal reading outcomes require reading opportunities with substantial time for students to experience, express, and discuss their personal responses to text and changes in their prior knowledge, perspective, feelings, and beliefs as a result of reading.

Personal reading is comprised of at least six major outcomes. These outcomes are presented in Figure 1-2, along with their instructional focus, suggested opportunities for reading, and related instructional strategies to facilitate their attainment.

Understanding that Reading is Part of the Total Communication Process

The attainment of the first outcome, understanding that reading is part of the total communication process, is crucial. Students must acquire the concept that language activities such as reading and writing are purposeful and interrelated. Instruction focuses on why writers write and why readers read. Developing this concept begins with opportunities to tell simple stories, write these stories down, and read the stories one has written. The Language Experience Approach is one of the most appropriate forms of instruction for attaining this outcome.

LANGUAGE EXPERIENCE APPROACH

In the Language Experience Approach or LEA, students use their own language and experiences to compose sentences, passages, or stories. Since there is no set of procedural guidelines to follow, teachers, through the years, have developed a variety of techniques for using students' own language contributions as the basis for their reading material. When used in conjunction with reading literature, the LEA is particularly useful. As a prereading activity, the LEA can be employed to generate purpose setting questions. After the class or group surveys the title page, studies the illustration, or reads a few opening sentences or paragraphs, the teacher can elicit questions they would like to see answered in the story to follow. These questions can be recorded in language experience chart format to use as guides for reading or listening to the selection. Figure 1-3 is a chart of sample questions raised by a group of students before reading the story, *King Bidgood's in the Bathtub* (Wood, 1985).

The language experience approach is particularly appropriate when used after the reading of a selection as well. An entire story can be reconstructed by individual student contributions and then displayed on chart paper, a transparency, or the blackboard. Begin by allowing students to make contributions about story events in any order that comes to their minds (see Part I of Figure 1-4). Permitting this freedom of recall coordinates with the current research that suggests that, because of divergent experiences, readers quite naturally remember different things after reading the same text. This practice supplants questions such as "Tell

> 1. Who is King Bidgood?
> 2. Is he a real king?
> 3. Why does he want to stay in the bathtub?
> 4. What does he do in the bathtub?
> 5. Does he turn wrinkly in the end?
> 6. Who gets him out of the bathtub?
> 7. Does he get out of the tub?

Figure 1-3
Language Experience Approach: Prereading Question Chart for *King Bidgood's in the Bathtub*

I. Free Recall Phase

2. King Bidgood plays war in the bathtub.
1. The Page can't get him out of the tub.
4. The Duke can't get him out of the tub.
7. The King danced in the tub.
3. The Queen told him to come to lunch but he wouldn't come.
8. The King got out when the Page pulled the plug.
9. The water went glub, glub, glub.
5. The King even went fishing in the tub.
6. The Court tried to get him out.

II. Reconstruction Phase

The story begins when the Page can't get the King out of the bathtub. It was time to go to battle but the King played war in the tub. The Queen told him to come to lunch but he ate in the tub instead. The Duke asked him to go fishing but he went fishing in the tub. The Court said it was time for the ball so he danced in the tub. Finally, the Page decides to pull the plug and the King got out. The water went glub, glub, glub down the drain.

Figure 1-4
Language Experience Story

us what happened in the beginning of the story when the giant first stopped the little boy, Tony." Here students are put on the spot and expected to remember and recall an event that may have had little or no meaning for them as opposed to contributing the event or events that trigger their interests.

After the teacher determines that the story events have been sufficiently recalled, the class is asked to tell what happened first, second, third, and so forth. Numbers can be placed next to the initial contributions. Disagreements regarding the correct order may occur as the students seek mentally to reconstruct the story line. Then the teacher, with the aid of the class, may choose to rewrite the sentences on another paper (see Part II of Figure 1-4), asking inferential questions and soliciting student reactions about characters, happenings, and the like.

Making and Confirming Predictions

Making and confirming predictions is the second outcome. We know that students use their prior knowledge to generate predictions. We also know that prior knowledge is a significant determinant of the comprehension of written material. As might be expected, instruction relevant to this outcome is aimed at getting students to relate their background of experiences to the text by having them make predictions. In making predictions, students place their attention on background experiences most relevant to comprehending the text. In addition, they have a personal investment in reading the material. The results are deeper processing of information and more personal responding to the text. Consequently, opportunities to make risk-free predictions before reading and to participate in discussions of whether predictions were confirmed or disconfirmed by reading, along with the evidence used, are essential. Instructional strategies such as Exchange-Compare, Possible Sentences, and What If are very effective in achieving this outcome.

EXCHANGE-COMPARE WRITING STRATEGY

One means for engaging students in the process of prediction simultaneously involves them in a writing assignment as well. The Exchange-Compare writing strategy (Wood, 1986, adapted from Shuman, 1977) takes place in the prereading phase of a lesson and uses strategically selected concepts from a selection to stimulate students' predictive thinking abilities.

The teacher begins by selecting ten to fifteen key terms from a story or portion of a selection (see Figure 1-5). Students are assigned to heterogeneous groups of four or five to discuss the terms, their meaning, and their

Runaway Marie Louise
Natalie Savage Carlson

mongoose	sugarcane field
Marie Louise	mama
thatched hut	Christophe the snake
Dabble Duck	Snapping Turtle
Banded Armadillo	Witch Toad
naughty	mud pies
	spanking

Students' Predicted Passage

Marie Louise had a pet mongoose who lived in a thatched hut with Banded Armadillo, Snapping Turtle, and Dabble Duck. One day Marie Louise was making mud pies with her four pets. Christophe the Snake was being naughty and slithered by, tracking mud all over. Marie Louise was going to run away to the sugarcane field so she wouldn't get a spanking. Witch Toad talked Marie Louise into going back home to her mama.

Figure 1–5
Exchange-Compare Writing

relationship to each other. Then the students are instructed to put their heads together in the construction of a single composition, predicting the content of the actual selection. Thus, the students are engaged in a "communal writing" activity that has several advantages. One advantage is that having heterogenous students work together on a single composition tends to minimize the differences in the ability levels of the students. Second, students learn from each other, and no one individual is asked to perform in isolation. Another benefit is that such an activity maximizes participation by involving everyone in a meaningful and manageable task in which all have input, no matter how minor the contribution may appear to be. Last, communal writing is expeditious; that is, it is convenient for both teacher and students in that it takes less time than assigning each student the task of writing a composition individually.

The teacher must circulate among the groups to provide assistance and monitor progress. If help with definitions is needed, the word can be used in a sentence to elicit students' ability to use context clues.

Since this writing assignment has many purposes, one of which is to stimulate students' ability to predict, the need to turn in a final, edited copy is not a necessity and should be left to teacher discretion. Requiring a polished draft often takes too much time and may diminish students' interest in the reading of the actual literary selection.

Next, have the groups volunteer to share their completed compositions with the class by reading them aloud. It is preferable (though not necessary) that the entire prereading phase from the presentation of the key vocabulary to the creation and sharing of the communal composition take no more than two-thirds of the allotted class time, or approximately thirty minutes. In this way, the students have the opportunity to at least begin the reading phase of the instructional lesson, which involves comparing the content from the predicted to the actual passage. While reading the story, students can be instructed to attend to the key terms, noting the context in which they are used. Afterward, as part of the postreading phase, the teacher can return to the key terms, asking the students to elaborate on their meaning given the story context encountered.

POSSIBLE SENTENCES

As was demonstrated in the previous strategy, the vocabulary of a selection can be used as a springboard for developing rich predictions before reading. In Possible Sentences (Moore & Moore, 1990), students use their prior knowledge to predict relationships between vocabulary terms chosen from a novel, short story, trade book, or excerpted selection. The strategy begins in the prereading phase with the development of predicted sentences based on key vocabulary terms (see Figure 1-6), continues through the reading phase as students confirm and disconfirm their predictions, and concludes in the postreading phase with a modification of the original sentences.

Specifically, the teacher selects approximately eight to ten key terms that reflect the content of the story and are worthy of emphasis. The students are asked to use two of the vocabulary terms in a sentence that

Unit 2
"Freckle Juice"

From: Judy Blume, "Freckle Juice"

I. Visually display significant vocabulary.

refrigerator	mayonnaise	greenish	gulped
absolutely	moaned	stomach	awful
mistake	vinegar	decorated	probably
ketchup	Andrew Marcus		

II. Have students predict possible sentences and use these to guide their reading.

1. Andrew Marcus probably put vinegar in the formula by mistake.

2. He put the secret formula in the refrigerator to keep the mayonnaise cold.

3. The freckle juice he gulped was greenish in color.

4. The recipe for freckle juice contained vinegar, ketchup and mayonnaise.

5. Andrew Marcus moaned after drinking the juice.

6. The juice he put in his stomach tasted absolutely awful.

7. Jars of mayonnaise and ketchup decorated the refrigerator shelves.

III. After reading, indicate "true", "false" or "don't know" beside each statement. Then modify the statements to reflect the actual content of the selection.

Before Modification		After Modification
F	1.	Andrew Marcus dropped a lemon seed in the formula by mistake.
F	2.	He found everything on the shelves except the lemon and onion which were in the refrigerator.
F	3.	Andrew turned greenish and felt very sick.
T	4.	The recipe for freckle juice contained vinegar, ketchup and mayonnaise as well as lemon, pepper, salt, olive oil, onion, grape juice and mustard.
T	5.	Andrew Marcus moaned after drinking the juice.
T	6.	The juice he put in his stomach tasted absolutely awful.
D.K.	7.	Andrew studied his reflection in the mirror and decorated his face with a magic marker.

Figure 1-6
Third Grade Possible Sentences

might *possibly* appear in the story to be read. Using their prior knowledge and predictive abilities, they are to develop possible sentences that they think might be included in the selection. The teacher writes these sentences on the board or an overhead projector as dictated by the students, even if the content is inaccurate.

The students then write the number of each sentence on their papers. As they read the story, their task is to determine if the possible sentences are true or false. They do this by writing beside each number a T if the sentence is true as reflected by the story content, an F if it is false, or DK for don't know, if the statement's content is not evident from reading the story.

Finally, the class or group as a whole responds by making the necessary revisions in the existing sentences to comply with the story content. In essence, the sentences are rewritten or modified to make them true.

In Possible Sentences, students exercise their abilities to make predictions and to confirm or refute their predictions while reading a literature selection. Thus, they receive practice in a number of skills traditionally associated with reading instruction. In this lesson alone, they practice the skills of a) using the context to determine word meanings, b) developing complete and logical sentences and c) interacting with new vocabulary in a meaningful way both in oral and written form.

WHAT IF STRATEGY

Another method for helping students make and confirm predictions as they read is the What If strategy (Pearson, 1982). The What If strategy begins with a line of prereading questions that, because students become personally involved in the reading, elicit deeper processing of the text. Before reading, responses are elicited from students about what they would do under certain circumstances that parallel events occurring in the selection to be read. The teacher informs the class that the protagonist in the story to be read will undergo similar circumstances and then asks them to predict what the main character may do. After the reading, the students discuss the protagonist's actions in conjunction with their predictions about what they would have done under similar circumstances.

Specifically, the teacher decides on a few key points in a selection (for example, the moral or theme, a motivating factor, a main goal of the protagonist, etc.) upon which to base a set of What If questions. An example for the chapter, "Beezus and Her Imagination" from *Beezus and Ramona* by Beverly Cleary might be:

Have you ever felt that a sibling, friend or relative had more talent in some area than you? Describe how you felt. Did it cause problems for you? What did you do about it?

Next, establish a set of predictions for the protagonist that parallel those set for the students. Older students may be asked to write out their predictions.

In this chapter, Beezus charms the adults around her with her lively imagination. How do you think her sister, Ramona feels? What do you suppose she does about it?

Have the students read the text with these predictions in mind, comparing their predicted behaviors with the actions of the character(s). A lively and interactive discussion typically follows this strategy since students now have a personal stake in the reading which comes from seeing what others (their classmates and "story mates" as well) might do when confronted with certain conditions. Students learn to apply their predictive abilities to real life situations, not just story events. In addition, they tend to remember, due to their extensive involvement, more literal and implied information after using this technique.

Reading to Gain a Broader View of the World

The next outcome, reading to gain a broader view of the world, has two instructional foci. First, reading is presented as a way of experiencing other people, places, things, events, and feelings without really being there. Second, emphasis is place on using reading as a way of developing insight into one's self and solving personal problems. Here, we want to take students beyond discussion about mere interpretations of what they have read and help them discover new ideas about themselves and the world. In other words, reading instruction should engage students in reading material in ways that change them a little, as children, as human beings. The Inquest Procedure and the Reaction Guide are two instructional strategies leading to this important outcome.

INQUEST PROCEDURE

The Inquest Procedure (Shoop, 1986) provides a systematic way for modeling the asking and answering of questions during reading by engaging students in spontaneous drama. Helping students develop sound self-questioning techniques aids them in processing story content in a deeper, more personal way. In addition, it helps them to view the world from other perspectives. In the Inquest Procedure, students engage in a series of oral language exchanges in the form of a news interview as they read a selection. In this way, comprehension is enhanced and students learn to question themselves mentally as they read future selections. Figure 1-7 shows how this strategy is applied to a literature selection appearing in a basal reader.

The teacher begins by explaining to students that they are about to become news reporters who are responsible for interviewing some famous characters in the story they are to read. To model this process, the teacher can have students watch a television news interview to note formal protocol and types of questions asked, or the teacher may play the part of a news reporter to portray the interviewing technique.

Next, select a story that has interesting character and plot development and determine at which points in the story to stop and conduct the interview session. Suggest that students think of questions they would like to ask a particular character as the story unfolds. Then, choose a volunteer (or volunteers) to play the character(s) to be interviewed. Other members of the group assume the roles of investigative reporters at a news conference. The student-character maintains the role in the story by using information revealed up to that point in the plot and elaborating with background knowledge. The student-reporters pose questions in interview fashion. Through this exchange, the story is embellished, interpretations are made, reflections and personal thoughts are elicited, and predictions are made about future events.

Be certain that students understand that effective questions (a) require longer, more reflective responses as opposed to yes/no responses; (b) elicit information, a reflection, an evaluation, or a prediction; (c) should be varied when conducting an interview; and (d) should be followed by Why if a yes/no answer is generated.

At the conclusion of the story, have students evaluate their question-answer exchanges. Explain to them the importance of internalizing good questioning routines as they read to strengthen their understanding of story content and to broaden their view and perspective on characters and events.

REACTION GUIDE

Questions are the typical vehicle for developing students' story understanding. Yet statements, strategically designed, can be a most

Read: "Winnie-the-Pooh, In Which Pooh Goes Visiting and Gets Into a Tight Place", by
A. A. Milne; from: <u>Journeys</u> - a basal reader (level 3/J) p. 354-65, Houghton-Mifflin
Co., Boston, 1986.

One place reading could be stopped to implement interview role-play is at the
point where Pooh tries to leave Rabbit's house and becomes stuck:

Student volunteers to act as Pooh and several reporters.

DIALOGUE:

Reporter A: Mr. Bear, you seem to be stuck. When did this happen?

Pooh: Just a few minutes ago.

Reporter B: How did it happen?

Pooh: I don't know. I was on my way out and suddenly I was stuck.
Rabbit's door must have shrunk.

Reporter C: Then how did you get <u>in</u> Rabbit's house?

Pooh: I just wiggled in like always. It must have shrunk while I was inside.

Reporter D: Did anything happen while you were in Rabbit's house?

Pooh: Oh, we just talked and ate.

Reporter D: You ate? Did you eat a lot - enough to make you fatter?

Pooh: Well, no - I didn't eat <u>very</u> much.

Reporter E: How does it feel to be stuck in Rabbit's doorway like that,
Mr. Bear?

Pooh: It feels tight, and I can't <u>do</u> anything and I'm scared.

Reporter E: Why are you scared?

Pooh: Because I might be here forever!

Continue with story - possibly stopping
once or twice more

At end: Evaluate:

Teacher Did you enjoy pretending to be reporters and the characters from the story?

Students: Yes.

It was fun!

Teacher: Do you think the reporters asked more than one kind of question?

Students: Yes

Teacher: What kinds of questions did they ask?

Students: "feeling" questions

"how" questions

"when" questions

Figure 1-7
Inquest Procedure Sample Lesson

effective way to help students think critically, analyze a problem from different perspectives, conjure up their prior knowledge on a topic, and experience issues from the point of view of their peers. The reaction guide (Bean & Peterson, 1981; Readence, Bean & Baldwin, 1989) uses statements that are generalized and somewhat ambiguous to which students must respond both before and after having read a selection.

The teacher begins by determining the most significant events or concepts in a story or portion of a story. Develop approximately five to eight thought-provoking and discussion-inducing statements with columns for responding both before and after the selection.

Distribute or display the statements on the board, overhead, or chart paper. Allow the students to work in pairs or small groups and tell them to take turns reading each statement out loud. After each statement is read, group members must respond orally, indicating if they agree or disagree with the statement. Partners or group members need not reach a consensus. In fact, more elaborate discussions often ensue when there is disagreement. To ensure that this assignment does not deteriorate into a simple true/false activity, insist that they substantiate their responses by elaborating and using their background knowledge. The teacher can circulate to each group to monitor student progress and clarify any concepts as needed.

After the groups have responded to the statements, the teacher can conduct an informal pool by asking how many class members agreed or disagreed with each statement. Request that volunteers explain the thinking behind their varied responses. Be sure to maintain a non-judgmental posture to create a relaxed, open and communicative environment.

Next, the students can read the selection with the statements as their guides, mentally or orally noting when they encounter the concept in the selection. Such a guide can serve as a purpose-setting device because it focuses students' attention on certain significant concepts (Blanton, Wood & Moorman, 1990).

Last, the students can return to their groups or, if time is a concern, can respond as a class to the statements in the "after" column. After each statement is read, the class can respond by elaborating and substantiating their answers with new information gleaned from the selection. In many instances, their answers may not change, but their knowledge base and view will surely broaden.

Figure 1-8 shows a reaction guide developed for a folk tale selection, "Arap Sang and the Cranes," which appears in a basal reader. This example

"Arap Sang and the Cranes"

An African myth retold by Humphrey Harman
in <u>Tales Told Near a Crocodile</u>
from the Houghton-Mifflin Reading Program

Directions: Before reading the story, read these statements and
decide if you agree or disagree with them. Mark the
BEFORE column with a (+) or (-). Then talk over the
reasons for your answers with a partner. Now read the
story using the statements as guides. Mark the AFTER
column and discuss with your partner how the statements
relate to the story.

<u>BEFORE</u>   <u>AFTER</u>

_____   _____   1. People will do almost anything to assist
                         their fellow man.

_____   _____   2. Gifts are the responsibility of the giver.

_____   _____   3. Rewards are a mixed blessing.

_____   _____   4. Good things always happen to good people.

Figure 1-8
Reaction Guide

illustrates how teachers can use creative and motivating strategies with the literature in basal reading programs to de-emphasize the skills strand and emphasize, instead, the personal dimension of reading. Then, Figure 1-9 depicts the use of the reaction guide with an expository book. Lapp, Flood, and Farnan in this text further explore how basals and literature can be used compatibly within a reading program.

Understanding Literary Genre and Text Structures Used by Authors in Writing Reading Material

Another outcome of reading instruction is understanding literary genre and text structures used by authors in writing reading material. Research

<u>Ducks Don't Get Wet</u>
by Augusta Goldin

<u>BEFORE</u>   <u>AFTER</u>

_____   _____   1. Bird and duck feathers are waterproof.

_____   _____   2. You can easily mix oil and water together.

_____   _____   3. Most ducks don't dive very deeply.

_____   _____   4. Ducks can swim the length of a city block.

_____   _____   5. Ducks can fly as fast as an automobile.

_____   _____   6. When ducks are hungry, they fly south.

Figure 1-9
Reaction Guide

(Armbruster & Anderson, 1980; Bartlett, 1978; Geva, 1983; Slater, Graves & Piche, 1984; Smith & Standal, 1981; Taylor, 1982; Taylor & Beach, 1984) indicates that students benefit from exposure to varied forms of literature and instructional strategies designed to teach text structure.

It is also known that accomplished readers possess a better understanding of how authors organize information in their writing than do poor readers (Meyer, Brandt & Bluth, 1980). This includes an understanding of the overall text design, such as how short stories, novels, plays, and poetry are organized, along with text patterns authors commonly use.

Most students come to basic reading instruction familiar with the organization of simple narrative text. If not, they tend to learn it more easily because it is similar to the structure of spoken language. Other text patterns, on the other hand, are more varied, complex, and difficult to learn. These complex text patterns are learned by some students merely by continued exposure. Some students experience difficulty in learning these patterns, which partially explains why they experience failure in reading different kinds of literature. Instructional strategies such as Probable Passages and Circle Stories are excellent for reaching this outcome.

PROBABLE PASSAGES

Probable Passages (Wood, 1984) is a strategy easily combined with a basal reading selection, trade book, or short story lesson that can be used as a means of (a) incorporating writing practice in an instructional lesson and (b) helping students understand how narrative text is structured. Using terms strategically chosen from a literature selection, the students categorize them according to the elements of a story frame, a sequence of spaces connected by key language elements (Fowler, 1982; Nichols, 1980). Students use the categorized terms to predict a story line and then insert the embellished terms into the story frame to develop a "probable passage." After reading the story, the students, with the aid of the teacher, modify the predicted passage to correspond with the content of the selection.

In order to construct probable passages, students must use their intrinsic knowledge of story grammar, the common elements that govern both a story's structure and a person's mental image of a story's structure. Mandler and Johnson's (1977) six major story elements are used here because they are readily understood by elementary level students. The six major elements are setting (introduction of characters, time, and location), beginning (a precipitating event), reaction (a main character's response to the beginning or the formation of a goal), attempt (plan to reach a goal), outcome (success or failure of attempt), and ending (long-range consequences). By engaging in the probable passage strategy, students learn about story grammar elements and how they are related to the composition of a coherent written passage.

In the preparation stage of the development of a probable passage, the teacher first selects concepts or terms to be emphasized from a reading passage. These terms are presented to the students on the chalkboard or on an overhead projector along with categories corresponding to the appropriate story frame. Next, the teacher displays the incomplete story frame, to be used before and after reading, on another section of chalkboard or on another transparency.

When the list of terms, categories, and the story frame have been presented to the students, the prereading stage begins. The teacher reads the list of terms and students repeat each word. The students are told to use the words to construct a story line mentally and to place each word in a category. Next, as a group activity, the students use the terms to fill in the story frame as a group activity, working together until a consensus is reached.

I. Lesson - words

Tomas	Mr. Tucker	delicious
doughnuts	jelly-cinnamon-honey	customer
bank loan	huge	Whirr!
flour	Buzz!	Clunk!
start button	Mr. Redstone	invented

II. Incomplete word frame:

Setting	Character(s)	Problem	Problem - solution	Ending

III. Incomplete probable passage:

The story takes place_____. _____is a character in the story who _____. A problem occurs when _____. After that, _____. Next, _____.
The problem is solved when _____. The story ends_____.

IV. Predicted word frame:

Setting	Character(s)	Problem	Problem - solution	Ending

V. Probable passage:
    The story takes place in a doughnut shop. Mr. Tucker is a character in the story who owns the store. A problem occurs when Tomas, a little boy, pushes the start-button. After that, the machine goes whirr, buzz, and chunk and a huge doughnut pops out. Next, a customer comes in. The problem is solved when they are given a bank loan and Mr. Tucker and Tomas invent the jelly-cinnamon-honey doughnut.

V. Actual passage:
    The story takes place in a doughnut shop. Tomas is the character who invented the jelly-cinnamon-honey doughnut. Mr. Tucker is the owner of the store. A problem occurs when Tomas pushes the start-button and can't figure out how to stop the machine. After that, he pushes all the buttons together; the machine goes whirr, buzz, and chunk and a huge jelly-cinnamon-honey doughnut pops out. Next, Mr. Redstone, a customer, comes in and buys all the doughnuts. The problem is solved when customers come from all around to buy the doughnuts and Mr. Tucker doesn't have to take out a bank loan. The story ends when Mr. Tucker lets Tomas have a free jelly-cinnamon-honey doughnut every day.

Figure 1–10
Probable Passages

In the reading stage the students read or listen to the selection with their predicted passage in mind. In the postreading stage, they reevaluate the original placement of the categorized words and make changes accordingly. Then the story frame is modified to reflect the content of the actual story. Within a single instructional lesson, students receive practice in writing coherent paragraphs; they engage in oral language activities; they develop and extend their vocabulary knowledge; and they improve their ability to comprehend and learn how stories are constructed and composed.

CIRCLE STORY

The circle story (Simpson, 1981) is a method effective with children in grades K-4 that enhances their ability to group story details into main events or scenes and allows them to demonstrate comprehension and recall. Students begin to see at an early age how stories are sequenced from beginning to end as they work in groups to verbalize and illustrate story events that are depicted in the selection heard.

The teacher begins by informing the students that they will reconstruct a selection using their own drawings of what has occurred. To model the process, and provide a mental framework, display a blank circle divided into four segments. Next, the teacher should recite a familiar nursery rhyme (e.g., "Little Miss Muffet") and then think aloud, with the aid of the class, what occurred in each episode and how these events might be illustrated.

Divide the class into small groups and provide them with white paper and crayons. After listening to the selected story, each group should be instructed to draw a large circle on the paper and make an illustration at the top of the circle to indicate the beginning and end of the story. The children then identify and discuss the scenes in the story and divide the circle into sections to correspond with the number of scenes they have identified. Next, they use the crayons, chalk, or paint to illustrate the scenes in the sections of the circle. Different interpretations of the story as represented by the illustrations make excellent material for discussion. The circle story is effective in the development of group circle stories and in aiding students to develop stories on their own.

Once children have practiced by retelling circle stories after listening to them, they can work as a group to compose their own stories. A series of planning questions can guide the students in developing the story, such as: Who or what should we have as our main character? What could be the

The Gingerbread Boy

Student Responses:

1. The little old man and woman were alone at the beginning and the end of the story.

2. The little old woman made a gingerbread boy, hoping he could be like their little boy.

3. The gingerbread boy ran away from everyone who wanted to eat him.

4. The fox tricked him and he got eaten anyway.

This illustration contributed by Michael Manuel, 4th grade, North Rowan Primary School, Spencer, North Carolina

Figure 1-11
Circle Story

second adventure? What could be the last adventure? Individual children can take turns telling parts of the story when discussion and planning are complete. During this phase, technical aspects of writing should be de-emphasized since the focus is on their own ideas and content. If, however, the teacher decides to publish the students' stories, the publication stage is the time to refine grammar, punctuation, and spelling. With additional practice in working in groups, students can then be given the assignment to develop a circle story on their own.

Children enjoy sharing their stories and hearing what others have written. A story could be read aloud to the class each day of the week, or if the children have published their stories, copies can be made available to other students in the class or to other classes. Not only does the circle story strategy help young students see how stories are structured, but it also engages them in the processes involved in the act of retelling and composing stories.

Using Reading as an Opportunity for Social Interaction

The next major outcome of reading instruction is using reading as an opportunity for social interaction. As noted earlier, a great deal of reading instruction in schools is oriented toward public responding. Students work in groups and are held accountable for answering questions correctly and making socially agreed upon interpretations of text. Students also need opportunities to explore their personal responses with others. When readers have an opportunity for collaborative group sharing of the images, feelings, fears, shocking discoveries, reflections, and appreciations stimulated by their reading, the potential for personal growth and development is increased. Consequently, instructional activities that maximize the opportunity for using reading as a means of social interaction among students is important. Group Retelling is an effective strategy for facilitating social interaction.

GROUP RETELLINGS

A universal need exists among all individuals to share what they have learned with others. Everyone has witnessed the joy on the faces of young children when they encounter a new discovery while reading or has experienced the desire to tell a partner an interesting anecdote from the morning newspaper. This need to relate our new learning to others can be capitalized on in the classroom as well. Activities that promote collaborative learning experiences can be readily employed in conjunction with the reading and teaching of literature. One collaborative learning technique that is particularly beneficial and expedient is group retellings (Wood, 1987).

Group retellings can be implemented during the reading phase of the lesson and is a welcome replacement for round-robin reading. After the activities of the prereading phase have been completed, the teacher can group students into threes (pairs or groups of four work well, too) and have them read a segment of the passage. For upper elementary students, this reading can be silent. For the earlier grades, students can engage in a number of oral reading strategies described in the literature (Wood, in press) including whisper reading, choral reading, mumble or four-way oral reading, to name a few.

After reading a designated number of lines, paragraphs or pages, group members tell, in their own words, what they just read. Students can elaborate with related information from their background of experiences, describe mental images they have created while reading, or offer specific details recalled. An example of just such a retelling is shown in Figure 1-12.

Much pleasure is derived from the sharing that takes place in group retellings. Likewise, students have the opportunity to receive other therapeutic benefits as they hear and react to the responses of their peers.

Developing an Appreciation and Joy for Reading

Our final outcome is developing an appreciation and joy for reading. The focus of instruction for this outcome is on developing the attitude that reading is more than just learning from school books. We want students to use reading as a leisure activity that can be used to break daily routines and get away from the humdrum of everyday life.

To reach this outcome, students need opportunities to select materials for themselves and read them at their own pace. At the same time, it is important for teachers to explain and model free reading for students. It is also helpful to hold group discussions about the enjoyable and recreational uses of reading. A widely recognized strategy for this outcome is Uninterrupted Sustained Silent Reading.

<u>Beans on the Roof</u>
Betsy Byars

Chapter 1 - "A Bean on the Roof"

Student A: The story begins with George telling Mrs. Bean that Anna is on the roof writing a poem. Mrs. Bean knows she's up there. I was up on our roof once when my dad was cleaning the gutters - scary!!

Student B: George was upset because they were told not to play there. He wanted to go up on the roof, too. Even if it meant he would have to write a poem.

Student C: His mother handed him a pencil and paper and told him to write at the table. He bit into his pencil and got real restless and told his mother that he just couldn't write at the desk.

Student A: Me either. I like to write in my bean bag.

Student C: Not me, I'd rather sit at my desk. It's in my room and my little brother won't bother me there.

Student B: I write on the coffee table while I'm watching TV.

Student C: It ended with his mother letting him go on the roof to write his poem. That's it.

Student A: No, then he breathes the good "roof air" and starts writing.

Teacher: Any ideas about what might happen next?

Student B: Each chapter starts with more beans on the roof. I'll bet more of their family goes up there to write.

Student C: Yeah, then they all must have a fight or something because there's only one bean on the roof.

Figure 1–12
Partial Transcript of a Group Retelling

UNINTERRUPTED SUSTAINED SILENT READING

Uninterrupted Sustained Silent Reading (USSR) refers to the time set aside in a classroom, or preferably an entire school, in which everybody reads. During schoolwide USSR or SSR, students, teachers, secretaries, custodians, and principals stop what they are doing and pull out a book to read. Thus, the excitement found in books is demonstrated for students as something adults do and want to do, not just an assignment given to students by their teachers. A more detailed description of SSR is given in Chapter 4, "Promoting Recreational Reading."

SUMMARY

One of our primary objectives in this chapter has been to familiarize teachers and teacher educators with the personal dimension of reading, the aesthetic side that is concerned with the reader's personal reactions, images, ideas, and sensations. Another objective has been to demonstrate practical strategies for accessing the personal dimension in a classroom setting. By implementing these strategies with literature, teachers are emphasizing the skills traditionally associated with reading instruction in a manner that is motivating, interesting, and respectful of students' idiosyncratic responses to their reading.

REFERENCES

Armbruster, B. B., & Anderson, T. H. (1980). *The effect of mapping on the free recall of expository text* (Tech. Rep. No. 160). Urbana: University of Illinois, Center for the Study of Reading.

Bartlett, B. J. (1978). *Top-level structure as an organizational strategy for recall of classroom text.* Unpublished doctoral dissertation. Arizona State University, Tempe, Arizona.

Bean, T. W., & Peterson, J. (1981). Reasoning guides: Fostering readiness in the content areas. *Reading Horizons, 21,* 196-99.

Betts, E. A. (1946). *Foundations of reading instruction.* NY: American Book.

Blanton, W. E., Wood, K. D., & Moorman, G. B. (1990). The role of purpose in reading instruction. *The Reading Teacher, 43*(7), 486-492.

Blume, J. (1971). *Freckle juice.* New York, NY: Four Winds Press.

Byars, B. (1988). *Beans on the roof.* NY: Delacourt Press, Inc.

Carlson, N. S. (1977). *Runaway Marie Louise.* New York, NY: Scribner's.

Cleary, B. (1986). *Beezus and Ramona: The Beezus and Ramona diary.* New York: William Morrow.

Fowler, G. L. (1981). Developing comprehension skills in primary students through the use of story frames. *The Reading Teacher, 36*(2), 176-179.

Geva, E. (1983). Facilitating reading comprehension through flow-charting. *Reading Research Quarterly, 18*(4), 384-405.

Goldin, A. (1989). *Ducks don't get wet.* New York, NY: Harper & Row.

Iser, W. (1978). *The act of reading: A theory of aesthetic response.* Baltimore: The Johns Hopkins University Press.

Mandler, J., & Johnson, N. (1977). Remembrance of things passed: Story structure and recall. *Cognitive Psychology, 9*(1), 111-151.

Meyer, B. J. F., Brandt, D. M., & Bluth, G. J. (1980). Use of top-level structure in text: Key for reading comprehension of ninth-grade students. *Reading Research Quarterly, 16*(1), 72-102.

Milne, A. A. (1986). Winnie the Pooh, In which Pooh goes visiting and gets into a tight place. In *Journeys,* basal reader. Boston, MA: Houghton Mifflin Co.

Moore, S. A., & D. W. Moore (1990). Possible sentences. In *Reading in the content areas: Improving classroom instruction.* (Third edition), edited by E. K. Dishner, T. W. Bean, & J. E. Readence. Dubuque, IA: Kendall Hunt.

Nichols, J. (1980). Using paragraph frames to help remedial high school students with written assignments. *Journal of Reading, 24*(3), 228-231.

Pearson, P. D. (1982). Asking questions about stories. *Ginn Occasional Papers.* Columbus, OH: Ginn and Company.

Purves, A. (1985). That sunny dome: Those caves of ice. In C. R. Cooper (Ed.), *Researching response to literature and the teaching of literature: Points of departure.* (pp. 54-69). Norwood: NJ: Ablex.

Readence, J. E., Bean, T. W., & Baldwin, R. S. (1989). *Content area reading: An integrated approach.* Dubuque, IA: Kendall Hunt.

Rosenblatt, L. M. (1978). *The reader, the text, the poem: The transactional theory of the literary work.* Carbondale, IL: Southern Illinois University Press.

Rosenblatt, L. M. (1988). *Writing and reading: The transactional theory* (Tech. Rep. No. 416). Urbana: University of Illinois, Center for the Study of Reading.

Shoop, M. (1986). Inquest: A listening and reading strategy. *The Reading Teacher, 39*(7), 670-675.

Shuman, R. B. (1977). Writing workshops and the teaching of reading. Presentation at the International Reading Association Annual Conference.

Simpson, M. (1981). Writing stories using model structures: The circle story. *Language Arts, 58*(2), 293-299.

Slater, W. H., Graves, M. F., & Piche, G. L. (1984). Effects of structural organizers on ninth-grade students' comprehension and recall of four patterns of expository text. *Reading Research Quarterly, 20,* 189-202.

Smith, E., & Standal, T. (1981). Learning styles and study techniques. *Journal of Reading, 24*(7), 599-602.

Taylor, B. M. (1982). Text structure and children's comprehension and memory for expository material. *Journal of Educational Psychology, 74*(3), 323-340.

Taylor, B. M., & Beach, R. (1984). The effects of textstructure instruction on middle grade students' comprehension and production of expository text. *Reading Research Quarterly, 19*(2), 134-146.

Wertsch, J. V. (1979). The concept of activity in Soviet psychology: An introduction. In J. V. Wertsch (Ed.), *The concept of activity in Soviet psychology,* (pp. 3-36). Armonk, NY: Sharpe.

Wood, A. (1985). *King Bidgood's in the Bathtub.* New York, NY: Harcourt Brace Jovanovich.

Wood, K. D. (1984). Probable passages: A writing strategy. *The Reading Teacher, 37*(6), 496-499.

Wood, K. D. (1986). Smuggling writing into classrooms. *Middle School Journal, 27*(3), 5-6.

Wood, K. D. (1987). Fostering cooperative learning in middle and secondary level classrooms. *Journal of Reading, 31*(1), 10-18.

Wood, K. D. (in preparation). Implementing cooperative learning strategies in elementary classrooms. In Flood, J., Lapp, D. & Wood, K. *Managing the community of readers and writers.* Newark, DE: International Reading Association.

2

Basal Readers and Literature: A Tight Fit or a Mismatch?

Diane Lapp, James Flood, and Nancy Farnan

INTRODUCTION

What is the state of the art in reading instruction? In addressing this question, the following two questions are often debated: Should works of literature provide the sole foundation for reading programs, making basals obsolete? Do basals have a place in state-of-the-art reading programs? This chapter has been designed to explore these pivotal questions as a means to enable teachers to accommodate the shifts that have occurred in the says the educational community has come to view the teaching of reading in the latter portion of the twentieth century.

Current views of reading, based on sound theoretical foundations that suggest that comprehension occurs as a transaction between a reader and a text (Iser, 1978; Rosenblatt, 1938; Tompkins, 1980), allude to the value of developing literature-based programs. According to the latest International Reading Association's (1988) definition of reading, comprehension is a result of interactions among a reader, the text, and a specific context. This definition implies a meaningful transaction between a reader's prior knowledge or schema and a text, a transaction also molded by the specific context (i.e., time, place, situation) in which it occurs. In other words, children learn to read by participating in meaningful transactions with print, transactions likely to be encouraged by quality writings appropriate for children's psychological and social development. Given this perspective, a persuasive case has been made for embedding literature as the core of the reading curriculum in order to promote reading in the context of what is meaningful and necessary for children's cultural as well as language literacy. The question, then, that arises is how to structure effective literature-based reading programs.

Finally, a timely issue for reading educators involves coming to grips with what represents a major shift in instructional views of language arts programs. This is a shift from treating the language arts (reading, writing, speaking, and listening) as separate skill areas to looking at them as language processes that are not only related but also are mutually enhancing. Thus, concerns we will examine in this chapter, as we attempt to shed some light on the major topic, "Basal Readers and Literature: A Tight Fit or a Mismatch," include (1) curriculum questions associated with use of basals, the primary question being whether or not works of literature should supplant basal programs; (2) a topic closely related to the first question, the role of literary works in the curriculum; and (3) instructional decisions associated with planning integrated language arts programs.

WHAT IS THE ROLE OF LITERATURE IN THE READING PROGRAM?

If we look at our goals for teaching reading, we might conclude that two objectives provide an overarching rationale. One is to teach children how to read, and the other is to instill in children a love for reading. Of course, we have managed, without intensive use of literature in classrooms, to teach many children how to read, but we have done less well in creating lifelong lovers of reading (Cullinan, 1987). Good literature provides a vehicle that can help us accomplish both goals.

Children come to school with well-conceived ideas of what a story should be. Anderson and Pearson (1984), like many other researchers, refer to this as their story schema. Children, by the time they are five or six, have expectations for stories, expectations that are not always met by the stories they encounter in school. Too often, stories presented to children in school have been more concerned with introducing words and sounds through controlled vocabularies than they were with fulfilling readers' expectations for a good story. Good literature presents compelling themes, engaging plots, fully developed characters, and realistic conflicts. It piques children's interest, eliciting interaction and involvement of their feelings, raising questions that they seek to answer, and causing them to care about what happens and why it happens. It does not spell out every motivation and event but leaves room for student's logical inferencing; it is artfully crafted in order to encourage them to predict and to think about conflicts, motivations, themes, and events. It does not insult them by making every turn of plot, character motivation, and theme explicit and thus immune to the excitement and thought engagement inherent in quality literature.

What does it mean when we say that children come to school with expectations for stories they will read and hear? One thing it means is that they come equipped with definite preferences for what they want to read. Yearly, the International Reading Association and the Children's Book Council survey approximately 10,000 children around the country to evaluate children's books published in a given year. From these surveys, a list of Children's Choices is published in every October issue of *The Reading Teacher.* (Survey results may also be obtained from the Children's Book Council, 67 Irving Place, New York, NY 10003.) In 1979 Sebesta undertook a project to cull from the books chosen what characteristics they contained that differentiated them from books not chosen. He was able to delineate the following commonalities from books chosen by these children as the best. Those chosen:

1. tended to have fast-paced plots.

2. covered a wide range of topics. No specific interest categories were evident. However, in the books chosen as best, topics were covered in rich detail and specifies.

3. had richly described settings so that children could get a sense of how they looked and felt.

4. tended to be upbeat with happy endings, not sad and pessimistic.

5. had varied plot structures. Children seemed to be interested in stories with flashbacks, cause-effect plots, and even plots that were not explicitly connected.

6. often taught a lesson. Evidently, a bit of didacticism did not interfere with student interest.

7. evidenced a warmth, especially among character relationships. Children liked books in which warm, caring relationships existed among characters.

What does this information offer to educators? Certainly, it can be helpful for teachers to use as a yardstick for determining which books and stories they might use in their classrooms. An understanding of what characteristics might appeal to children will help teachers find books that will meet children's expectations for stories. As Cullinan (1987) suggests:

> Since comprehension is shaped by the reader's schema — the knowledge already stored in memory about what should be — it stands to reason that

when new material conforms to expectations, it is easier to understand. . . .
Good stories provide reading teachers with the right materials to teach
reading comprehension (p. 3).

In addition to bringing to school expectations for what they will find in
stories, Applebee (1978) found that children's sense of story grows as they
mature. He discovered that children begin by telling stories in disconnected
strings, beginning later to incorporate what he refers to as "story markers."
These include putting titles on their stories, using such phrases as "once
upon a time," using past tense when telling a story, and changing their
voices to accommodate differing characters. The progressive evidence of
these story markers in their oral language illustrates the power of literature
to affect children's language development.

Books can be catalysts for children at any age in their language as well as
cognitive and social/moral development, as they become immersed in
language through reading and responding to what they read. Understanding
the role of literature in cognitive development stems from our knowledge
of schema theory. According to Piaget, our prior knowledge and experiences
are what make up our schemata, the cognitive structures that represent
conceptual frameworks through which we understand our world. Through
the processes of assimilation and accommodation we either assimilate
information, which we already have stored, into existing structures, or we
accommodate new information by modifying existing structures to take
into account continually evolving views of the world. Literature can provide
rich experiences through which we consistently broaden our conceptual
frameworks.

Finally, we can see the value of literature as it contributes to children's
social and moral development. Learning is a social activity dependent upon
constructive interactions. Children develop feelings and understandings
about themselves through not only their experiences with literature but
also their interactions with others as they respond to and share what they
have read. For example, children in the intermediate grades get a chance to
experience in *Stone Fox* (Gardiner, 1980) the loneliness and responsibility
of Willy, a ten-year-old boy who fights to take care of his ill grandfather and,
with the help of his beloved dog Searchlight, to save their farm from being
sold. Children experience his feelings for his grandfather, who is suddenly
bedridden and unable to talk; for Doc Smith, who offers a helping hand but
not an acceptable solution to his problem; and for Stone Fox, who offers the
seemingly unsurmountable obstacle that Willy must overcome if he,
Searchlight, and his grandfather are to maintain their home together. How

Willy handles the situation and how the other characters react to his efforts constitute an experience that can broaden children's social as well as their moral perspectives. Additionally, as children respond with others to ideas such as what the book reminds them of in their own lives and to questions such as what would you have done if you were Clifford Snyder, the bill collector, they internalize various perspectives that help them develop their own points of view.

What is the role of literature in the reading program? We have examined this question from multiple avenues, from the importance of children developing a lifelong love of reading to providing them with experiences to support their language development, cognitive growth, and social/moral development. Having provided support for the contribution that literature can make in reading programs, it is important to move into an arena of debate: Should works of literature replace the use of basal readers?

ARE BASALS AND LITERATURE-BASED PROGRAMS COMPATIBLE?

We could keep you in suspense, until our discussion led you to conclude our answer to the above question. Instead, we will begin this portion of the chapter by saying that we believe the answer is an unqualified yes. Reasons for this perspective include a concern for the myriad decisions and challenges that teachers of reading face routinely in their programs, such as goal-setting responsibilities, the necessity for designing instruction that encompasses the complexity of reading processes, and meeting the multiple needs of diverse learners who bring a variety of interests and capabilities to the classroom. Given the complexity of the task, which is to design and implement curriculum and instruction to help students not only learn to read but also read to learn, it would be inhumane to expect teachers to teach without thoughtful, current guidelines and materials to provide support for their endeavors. It is that invaluable support function that current basal readers provide for teachers.

Major changes have been implemented in basals during the latter part of this decade, changes that reflect current understandings about reading. It is not the change that is new but the direction that the changes are taking. A historical glimpse at basals reveals that they have continuously evolved over the past 300 plus years, supplying a mirror for society's fluctuating views of itself, its children, and schooling. Venezky (1987) has described these changes with particular attention to the multiple factors influencing the development of reading texts. Factors that include society's attitudes toward children and education, changing demographics, and psychological research have guided what was taught and how it was taught. For example, in colonial times, literacy was not the desired goal of reading; instead, the purpose of reading, often directed toward memorization of verse and treatises, was the garnering of appropriate religious attitudes believed to fulfill religious responsibilities and ensure salvation. Obviously, purposes for reading instruction today are vastly different. Informed by psychology, linguistics, and sociology, reading is seen as a process whereby meaning is constructed, with the end result being enhanced literacy development. Embedded in the concept of literacy development are the ideas of increased knowledge and understandings, understandings of the world, those around us, and ourselves, accompanied by feelings of pleasure associated with reading.

It is easy to see, therefore, why literature has been placed in a central position in reading/language arts programs. It is also easy to understand why basal reading programs, particularly those copyrighted in the late 1980s, have begun to select quality literature from diverse ethnic sources to be central to their programs and to design instruction whose goals are to promote literacy and increased student interest in and appreciation for reading.

However, basal instruction of the 1960s and 1970s, in the minds of many people, still represents the traditional basal program, therefore making basals antithetic to the notion of meaning-centered, literature-based instruction. These individuals are partially right. Thirty years ago, the basal did represent views that are antithetical to today's conceptions of reading. Basal instruction followed recommendations for increased and earlier attention to phonics and instruction that emphasized attention to sounds and blending of sounds to form words (Durkin, 1987). One form this took was the linguistic approach (Fries, 1962), in which sounds were presented within the context of words, resulting in stories that included rigidly controlled vocabularies with sentences formulated around a series of words such as *at, pat, sat,* and *hat.* The 1970s further fragmented language instruction with management systems designed to address issues of accountability, behavioral objectives, and mastery learning. Therefore, a subskill approach to reading instruction was further ingrained, exemplified by the "*Wisconsin Design* (Otto, et al., 1977), considered by basal companies to be the most threatening competitor" (Durkin, 1987, p.335), with 309 subskills. Consequently, it is not surprising that many educators see basals and literature-based programs as being at opposite ends of an instructional continuum, a perspective that places basal readers in the same category as workbooks, skills sequences, and practice worksheets.

A perception of those who espouse a totally literature-based approach is that basal instruction has taken meaningful reading out of reading instruction. Fortunately, this viewpoint is not reflective of the changes that have occurred in basal programs. Although most basal programs still provide skill-based instruction, incorporating phonics particularly in the primary grades, changes have been made that also acknowledge the importance of literature and the fact that reading is more than the sum of a component number of subskills that, if learned, will equal proficiency in reading.

However, basals also reflect research in reading that has shown that skill-based instruction is important to a well-rounded reading program. Seventy years' research, some of which is presented in *Becoming a Nation of Readers: The Report of the Commission on Reading,* makes the point that "classroom research shows that, on the average, children who are taught phonics get off to a better start in learning to read than children who are not taught phonics" (Anderson et al., 1985, p. 37). Also, research suggests that direct instruction of comprehension skills (or we can call them strategies) does result in increased comprehension abilities (Gersten and Carnine, 1986; Palincsar and Brown, 1986); in other words, skill-based instruction does result in increased skill attainment. Based on an extensive body of data, Helmsfeld (1989) rightly contends that abandonment of what has been effective in traditional, skill-based instruction "does a disservice to students. Written language is like a safe-deposit box: more than one key is needed to unlock it, and children need all the keys we can give them" (p. 65). Similarly, Stahl and Miller argue that "quality phonics instruction need not be synonymous with excessive worksheets, nor must it exclude the use of quality literature" (1989, p. 109).

Given these changes in basals, it is our contention that the best reading programs are structured on a foundation of complementary instruction both from basal reading programs and from other sources of quality literature. Basal programs have the potential for providing a framework and organization for teachers, allowing them to enhance and expand basal instruction without having to invent and implement a reading program entirely from scratch. This is not to suggest that totally building a reading program is beyond the capabilities of talented teachers. It is not. However, teaching is an almost incomprehensibly complex task, requiring the individual to be an instructional expert, a curriculum specialist, a specialist in learning theory, an expert classroom manager, an authority on multi-cultural issues, an expert diagnostician, and many others. Basal programs that have been designed to approach reading as a complex process of meaning construction can provide invaluable guidance to teachers as they design programs goals, select useful curriculum, design effective instruction and assessment, and work to meet the needs of diverse learners. The word *guidance* is important in the preceding sentence for it implies that teachers are the final decision-makers, for only they work with their students and know intimately their needs and problems.

The question we believe teachers should be faced with is not whether to use the basal or literature but rather how to use the basal and outside literary sources as complementary partners in a well-rounded reading program. Curriculum and instruction, then, can move in two directions, exemplified below, with the basal providing a foundation and impetus for additional work in other resources, while, at other times, units and lessons might begin with a work of literature, incorporating ideas, activities, and readings from the basal as support material.

HOW CAN TEACHERS USE BASALS AND WHOLE WORKS OF LITERATURE TOGETHER?

Thematic units have been popular for years among teachers, for good reason. They provide a foundation upon which teachers can incorporate multiple readings and instructional strategies that capitalize on the best of what basals and other sources of literature have to offer in reading programs. In the most effective programs, teachers use this foundation as a vehicle for encouraging reading from many sources, sources that provide opportunities through which teachers can apply principles of effective reading/language arts instruction, such as activating prior knowledge, modeling competent reading strategies, incorporating all language skill areas, and encouraging personal explorations and connections with text.

Organizing themes can come directly from concepts embedded in basals or works of literature, such as themes organized around authors, illustrators, informational and story themes, and literary genres. Themes can also be generated from the world at large, concepts such as pets, travels, friends, and many others, that are then related to basal and other literary readings. Students, with a natural curiosity of the world around them, can also generate ideas for themes, giving teachers insights into students' interests and providing a variety of ideas around which to build one or two thematic units a year.

THEMATIC UNIT: CHARACTERS I'LL REMEMBER

As an example, we will present basal and literary works, with some activity suggestions, that center on two related thematic ideas, people; and places. One unit, designed for students at the upper elementary levels, centers on characters I'll Remember, with the first work being "Sequoyah: The Indian Who Captured Words," found in *Connections* (1989) by Macmillan.

One way to begin this unit is through modeling the thinking that might occur prior to reading Sequoyah. The teacher sets the stage for purposeful reading in a way that activates students' prior knowledge about the genre of historical fiction. That modeling might be similar to what follows on page 44 in Figure 2-1.

Of course, throughout the reading, this modeling can continue, with the teacher sharing how he or she might do such things as integrate new ideas with old information, monitor comprehension, and check for understanding. For example, when Sequoyah faced the problem of how he could create pictures to represent his new words, a teacher might model the thoughts shown in Figure 2-2 on page 45.

As they begin reading, students can be directed to think about what they believe are the most important events in the story and to construct a timeline that represents these events. Timelines help students identify text structure, which in this story is temporal sequence. With this story, asking students to construct a timeline around important events helps students understand not only the sequence of events, but also to engage in evaluation as they make selective decisions about which events to include. Productive discussions can center on why students would identify some events as being more significant than others. A timeline for "Sequoyah" might look something like the one shown on page 46

After reading "Sequoyah," other works such as *Johnny Tremain* (1946), another work of historical fiction; *Petronella* (1980), a fairy tale;

Modeling: Sequoyah

BUILD BACKGROUND ——— I know that a biography is the story about a person's life. It is like a story because it tells about events that happen in the order in which they occur. It is unlike just any story in that it tells facts about the life of just one person and it is always true or based on true events in the person's life. I also know that biographies are mostly written about famous people and what they did that made them famous.

SETS PURPOSE AND When I make a guess about what will happen next in a story, I am making predictions. Making predictions
MAKES PREDICTIONS ——— before I read and checking to see if they are correct after I read helps me to understand the story better. If I understand it, I will enjoy it more. *To make a prediction, I will use my own knowledge and any clues that the writer gives.*

First, I am going to read the titles of the story to see if it gives me an idea of what will happen in this story.

"Sequoyah: The Cherokee Who Captured Words."

——— "Sequoyah must be the person's name. I know that Cherokee is the name of a tribe of Native Americans or Indians because my great grandmother was a full-blooded Cherokee Indian from Oklahoma. Sequoyah must have been a Cherokee Indian. It also says the Cherokee who captured words. Capture means to catch something and put it in a cage or jail. If Sequoyah captured words, maybe he put words somewhere to keep them or work with them. *When I write, I cluster words to give me ideas. That is sort of like capturing them.* Because of this, I predict that he was a writer and he wrote something important, like a book or a document like the Constitution or something.

Next, I am going to look at the pictures to see if I can find some more clues so I can predict why this person, Sequoyah, was a famous person. I notice that the pictures show what appears to be a man wearing a strange looking headpiece, like a turban with feathers sticking out the bottom. That must have been what the Cherokee Indians wore at one time. In several pictures, he has something in his hand that looks like a paintbrush or a stick with a sharp blade at the end. I wonder if he was an artist or a writer. I also see what looks like a strange alphabet on a paper or skin of some kind. Maybe he wrote these funny looking letters. Now I *predict* that this is what he wrote. I still think that it must be a famous book or document, but in another language.

Now, I am going to read to find out if my predictions are correct and learn who Sequoyah was and what he did that made him a famous person. I am going to use a time line to help me put the events of his life in order. Then I can use it to help me summarize the story of his life.

Figure 2–1
Modeling: Sequoyah

CHECK FOR
UNDERSTANDING ——————— I am thinking about the problem that
Sequoyah ran into. It matches a thought I
had at the beginning about how could
Sequoyah draw a picture for every word.
As I look at the little pictures at the bottom
of the page, I can see that they represent
objects. But words like good and bad,
today and tomorrow have no real pictures
to represent them. He solved the problem
by creating symbols for many of the
words. I am going to add this to my time
line since it seems like he is making
progress in developing his written
language. This also created a new
problem. He had so many symbols that he
began to forget which ones stood for
which words.

Figure 2-2
Modeling: Check for Understanding

and *Island of the Blue Dolphins* (1960), another fictionalized account based on a true event; can extend the theme of Characters I'll Remember. Literature charts, along with myriad other activities, can serve to highlight the thematic concept throughout the reading of these additional works. Literature charts function to:

1. provide a forum for conversation and discussions.
2. preserve children's thinking and language development.
3. make links between books, ideas, and concepts.
4. encourage organized creative thinking.
5. develop reading strategies.
6. illustrate genre structures.

The chart on page 47 provides an illustration. Notice that this sample encourages students to recall or record literal information as well as to evaluate character's significance and to relate actively their prior knowledge and experience to what they know about these characters.

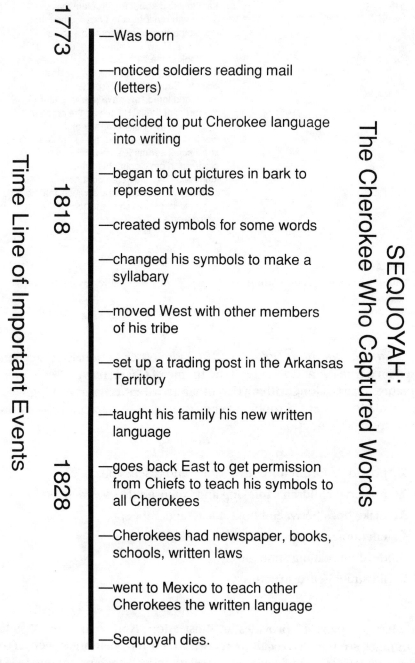

SEQUOYAH: The Cherokee Who Captured Words

Time Line of Important Events

1773 —Was born

—noticed soldiers reading mail (letters)

—decided to put Cherokee language into writing

—began to cut pictures in bark to represent words

—created symbols for some words

—changed his symbols to make a syllabary

—moved West with other members of his tribe

1818 —set up a trading post in the Arkansas Territory

—taught his family his new written language

—goes back East to get permission from Chiefs to teach his symbols to all Cherokees

1828 —Cherokees had newspaper, books, schools, written laws

—went to Mexico to teach other Cherokees the written language

—Sequoyah dies.

Figure 2–3
Time Line

		CHARACTERS I'LL REMEMBER		

NAME	Sequoyah	Johnny Tremain	Petronella	Karana
WHERE WE MET	Connections Basal Factual/Fiction	Historical Fiction	Fairytale	Fiction / Factual
TITLE	Sequoyah: The Indian Who Captured Words	Johnny Tremain	Petronella	Island of the Blue Dolphins
AUTHOR	Lillie Patterson	Esther Forbes	Jay Williams	Scott O'Dell
WHERE/WHEN THEY LIVED	West/East 1773 / 1828	Boston around 1774		
WHY THEY ARE SIGNIFICANT TO ME				
OTHERS LIKE THEM	Little Tree		Sleeping Beauty	
I'M LIKE THEM				

Figure 2-4
Characters I'll Remember

THEMATIC UNIT: PLACES

After reading in "Sequoyah" and *Johnny Tremain* about our country in another time, it might be appropriate to explore further the America that existed before the twentieth century. All stories take place in a certain time and place. Laura Ingalls Wilder portrays the life of a family as they help settle the American West. Her "Little House" series, made into a long-running television show, has delighted many elementary school children. Her books, of which the first of eight is *Little House in the Big Woods* (1953), make excellent material for reading aloud to students. *Sarah Plain and Tall* (1988) by Patricia MacLachlan, a fifty-eight page Newbery Award winner, continues this theme in a small, sod house on the Nebraska prairie.

As a complement to these novels, the basal, *Connections,* contains an excerpt from *Caddie Woodlawn* and an informational piece entitled "Frontier Schools." Although *Caddie Woodlawn* takes place in Minnesota and not the old West, it takes students to a similar time when settlers were just beginning to populate the outlying regions of the United States. Geography study can be included as students identify the various regions and the different conditions found in each. Students can complete literature charts, similar to the one on page 49, for each of the pieces read.

"Frontier Schools" takes a look at a specific slice of life on the American frontier, life in the schoolhouse. The teacher can prepare students for this reading by modeling the thought processes of an effective reader (see page 50).

The literature chart for this particular piece might look something like the one on page 51. This handout, or one similar to it, can be given to students to complete as they read and discuss this work, comparing schools of 100 years ago to their experiences in schools today.

A rich addition to this unit is a work such as Shirley Glubok's *The Art of the Old West* (1988). The art of a time and a place is often overlooked in reading/language arts programs. However, it provides a valuable complement to works of both fiction and nonfiction.

Numerous similar elements, such as emphasis on comprehension skills and use of all four language skill areas, are evident in the thematic units described. with the most obvious being the complementary nature of the basal reader and works of literature. We have only offered a glimpse at how basals and literature can be combined to produce a cohesive program; the possibilities for integrating literature into the reading program are virtually endless.

WHY IS THERE A NEED FOR A UNIFIED LANGUAGE ARTS CURRICULUM?

Several elements were purposefully incorporated into the sample units that we have described in this article. Besides using to the fullest extent

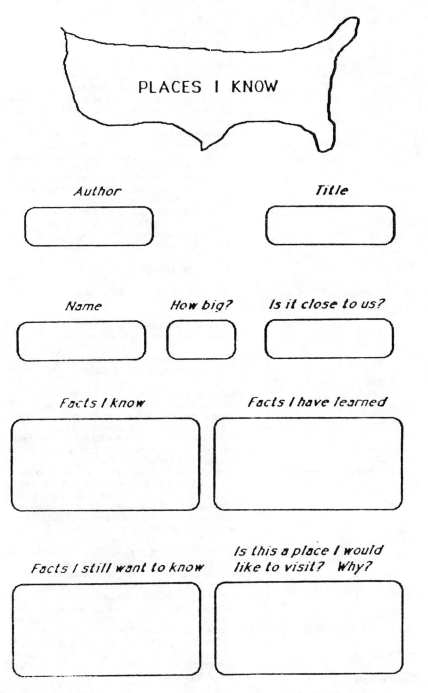

Figure 2-5
Places I Know

A: Modeling

Frontier Schools

Take a moment to look at *just* the title and pictures in this selection. What pictures or words caught your attention? Why? [Discuss] As I'm looking at the the title and pictures in this text, I'm wondering what it would have been like to attend school over one hundred years ago. If someone asked you to describe a school one hundred years ago, what do you think it would have been like? [List predictions on butcher paper chart. Include a fact column.] When we finish we can check the facts from the story with our predictions. Now take another minute to look at the section heading in blue letters. Which one of the headings are you most interested in finding more information on? [Discuss] How do these pictures and headings help us know what we will be reading about? How do you think this selection will be different from a "story"?

PREVIEW/ PREDICTION

Discuss the following:

1. Unlike a story which has characters, this text does not.

2. This text is divided into sections whereas a story is usually continuous.

3. This text is based on historical facts alone Stories are often fictional.

BUILDING BACKGROUND

I already know some facts about frontier life. I wonder if these will be discussed in the text. The central town usually had a blacksmith, restaurant, a saloon, a general store and a one room schoolhouse. I wonder how school was different from our school today, and if there are any similarities. I am going to read this to compare and contrast education then and now. Please follow along in your books as I read aloud. "When the first pioneer families settled in a new area, there were no schools of any kind. Young children were sometimes taught at home in spare moments by an older brother or sister. . . ."

SETS PURPOSE

Raise your hand if you see differences already. As I'm reading this, I am already finding several differences, and I need to start listing some of these on my chart. [Use butcher paper for modeling.] Because there seems to be so much information given, you will find it helpful to write it down on your chart also. What, if any, differences can you see thus far? [Discuss] and list on chart.] I'd like you to work with your partner for the next 15 minutes. Complete as much of the chart as you can in that time. Remember to look for similarities and differences.

CHECK FOR UNDERSTANDING

Figure 2–6
Modeling: Frontier Schools

Frontier Schools

	Present	Both	Past
The School house	1. Not taught at home 2. Taught by cert. teacher 3. Blackboard, overhead, dry erase, computers 4. Brick or cement 5. Desks and tables 6. Modern utilities 8. Drinking fountain 9. Few chores before school 10. To school by bus or car 11. Automatic buzzer	4. Few or no windows 7. Crowded 8. Walk	1. Taught at home 2. Taught by brother, sister, neighbor 3. Dirt and stick 4. Wood or sod 5. Benches - no desks 6. No electricity plumbing, water, etc. 8. Bucket and dipper 9. Did many chores before school 10. Walk long distance, horseback. or wagon 11. Iron bell rung by teacher
Subjects	13. Separate grades 14. Large groups 15. Many textbooks 17. Do math on paper 18. Geography text, films, videos, maps, globes	12. Same subjects 16. Spelling bees 19. Recitation	13. All grades 1-8 14. Teacher worked with a few at a time 15. Few texts; brought books from home 17. Mental math 18. Geography taught by singing; no maps
Teachers	22. Teach ten months 23. Have own homes 24. Have much training and education	20. Hard to find 21. Low pay	22. Taught 3-4 months 23. Boarded at student homes 24. Little training; few requirements

Figure 2-7
Frontier Schools

what is available in the basal and outside sources, such as stories, novels and magazines, these units include attention to all of the language arts: reading, writing, speaking, and listening. This integration seems logical to many professionals who have always understood the interrelationship among the language arts processes. These connections have long been recognized in the language skills of reading and writing: (1) as two sides of the same coin (Squire, 1983); (2) as similar language processes that structure and produce print (Flood, Lapp & Farnan, 1985); (3) as communication processes through which we function within the world, exercising control and promoting social interactions (Anderson & Lapp, 1988); and (4) as natural extensions of children's lives (Froese, 1989).

In addition, educators have begun to acknowledge that all four language arts processes are interrelated communication processes, through which learners gain as well as give information. In other words, they all relate to the individual's proficiency as a language user and contribute to overall literacy development. Therefore, if these processes are to be developed by all learners, instruction must be developed that allows students to use actively and meaningfully their reading, writing, speaking, and listening skills.

HOW DOES THE BASAL READER COMPLEMENT AN INTEGRATED LANGUAGE ARTS PROGRAM?

The creation of an integrated language arts program depends upon appropriate use of time, texts, tasks, and tests.

Time

As Thonis (1983, p.235) suggests, development of effective literacy processes takes time for all students in any language. Students need to be given ample time to participate in meaningful reading, writing, listening, and speaking experiences. Time for language learning means time for interacting, evaluating, and producing the language of understanding, skepticism, irony, doubt, and passion through fiction, history, science, poetry, and political science. An educated individual is one who is versed in both narrative and expository text. If a basal meets specified selection criteria for varied explorations, it should provide a productive avenue for development of all language skills in a variety of content areas.

Anderson, Wilson, and Fielding (1988) found that there is a clear relationship between leisure-time reading and achievement. Children who spend time reading become better readers. This should not be surprising, since this is true of most of life's activities. We get good at what we do, and we are motivated to do that at which we do well. Morrow and Weinstein (1986) also suggest that children should have the opportunity to select some of their reading materials. Therefore, a wide variety of materials should be available to them, whether these materials are collected and placed in the classroom or are available at other sites, such as school libraries.

While it is crucial that we delete from our curriculum the mind-numbing repetition of worksheets devoid of meaningful instruction, independent activities that allow time for rehearsal and reflection are definitely necessary. Many such activities are provided in teacher's manuals of basals readers, and it is time efficient to use these manuals rather than working to recreate them. For this reason, teacher's manuals should be carefully examined to glean the language rich experiences, and time should be set asked for their inclusion in a unified curriculum.

Texts

As we have already discussed, materials appropriate in a unified language arts curriculum should be rich with good literature and meaning-ful language activities. In evaluating the place of the basal in such a program, the teacher needs to ask whether the contemporary basal contains a wide range of readings and activities that ensure students' active participation in listening, speaking, reading, and writing activities. The answer will be yes, for the newest basals provide a well-integrated language arts foundation that includes a variety of literary genre.

These basals have been designed to create a balance between fiction and nonfiction works and to provide a broad spectrum of text types. As Heymsfeld (1989, p. 68) notes, "Basals today are not the rigid, poorly written exercises some . . . would have us believe. They include favorite poems, excerpts from fine children's literature, and well-written nonfiction."

Tasks

Only through a range of language experiences will we be able to help students not only to read history, literature, and science but also to talk and write about their perspectives on an issue or event; to view it from a different angle; to question assertions, works, and issues; to formulate and test hypotheses for alternative solutions; and to listen to and alternatively respect and question the thoughts of others. Only through a variety of language tasks can students explore their world and come to a better understanding of it and themselves.

Personal growth becomes reality through the varied language tasks found in contemporary basals, as students are engaged in reading quality works and in listening, speaking and reading activities before, during, and after reading. An integrated approach is fostered because these language skills cannot be developed apart from one another. Students need practice sculpting thoughts through all language processes; and ideas are shaped as they are shared, challenged, and refined.

In a unified, language-rich classroom, students are given the opportunity to respond through talk and writing to the myriad ideas encountered in their reading and shared conversations. Student response should be valued and encouraged, since facility with language in all of its forms ensures communication. When students share their responses, they are not only put in the position of having to clarify thoughts and ideas in order to communicate them to others, but also have their ideas molded by the responses of others.

Tests

Evaluation in a unified language arts program must include multiple measures and forms of feedback. "A single score, whether it is a course grade or a percentile score from a norm referenced test, almost always fails to accurately report students' overall progress" (Flood & Lapp, 1989). Reliance only on paper and pencil assessments with pass or fail feedback are as outmoded as using one text with only one type of instructional activity. Flexible evaluation, offering informational feedback, must be used to assess students' accomplishments, their growth, and their needs. A single measure of performance is an unacceptable measure of whether or not learning has occurred. Instead, language development must be assessed continuously, with teachers continually directing and redirecting classroom activities to provide growth opportunities for all students. Teachers must be keen observers of student growth, for one of the most reliable indicators of student development is the judgment of an informed teacher. This is not to suggest that paper and pencil tests can never be useful; however, as single and definitive indicators of student progress, they are inadequate.

Educators who are attempting to select texts and tests that complement the goals of a unified language arts curriculum will find today's basals provide significant help in meeting this challenge, for contemporary basal programs present testing as synonymous with performance and learning. They encourage assessment to become a part of every lesson, since continual evaluation is a factor in providing effective instruction for all students.

WHAT IS THE ROLE OF LANGUAGE ARTS IN OTHER CURRICULUM AREAS?

Now that we have discussed the efficacy of an integrated language arts program, the next point to explore is the challenge of integrating a unified language arts approach throughout the entire curriculum. Language arts instruction must permeate all classroom experiences, not just one class period per day. The reason for this is apparent as we observe the routines of students on any given day. When students participate in science, math, or social studies activities, they employ all of the language arts processes. They often *listen* to ideas being shared; they *speak* about their ideas; they may be involved in the *reading* of these content materials, as well in the *writing* of reports, journals, and notes. All of the language arts processes are natural components of all subjects across the curriculum.

A unified language arts approach can be illustrated in the following way:

Students are encouraged to respond and react to literature and real-life experiences through writing. Writing suggestions range from structured composition activities using a process approach, to informal reporting in a reading/writing log, written responses to questions, and personal reactions to selections. Basic to the development of success in reading and writing is fluency in speaking and listening. By participating in individual and group oral language and listening activities, students share background information, compare and analyze the themes and values revealed in selections, dramatize and create oral presentations (Arnold, Smith, Flood, & Lapp, 1988).

CONCLUSIONS

No one source, activity, or strategy will address the needs of all of our students. Although instruction may have been approached at one time as if one text would provide all necessary curricular selections and instructional suggestions, if that were ever the case, it is certainly not so today. The works of literature we choose for our classrooms, on their own, may not always be appropriate to address all of the issues that are relevant to our students' needs. On the other hand, no basal collection provides instruction through which all skills will be taught as we think they should be, nor will all basal reading selections be adequate for our particular goals and needs. This is why every classroom should be supplied with two integral components: a wide array of materials from which to choose, including an up-to-date basal reading program that contains a supply of good literature, and an informed teacher/decision-maker.

REFERENCES

Anderson, P., & Lapp, D. (1988). *Language skills in elementary education,* 4th ed. New York: Macmillan Publishing Co.

Anderson, R. C., Hiebert, E. H., Scott, J. A., & Wilkinson, I. A. (1985). *Becoming a nation of readers: The report of the commission on reading.* Champaign, Illinois: Center for the Study of Reading.

Anderson, R. C. & Pearson, P. D. (1984). A schema-theoretic view of basic processes in reading comprehension. In. P. David Pearson (Ed.). *Handbook of reading research.* New York: Longman.

Anderson, R. C., Wilson, P. & Fielding, L. (1988). Growth in reading and how children spend their time outside of school. *Reading Research Quarterly, 23*(3) 285-303.

Applebee, A. N. (1978). Studies in the spectator role? An approach to response in literature. In C. R. Cooper (Ed.). *Researching response to literature and the teaching of literature,* 92-99. New York: Atheneum.

Arnold, V., Smith, C., Flood, J., & Lapp, D. (1988). *Connections: Language arts/reading program.* New York: Macmillan Publishing Co.

Connections. (1989). New York: Macmillan.

Cullinan, B. E. (1987). Inviting readers to literature. In B. E. Cullinan (Ed.). *Children's literature in the reading program,* 2-14, Newark, Delaware: International Reading Association.

Durkin, D. (1987). Influences on basal reader programs. *The Elementary School Journal, 87*(3), 332-341.

Flood, J., & Lapp, D. (1989). Reporting reading progress: A comparison portfolio for parents. *The Reading Teacher, 42*(7), 508-515.

Flood, J., Lapp, D. & Farnan, N. (1985). A reading-writing procedure that teaches expository paragraph structure. *The Reading Teacher, 39*(6), 556-563.

Forbes, E. (1946). *Johnny Tremain.* Boston: Houghton Mifflin.

Fries, C. C. (1962). *Linguistics and reading.* New York: Holt, Rinehart, and Winston.

Froese, V. (1989). A special issue of empowerment through literacy. *The Reading Teacher, 42*(8), 559.

Gardiner, J. R. (1980). *Stone fox.* New York: Harper & Row.

Gersten, R., & Carnine, D. (1986). Direct instruction in reading comprehension. *Educational Leadership, 43*(7), 70-78.

Glubok, S. "The Art of the Old West" (1988) in *Connections: Language arts/reading program.* New York: Macmillan Publishing Co.

Heymsfeld, C. (1989). Filling the hole in whole language. *Educational Leadership, 46*(6), 65-68.

New directions in reading instruction. (1988). Newark, Delaware: International Reading Association.

Iser, W. (1978). *The act of reading: A theory of aesthetic response.* Baltimore: Johns Hopkins University Press.

MacLachlan, P. (1985). *Sarah, plain and tall.* New York: Harper & Row.

Morrow, L. M., & Weinstein, C. S. (1986). Encouraging voluntary reading: The impact of a literature program on children's use of library centers. *Reading Research Quarterly, 21,* 330-346.

O'Dell, S. (1960). *Island of The Blue Dolphins.* Boston, MA: Houghton Mifflin.

Palincsar, A. S., & Brown, A. L. (1986). Metacognitive strategy instruction. *Exceptional Children, 53*(2), 118-124.

Rosenblatt, L. (1938, 1976). *Literature as exploration,* 3rd ed. New York: Noble and Noble Pubs, Inc.

Sebesta, S. L. (1979). What do young people think about the literature they read? *Reading newsletter, 8,* Rockleigh, New Jersey: Allyn & Bacon, Inc.

Stahl, S. A., & Miller, P. D. (1989). Whole language and language experience approaches for beginning reading: A quantitative research synthesis. *Review of Educational Research, 59*(1), 87-116.

Squire, J. (1983). Composing and comprehending: Two sides of the same basic process. *Language Arts, 60*(5), 581-589.

Thonis, E. (1983). *The English-Spanish connection.* New Jersey: Santillana Publishing Co.

Tompkins, J. P. (Ed.). (1980). *Reader response criticism: From formalism to post structuralism.* Baltimore: Johns Hopkins University Press.

Venezky, R. L. (1987). A history of the American reading textbook. *The Elementary School Journal, 87*(3), 247-265.

Wilder, L. I. (1953). *Little house in the big wood.* New York: Harper & Row.

Williams, J. (1980). Petronella. In W. Dun (Ed.). *Weavers.* Boston, MA: Houghton Mifflin Co.

3

Technology in the Teaching of Literature-based Reading Programs

Robert J. Rickelman and William A. Henk

As the thrust of this volume clearly indicates, many educators now place high quality children's and adolescent literature at the very heart of reading instruction. They have come to believe that first-rate reading fare, with its vivid descriptions, riveting plot lines, and fascinating characters and themes, will literally mesmerize young readers. Once captivated and spellbound, these children will revel in the exhilaration that good literature provides, all the while laying the foundation for a lifetime of successful, gratifying, and pleasurable reading experiences (Lamme, 1987; Newman, 1985).

Along with this welcome trend toward literature-based reading curricula, educators find themselves immersed in a veritable explosion of technology. Microcomputers of the recent past have rapidly given way to newer models whose speed and memory capacities rival larger mainframe computers. CD-ROM (Compact Disc-Read-Only Memory), hard disk, and optical disk technologies, when used in conjunction with microcomputers and their accompanying software, offer far more powerful and exciting applications. In fact, the realm of microcomputing now includes interactive text adventures, creative writing and editing programs, HyperText, speech production, sophisticated color graphis, and highly efficient database searches.

Despite the intimidating ring of this specialized jargon, educators need not be overwhelmed by the possibilities technology offers. On the contrary, the premise of this chapter, that teachers can use technology to enhance literature-based reading instruction, stems mainly from our belief that technology is no longer reserved exclusively for the obsessed or technically inclined educator. Like countless other consumers, teachers have felt the impact of various media technologies in their personal lives. Our automobiles and homes boast audio cassette and compact disc (CD) players. Video cassette recorders (VCR), stereo televisions, personal computers, video cameras, and advanced audio systems literally abound. Yet, as consumers, we remain poised to purchase the next piece of technological gadgetry that grabs our fancy.

The unprecedented growth in both instructional technology and literature-based reading curricula is encouraging, but beyond similar timing, what do these emerging trends have to do with one another? Can the two be integrated functionally? Will attempts to merge technology with high quality literature either taint the magical appeal of the literature or limit the natural fascination generated by the hardware? Can technology possibly enhance and expand the impact of a literature-based reading program?

In this chapter, we address these and other questions related to the relationship between technology and a literature-based reading curriculum. To do so, we have adopted a broad definition of technology that includes a spectrum of hardware and accompanying software. Besides devoting considerable attention to microcomputer-related topics, our discussion includes more familiar technologies such as audio cassette recorders, compact disc players, filmstrip and film projectors, and videocassette recorders.

The discussion begins with a general description of how technology can be integrated into literature-based reading approaches. Then we address the impact of various technologies on the literature-driven reading curricula. More specifically, we provide a brief history of effective past applications, describe current uses with recommendations for practice, and, finally, attempt to give educators a glimpse of exciting future instructional possibilities.

TECHNOLOGY AND LITERATURE: AN UNCOMFORTABLE MARRIAGE?

On the surface, the union between technology and literature would seem to be fraught with problems. Literature is a decidedly intimate medium, intended to stimulate, stretch, and satisfy the human imagination. By contrast, the connotation of technology is cold and machinelike, linear and uninventive, the very antithesis of humanism.

Technology and literature, however, share some important common ground. When used creatively by teachers, both offer near limitless possibilities for expanding students' minds. In this context, both technology and literature can be viewed as vehicles that allow participants to experience imaginative and bold new worlds. And in each instance, the greatest potential threat to instructional effectiveness is a failure to exploit the medium's limits. Likewise, the ideal integration between technology and literature-based reading curricula will require creativity, inspiration, insight, and conviction.

HOW CAN TECHNOLOGY AND LITERATURE BE MERGED?

In our minds, reading educators can learn to use technology as a means to enrich and cultivate the already provocative powers of high quality literature as an instructional medium. They must first, of course, be intimately familiar with the literature they choose to anchor their curriculum. Similarly, they must be highly aware of the range of various technologies, their respective capabilities, and the availability of accompanying software. Finally, teachers must be able to envision the general role each technology will play in their literature-based curriculum as well as the specific role each might serve with regard to individual stories.

Teachers must approach the use of technology in literature-based instruction much like conductors of symphonies would orchestrate the relative contributions of the many instruments at their disposal. Individual teachers will show preferences for certain technologies over the others. Some will be used habitually; others will never be used. On occasion, a certain story might lend itself to a particular technology or combination of technologies. Here the teacher is seen as an informed decision-maker, empowered by credible knowledge of both the nuances of the literature and the capabilities of the technology.

COMPUTERS IN THE LITERATURE-BASED PROGRAM

No other form of technology has been as predominant in the schools in the past ten years as computers. Most school districts have invested heavily in microcomputer hardware and software. However, relatively few have made a major commitment to training teachers in how to integrate computers into their classroom teaching. Coupled with the strong acceptance of computers in the public sector, this trend toward computer-based technology can, at times, seem overwhelming.

Many educators just now seem to be coming to terms with computers in the school curriculum. Some are discovering that it is difficult to integrate available computer program into more traditional text-based lessons. Some fail to realize that, in spite of exaggerated claims, computers in the classroom are only as effective as the humans controlling them. Therefore, it makes sense for teachers to become familiar with the possibilities computers offer to developing a strong, literature-based curriculum.

Today's teachers who wish to use computers in a literature-based reading program have two major choices. First, they can use software that has been designed to be used in conjunction with well-known children's literature books. Second, teachers and students can use different software that would allow them to develop their own material. Each of these choices offer some important challenges to teachers using computers in the classroom.

Using Existing Software

In the past few years, software publishers have begun to develop programs specifically meant to be used in conjunction with children's literature books. Typically, the books chosen are award winning stories or those judged by many to be "good" literature. In some cases, familiar nursery nursery rhymes or children's songs are used.

There are two kinds of programs that teachers can use in conjunction with children's books. One type, often used with younger readers, uses synthesized speech to read stories to children. Synthesized speech allows the computer to talk. The quality of the speech can vary from a dull monotone to speech almost indistinguishable from the real human voice. The *Talking Text Library,* published by Scholastic, is a typical program of this type. Colorful graphics, intended to motivate the students, are combined with text. As each screen of the story is viewed, the text appears at the bottom. The computer highlights each word as it is spoken by the computer. The program also has printer capabilities, so that the stories can be reread at a later time away from the computer. A special speech synthesizer chip or card is needed with most computers in order to use this program. Stories available in this series include *The Three Billy Goats Gruff,*

The Three Bears, and *Sleeping Beauty.* Not only will this type of program allow children to practice learning to read, but it will also give them listening practice using well-known stories.

The second type of software that teachers can purchase assumes that children have already read a book, and it includes exercises focusing on skills and promoting further enjoyment of the book. Sunburst Communications has adopted several Newbery Award winners to this format. Students work on various comprehension and vocabulary skills as they view graphics related to books such as *Charlotte's Web, Mr. Popper's Penguins,* and *Island of the Blue Dolphin.* Mindscape Inc. has also developed a similar set of programs in its *The Reading Workshop* series, intended for Grades 4-9. These programs could be used individually for students who particularly enjoyed the story, for poor readers who wish to practice related skills, or by the whole class as a means of enrichment.

When judging the value of these programs in the literature-based curriculum, we think it makes sense to ask several questions before purchasing them. First, is the story basically true to the original version? Most of the programs condense the story in order to create manageable lessons. The integrity of the story needs to be maintained. Second, does the program utilize the unique capabilities offered by the computer? Some teachers have rightfully complained that a program achieved little more than what could just as easily be accomplished on paper, or with more traditional audio-video equipment. While just using the computer is motivational for some students, the software should promote both learning about and the appreciation of good, quality literature. Third, do the activities used in conjunction with the story extend or enhance the curriculum set forth by the teacher? It is important that teachers use the computer in a way that fits into the curriculum plan, not change the curriculum in order to make a computer program fit. Overall goals of a literature-based reading curriculum should be decided on before any investment is made in computer material, and they must be maintained throughout every dimension of the program.

Another type of readily available software that allows a student access to literature is the interactive text adventure (Layton, 1986). In these programs, students must make decisions throughout the text that directly affect the outcome of the story. Often these programs are fantasy adventures in which the student using the program is one of the main characters. The student must be able to follow the story line and write the next action to be taken. Each time the story if read, different actions could lead to a different story line. A major strength of this kind of program is that a student can use the program many times to create many stories. Thus, one program could maintain student interest for an entire school year. A weakness of interactive text adventures is that few of the programs now available would be considered quality literature. Still, students with a negative attitude toward reading are often willing to read these interactive stories, even though many are written at a relatively difficult reading level.

Creating Your Own Software

While there are relatively few programs available for the teacher to use that directly relate to children's literature, there are many options for teachers and students to create their own stories to be read by others. It is in this area that a resourceful teacher can push students to the limit in creativity and foster enjoyment and appreciation of both reading and writing.

There are several different kinds of programs that allow teachers and students the opportunity to become involved in the writing process. Some are very structured, in that the user follows a set procedure in order to generate text within a limited framework. Others are very unstructured, allowing for more flexibility in design and use. Several of the more popular programs currently available will be discussed.

Writing Assistance Programs

Writing assistance programs provide the students with a guide for writing and often illustrating an original story. Some of these programs offer prewriting activities to help the student brainstorm, plan, and organize a story. Others allow students to use and modify provided graphics to create an original illustration and then write a story to go with it. In either case, a major goal is to get students involved in writing activities, often a difficult goal.

An example of a program that allows students to create an illustration and then to write about it is *Creation* (Pelican), available from Scholastic. The student begins by selecting a background for the story from those provided by the program. Examples include a cave, a street scene, and a castle atop a big mountain. Once the background is set, students can choose props to impose onto the background. Props could include odd characters, animals, furniture, and assorted vehicles. Students decide where on the background to put the items chosen. Once the illustration is completed, the student can write about the illustration, making up stories to go along with the strange creatures created. These stories and illustrations can then be printed and put into an individual or class book. These books could then be placed in a classroom or school library for others to read.

Story Tree (Scholastic) is a program that allows students the opportunity to create interactive stories. Unlike *Creation,* which is limited in the sense that students must choose material provided in the program, *Story Tree* operates on the principle of frames. A frame is a single screen from a computer monitor. In creating each frame, students must provide their own text and then create options for the reader to choose after reading the frame. One option is for the reader to continue on to the next frame. Another option is for the writer to give the readers up to four choices. Each choice will send the story on a different path. For instance, a frame might ask the reader, "Do you want to open Door A, Door B, or Door C?" As readers choose different doors, the plot can go in multiple directions. A third option allows the writer to create two choices for how the story will continue and to assign a percentage value designating how often the computer will automatically pick one choice compared to the other. Thus, even though a story has been read previously, it can change during subsequent reading without the reader making any different choices! One advantage of this program is that a class could work on an ongoing story, with the reader becoming the writer when coming to an unresolved story line.

For nonreaders, *Talking Text Writer* (Scholastic) is a talking word processor, which can orally read back anything typed into a file. In addition to creating children's books that form a classroom library of student works, it could also save stories in files that could be listened to and simultaneously read on the screen. Older authors could share their stories with younger readers without concern for reading ability.

With the popularity of the Apple IIGS in many classrooms, more programs utilizing the outstanding speech capabilities of the computer will be forthcoming. These programs will be quite different from those currently popular in many schools. As these programs are introduced, it is important for teachers to be aware of their availability and potential. Several excellent resources are:

Instructor (Scholastic Inc., P.O. Box 3018, Southeastern, PA 19398-3018)

The Computing Teacher (ICCE, University of Oregon, 1787 Agate St., Eugene, OR 97403)

Technology and Learning (Peter Li, Inc., 2451 East River Road, Dayton, OH 45439)

Microcomputers in Reading Special Interest Group, International Reading Association (c/o Dr. Kent Layton, Department of Elementary Education, Arkansas State University, State University, AR 72467-0940)

FrEdWriter

FrEdWriter (Free Educational Writer) is a word processor for the Apple computer that has several advantages over more traditional word processors (Starshine, 1990). First, once the first copy is purchased for $20 from Computer Using Educators (CUE), the user is free to make additional copies for no charge. Second, the program only takes up part of the disk so that room is available for students to store files on their own copy of the disk. Thus, using a computer with only one disk drive does not necessitate constant disk swapping, which can be annoying, confusing, and sometimes costly. Third, a Spanish version of FrEdWriter is available for ESL students who speak Spanish or for those interested in writing in Spanish. Finally, this program allows the teacher to insert prompts into a file, messages that are only seen by the writer and are not printed. Thus, a teacher writing prompts could help the student by providing a step-by-step outline to be used for writing creative stories or poetry or by asking the student to provide information relating story structure elements or other specific information.

Databases in the Literature-based Classroom

While many teachers have learned to use the word processor, relatively few have mastered the database. Databases offer flexibility in terms of managing children's books in a classroom library and offer students a way to organize, search, and recall information related to books they are reading.

One way in which databases may be used is to help organize a classroom library of children's books. The first step in constructing a database is to decide on categories of information to be logged for each entry. An example of a database framework using Appleworks is seen in Figure 3-1. Using this form, teachers and students could categorize each book according to descriptors agreed upon by the class. The power of databases is in searching for information once the database is completed. Individual books could be searched, as well as books which meet a certain criteria. For example, if a student wanted to see some information on *Dear Mr. Henshaw* that record could easily be found if any information about the book is known to the

File: Lit   **CHANGE NAME / CATEGORY**   Escape: Review/Add/Change

Category names

Title	Options:
Author	
Publisher	Change filename
Illustrator	Return Go to first category
Year Published	
Topic	
Copies Available	
Grade Level	
Interest Level	
Comments 1	
Comments 2	
Comments 3	
Comments 4	

Type filename: Lit   **1022K Avail.**

Figure 3–1
Database Form for Children's Books

student (see Figure 3-2). If a teacher or student wanted to find a list of books written by Beverly Cleary for the fourth grade reading level, a list could be retrieved and printed. If a student knew the name of an illustrator that he or she particularly appreciated, a quick search would easily yield that information. As students read different books throughout the school year, information about the book, including the names of the children who had previously read it, could also be entered. By the end of the year, a complete listing of all books read by students within a particular class could be generated. In this way, it would be simple to see which student read the most books, which author was the most popular, and which topics that seemed to appeal to the class the most.

Another use for databases would be as a means to allow a student to store comments about a certain book after reading it. Once the comments are typed into the databases program, other students could easily retrieve a record of the book, read peer evaluations, and then add their own comments after they have finished reading.

Databases can offer a lot of flexibility in the literature-based classroom. Students and teachers who save and retrieve relevant information about

File: Lit   REVIEW / ADD / CHANGE   Escape: Main Menu

Selection: All records

Record 1 of 1 (1 selected)

Title: Dear Mr. Henshaw

Author: Beverly Cleary

Publisher: Morrow

Illustrator: Paul O. Zelinsky

Year Published: 1983

Topic: Troubled boy writes to author and diary

Copies Available: 5

Grade Level: 4

Interest Level: 3-6

Comments 1: Begins with Leigh's letters to children's author

Comments 2: Moves to diary writing

Comments 3: Comments on absent father, lunch bag thief

Comments 4: -

Type entry or use @ commands   @ - ? for Help

Figure 3–2
Database Record for Individual Book

books to be used at a later date are using the computer to help manage information and to make it easily accessible.

AUDIO TECHNOLOGIES AND LITERATURE-BASED READING INSTRUCTION

For children's literature to qualify as outstanding, it must combine superior visual *and* auditory elements. In fact, the rhythm, sound, and flow of the text affects the overall quality of a story more than the accompanying artwork. A weak story with uninspired word choice remains second rate at best regardless of how well illustrated it might be. On the other hand, strong, skillfully narrated story scripts can stand alone. A talented author's masterful weaving of words can grab and hold the reader's attention, elicit elaborate pictures in the mind, and arouse the powers of imagination (Cullinan, 1987; Stoodt, 1988).

The importance of the audio portion of the story explains why oral storytelling is such a revered art form. Without the benefit of illustrations, an accomplished storyteller or narrator can nonetheless hold children captive. Add an inspired musical score and realistic sound effects as a background and the result can be enchanting.

In this section audio technology and its role in a literature-based reading curriculum will be discussed. Our belief is that audio media can heighten children's appreciation of literature and lay the cognitive groundwork for story comprehension during reading (Anderson, Hiebert, Scott, & Wilkinson, 1985; Cohen, 1968; Wells, 1986).

To some educators, the use of audio media may pale in comparison with the intimate narration a teacher can provide. In some respects, however, audio media may offer some advantages over teacher narration. First, recorded audio can be played over and over again, thereby allowing the teacher to devote time to other instructional activities. Through audio technology, children can be repeatedly exposed to a fluent model of reading that helps them to grow in confidence and push toward independence (Chomsky, 1976; Samuels, 1985). Second, beginning and at-risk readers, students learning English as a second language, and even good readers merely wishing to savor a book can all benefit from listening or following along in the accompanying texts. Third, because the narration of audio media is professionally recorded, it tends to be as error free as possible. Even the most adept storytellers and oral readers tend to falter on occasion. Reading, phrasing, and intonation errors are more likely since the teacher must read the book "off to one side." Fourth, recorded media allow for the effective use of sound effects and background music. The highest quality audio media showcase a precise and compelling mix of narration, sounds, and music whose collective intent is to create the finest possible ambience for appreciating the literature.

Our focus on audio media centers primarily on the use of cassette recorders and compact disc players and their respective software. Admittedly, the selection of quality phonograph recordings that can be used in conjunction with story books is considerable; however, phonograph use in schools is nearly obsolete. Most material previously available on phonographs has been converted to cassette tape. Although only a limited number of literature-related compact discs are presently available, this situation is likely to change with the rapid surge in CD player sales and resulting price reductions that make them increasingly affordable for schools.

With their high-speed search capabilities, both cassettes and CDs offer greater accuracy and flexibility in locating specific parts of the story for playing or replaying. Consider also that if, during the playing of a story, the teacher finds it necessary to provide elaboration or to respond to a question, a phonograph becomes unwieldy to use. Cassette tapes and CDs can be stopped and restarted much easier than phonographs. In fact, optional remote control units permit teachers to operate the technology from anywherein the room.

Still another consideration is that both of these newer formats are far easier for children to use without incident. A scratched or heavily fingerprinted record is ruined. Cassettes and CDs, on the other hand, resist children's mishandling. CDs are actually more durable than cassettes and, ultimately, more cost effective. Because their sound reproduction is also superior, CDs become more desirable from an aesthetic standpoint as well.

Instructional Considerations for Using Audio Media

Standard speaker arrangements can project literature-related cassettes and compact discs to any size group of students. When trying to limit any distraction that the cassettes or CDs might create, teachers can choose listening centers with headphones. Besides advocating CD players, our most novel suggestion would be to consider the use of portable component systems, or boom boxes. Because all of the components are housed in one movable unit, boom boxes are extremely convenient. They can be used effectively with large and small groups of students, and they typically have individual or dual headphone capabilities as well.

As with the phonograph format of years past, cassettes and compact discs can be played either alone or in conjunction with the visual presentation of a story book. In many books appropriate for the early grades, pictures play an intentional and sizable role in establishing a visual context for interpretation. When this is the case, children should view the illustrations.

There are three basic forms of audio-supported visual presentation of story books. In the first form, the teacher holds the book open and turns the pages to correspond with the timing of the narration. This approach tends to work effectively with small groups of students since the pictures are difficult for all students to see. The renewed interest in Big Books has reduced this problem.

The second audio-visual presentation technique involves having a student read independently in a copy of the story book as the audio plays. For younger children, it is beneficial for a sound like a beep or a chime to signal that the page should be turned. In this approach, children must be able to keep track of the match between the narration and the text. This matching requires that the narration is reasonably paced and that the pictures are not distracting.

The third way audio technology supports visual presentation occurs with the use of filmstrips. Once again, the audio source, normally a cassette tape, includes signals to indicate a change of frame. Some projectors will advance the filmstrip automatically using a prerecorded signal that may be inaudible. This application generally is used with larger groups.

Sources for Literature-based Cassette Tapes and Compact Discs

Experience points to three very useful sources of literature-based audio and visual technologies: *Windham Hill Records, Opportunities for Learning, Inc.,* and *Weston Woods.* In this section, we focus on audio products.

Windham Hill offers exceptionally high-quality, literature-based recordings in phonograph, cassette, and compact disc formats. All of the titles come under the heading of their *Rabbit Ears "Storybook Classics"* collection. To ensure top caliber recordings, Windham Hill has enlisted narrators including Meryl Streep, Holly Hunter, Robin Williams, Jack Nicholson, Cher, Glenn Close, Kelly McGillis, and Jeremy Irons. This talent is expertly combined with the original scores and performances of several outstanding recording artists such as George Winston, Ry Cooder, Bobby McFerrin, Mark Isham, Tim Story, and Michael Hedges.

At the heart of the Windham Hill audio line are the stories themselves, a rich collection of classic literature that includes:

The Velveteen Rabbit
The Legend of Sleepy Hollow
Thumbelina
Santabear's First Christmas
The Elephant's Child
How the Rhinoceros Got His Skin
The Emperor and the Nightingale

How the Camel Got His Hump
The Tale of Peter Rabbit
The Steadfast Tin Soldier
The Ugly Duckling
Pecos Bill
The Tailor of Gloucester

The beautifully illustrated books that accompany the Windham Hill audio line are the work of the *Picture Book Studio.*

The exceptional craftsmanship and artistic expression of the audio series recently garnered the label two consecutive Grammy awards in the category for Best Children's Recording (*The Elephant's Child* and *Pecos Bill*). Interestingly, four Windham Hill titles were nominated in one year. Reviewers, consumer groups, and the music industry recognize the extraordinary caliber, content, and delivery of Windham Hill's line of children's recordings.

Perhaps the most extensive selection of literature cassettes is available from Opportunities for Learning, Inc., a distributor of reading, literature, and language materials. Several of the series they distribute come in a read-along format while others are intended for listening only and do not include copies of the original books. The selections range in difficulty from beginning reader to young adult levels. Representative series and titles are:

Junior Cassette Libraries
Frog and Toad
Amelia Bedelia
Little Bear

Young Adult Cassette Libraries
The Outsiders
Are You There God? It's Me, Margaret.
Pippi Longstocking

Pocket Classics Read-Alongs
Dr. Jekyll and Mr. Hyde
Moby Dick
The Call of the Wild

Elementary Paperback Read-Alongs
The Emperior's New Clothes
Come Back, Amelia Bedelia

Folk Tales Books and Cassettes
Jack and the Beanstalk
Little Red Riding Hood
Stone Soup
The Three Billy Goats Gruff

Cassette Bookshelves
Hemingway Short Stories
Poe Short Stories

O. Henry Short Stories
Bradbury -Tales of Fantasy

Classics on Cassettes
The Martian Chronicles
The Great Gatsby
The Red Badge of Courage

Walt Disney Read Alongs
Snow White and the Seven Dwarfs
Pinocchio
Cinderella
Winnie the Pooh and Tigger Too
Lady and the Tramp
Sleeping Beauty

Read-Along Books on Cassettes
Huckleberry Finn
Black Beauty
Little Women

The audio materials distributed by Opportunities for Learning, Inc. hail from several different companies including Audio Language Studies, Inc. (ALS), Listening Library, and Random House. As a result, overall generalizations about the full range of materials would be difficult to make. However, the narration, done by the authors of the stories themselves or professional actors and actresses, seems to be consistently well done. Many of the tapes begin with clear directions to children that explain how to read and follow along as well as how to use the recorder. Some of the read-along tapes distributed by the company have no musical accompaniment and limited or no sound effects, aspects that prospective buyers may want to inquire about in advance.

For over 30 years, *Weston Woods* has produced consistently superb literature-based media for children. Under the dedicated and conscientious leadership of Morton Schindel, the company consistently generates materials that serve as industry standards. In the realm of audio technology, the company presently offers thirty-six Read-Along Book/Cassette Packages. Some of the titles available are:

Beauty and the Beast   Caps for Sale
Blueberries for Sal   Danny and the Dinosaur

Doctor DeSoto	Pinkerton, Behave
Goodnight Moon	The Snowy Day
Homer Price Stories	A Weekend with Wendell
In the Night Kitchen	What's Under My Bed
Max's Christmas	Where the Wild Things Are

Like all Weston Woods audiovisual media, the read-along book/cassette packages are excellent. The books are original award winning versions, the narration is inspired, the sound effects are realistic, and the finely crafted original music matches the mood of the stories beautifully.

VISUAL TECHNOLOGIES AND LITERATURE-BASED READING INSTRUCTION

The key element in converting high quality literature into visual media such as films, filmstrips, and videocassettes is keeping the presentation faithful to the original work. Adapted visual media should not depart so dramatically from the book that its artistic flavor is somehow compromised. The new visual medium should elaborate upon the original, never supplanting the qualities that made the book a classic in the first place. To do so, producers must insist that any additional artwork be true to the original in every respect. The new media should allow viewers to experience the same wonder and delight that the original book engenders.

Visual presentation of literature can take four basic forms: *filmstrip, iconographic, full animation,* and *live action.* In the past, iconographic, animated, and live action forms were delivered exclusively via motion picture technology. Now, many of these same 16mm motion pictures appear in a videotape format. It is likely that new adaptations of other stories will follow suit.

Filmstrip presentation lends itself to the task of adapting high quality literature for group use. It creates a bigger-than-life atmosphere for viewing since illustrations can be projected on a large scale. When the room lights have been dimmed, the bold and colorful images demand children's attention even more than the original book could have.

Generally, filmstrip preparation involves photographing each page of the original book onto a single frame of the filmstrip. Some productions go no further. In others, these photographs serve as a general framework into which several new drawings not found in the books are created, photographed, and inserted. Both the original and the additional illustrations are often adapted to conform more effectively to the horizontal frame of the filmstrips. Other modifications include adding color to the white backgrounds for dramatic effect and occasionally taking some liberties with the text.

The frame by frame presentation of a filmstrip is usually accompanied by taped oral narration. Some producers choose not to superimpose the text over the pictures as a way of maintaining fidelity to the original. Children study the images of the filmstrip as they actively attend and listen to the sound track. Although the visual images of a filmstrip predominate the presentation, producers exert their greatest creative impact on the audio portion. They must skillfully blend the narration, the musical background, and a series of recreated sound effects into a unified whole whose pace, texture, and intensity precisely matches the mood of the story.

Iconographic films, an innovative medium developed by Morton Schindel, create the illusion of motion in still pictures. Here the apparent movement of the camera over the original pictures simulates the way a child's eyes might examine the illustrations. Actually the camera is stationary; the picture itself moves on an automated easel that presents the elements of the picture to the camera in such a way that the total composition can be appreciated. By carefully controlling the size of the field, the light intensity and perspective, the speed and direction of movement, and the pace of cutting and dissolving, producers capture the mood and action of the original book (Schindel, 1981). This iconographic technique has been used successfully for several years to transpose literature in audiovisual formats suitable for group presentation.

Compared to iconographic films, *full animation* requires the creation of thousands of new illustrations. To create the illusion of movement, animators must generate about twelve drawings per second of film time. Each drawing is photographed twice so that twenty-four frames (or cels) per second pass the viewer's eyes. A ten-minute fully animated film rendition of a children's book, then, requires at least 7,200 drawings, not including revisions. It appears that the trend in translating literature to audiovisual media is clearly moving toward full animation videocassettes.

Live action literature-based films use actors and actresses and real settings to bring stories to life. In this medium, the cast is chosen for their resemblance to story characters in appearance as well as assumed mannerisms and speech. Scenes are shot in natural or contrived settings that reflect the backdrop maintained in the book. On the whole, live action literature-based films are not prevalent.

INSTRUCTIONAL CONSIDERATIONS FOR USING VISUAL MEDIA

As Schindel (1968) suggested, each visual technology has its own traditions, peculiarities, advantages, and disadvantages. Filmstrips encourage children to use their imaginations to complete the gaps between frames. Iconographic films give children a feel for the original book by simulating the way they might view it. Animation brings the characters as close to life as illustrations permit. Live action films bridge the domains of fantasy and reality.

The kind of visual media a teacher chooses depends on several factors including instructional purpose, thematic and aesthetic appeal, cost, availability, and story length. By previewing the various media, teachers can develop a sense of which will work best with their children under certain circumstances. We believe that the most important consideration to recommend a particular visual media is its ability to motivate children to read the original book.

Generally, teachers can approach the use of literature-based visual media in two ways: formally or informally. Formal activities could be conducted much like a typical reading lesson. The introductory step would involve activating relevant background knowledge, generating interest in the themes, setting a purpose for viewing, and encouraging predictions of possible story content. At various points during the playing of the media, teachers can stop and ask children to predict what they think will happen next and why they think so. Discussions can focus on the accuracy of predictions and how they must be revised according to story content.

Misunderstandings can be clarified and fix-up strategies can also be modeled. Following viewing, children can select or produce the best summary for recounting the story to a friend. Many critical and evaluative viewing activities are also possible after the visual media has concluded.

Informal uses of literature-based visual media may be even more important. Here children view the media strictly for enjoyment. No strings are attached to the viewing; accountability need not be demonstrated. This risk-free viewing helps to develop a pressure-free, lifelong love for literature.

Sources for Literature-Based Visual Media

Our recommended sources for literature-based visual media again include Windham Hill, Opportunities for Learning, Inc., and Weston

Woods. In particular, Weston Woods has been the principal innovator in the translation of picture books into audiovisual media. Their film and video products reflect meticulous attention to detail and what amounts to a labor of love.

Our three primary sources of literature-based visual media differ in terms of production responsibilities. Weston Woods oversees and orchestrates all aspects of film and video production. Opportunities for Learning, on the other hand, distributes videocassettes created by other companies. Windham Hill markets videocassettes, but, in actuality, their responsibility is mainly the production of the audio portions. The videos are expertly prepared by Sony Video Software.

Most audio products from Windham Hill are also available in videocassette form. Only *Thumbelina, The Three Billy Goats Gruff, The Three Little Pigs,* and *Santabear's First Christmas* are not available in a video format at this time.

Opportunities for Learning, Inc. markets several literature-based videocassette series encompassing nearly seventy titles. A partial listing of series and representative sample titles are:

Newbery Video Collection
  Mrs. Frisby and the Rats of NIMH
  Call It Courage

Caldecott Video Collection
  If I Ran the Zoo
  The Bremen-Town Musicians

Primary Caldecott Award Collection
  Hansel and Gretel
  Rumpelstiltskin

Newbery Award Collection
  Sarah, Plain and Tall
  Across Five Aprils

Video Double Classics
  Robert Louis Stevenson Classics
  Mark Twain Classics
  H. G. Wells Classics
  Charles Dickens Classics

The Adventures of Peter Cottontail and His Friends
  Spring Comes to Green Forest
  Peter Changes His Name

Literature Into Film Series
My Side of the Mountain
Romeo and Juliet

Our final source, Weston Woods, creates and distributes over 330 filmstrips as well as 37 animated, 39 iconographic, and 8 live action motion picture and videocassette products. Listed below are just a few of the numerous available titles:

Caps For Sale	Pierre
Curious George Rides a Bike	The Snowy Day
The Emperior's New Clothes	Where the Wild Things Are
The Doughnuts	Stone Soup
The Five Chinese Brothers	The Very Worst Monster
Georgie	Make Way for Ducklings
The Owl and the Pussycat	A Weekend with Wendell
The Most Wonderful Egg in the World	Mufaro's Beautiful Daughters

Many of these titles are available not only as filmstrips, but also as 16mm motion pictures or VHS videocassettes. The company has also entered the personal video market with their *Children's Circle Home Video* series. Each of the series' fourteen videocassettes contains film adaptations of three or four award-winning children's books.

ONWARD TO THE FUTURE

As you can see, technology and children's literature complement each other in many ways. The determining factor in the success or failure of using technology in a literature-based program is the teacher. Only the teacher can see the big picture. Only the teacher can informally assess students' abilities and interests. Only the teacher can determine how well students learn and enjoy literature using different media.

As we look into the future, technological advances should continue to have an impact on the literature-based curriculum. There are two areas we would like to highlight to provide a sample of future possibilities! HyperText and holography.

HyperText

HyperText is a fairly new operating environment first used on an Apple Macintosh computer. It consists of the programmer using *cards* and *stacks* to present information. A card is an individual screen, including graphics, text, sound, or even animation. A stack is a set of related cards. The power of HyperText is in how stacks are interrelated and controlled. By using a computer to control choices given by a programmer, a user can go from stack to stack, or go up or down a hierarchy of cards within a stack.

In a literature-base program, a HyperText format could be used to enhance reading enjoyment by allowing multiple options during reading. For instance, HyperText could be used to explain confusing concepts or provide readers background knowledge essential for story development. If a student is reading a book on slavery during the Civil War and has a problem understanding how slavery began in the United States, he or she could ask for additional information at that point in the story. The text could be written at many different levels of complexity and understanding. If, for instance, a gifted student understood the major concepts presented but desired expanded information about the Underground Railroad, HyperText would allow that student to independently explore, coming back to the story when desired. On the other hand, the reader could have the background necessary to understand the story, in which case the story could be read from the beginning to end with little or no information requested.

HyperText stacks could also be linked to audio and video technologies. For instance, a videodisc or CD-ROM could be used to store images, sound, or both. Thus, a student reading about slavery could ask to see a photograph of Abraham Lincoln or a map of free versus slave states or to hear one of the Lincoln-Douglass debates while viewing photographs of the two statesmen.

HyperText, therefore, allows reading to occur at many different levels, giving the reader the option to request additional information at any point. Thus, the reading becomes three dimensional in the sense that it now also has depth. The reader controls how brief or expanded the text will be, and can ask only for information needed for full understanding and enjoyment. Thus, the effect would be similar to having an expert at hand at all times. A knowledgeable reader would request only minimal information related to a plot if he or she were already familiar with the text material.

Holography

Holography is a process that allows artwork that looks three dimensional to be printed on a two-dimensional medium. Many credit cards now include a holograph, since they are difficult to forge. As you look at a holograph and move it sideways in the light, it appears to be jumping off the card. This technology can also be projected, allowing what appears to be a three-dimensional object to appear in space. Brand (1987) presents an interesting discussion of how holography may be used to design automobiles in the future.

In a literature-based curriculum in the future, holography may allow students to view stories in three dimensions. Characters will literally come alive before the readers' eyes. Readers could even interact directly with the images of the characters, moving around a room to view different angles of their favorites! Since holography will be computer controlled, a favorite section could be replayed or perhaps modified to meet the readers' needs. While this technology is relatively new, it offers exciting possibilities in education.

In spite of all of the promise technology can offer, we believe that the teacher remains the key to the quality and quantity of learning. Technology in the hands of a creative and innovative teacher can foster classrooms where learning is both fun and informative. Used in conjunction with a literature-based reading program, technology can allow teachers to challenge the creativity and curiosity of students.

PUBLISHER'S ADDRESSES

Computer Using Educators (CUE)
P.O. Box 271704
Concord, CA 94527-1704

Mindscapes, Inc.
3444 Dundee Rd.
Northbrook, IL 60062

Opportunities for Learning, Inc.
20417 Nordhoff Street
Department K A 2
Chatsworth, CA 91311

Scholastic Software
2931 East McCarthy Street
P.O. Box 7502
Jefferson City, MO 65102

Sunburst Communication, Inc.
39 Washington Ave.
Box 40
Pleasantville, NY 10570-9971

Weston Woods
Weston, CT 06883-1199

Windham Hill Records
P.O. Box 9388
Stanford, CA 94309-9388

REFERENCES

Anderson, R. C., Hiebert, E. H., Scott, J. A., & Wilkinson, I. A. G. (1985). *Becoming a nation of readers: The report of the commission on reading.* Washington, DC: National Institute of Education.

Brand, S. (1987). *The Media lab: Inventing the future at MIT.* New York: Viking.

Chomsky, C. (1976). After decoding: What? *Language Arts, 53*(3), 288-296, 314.

Cohen, D. (1968). The effect of literature on vocabulary and reading achievement. *Elementary English, 45*(2) 209-213, 217.

Cullinan, B. E. (1987). Inviting readers to literature. In Cullinan, B. E. (Ed.), *Children's literature in the reading program.* Newark, DE: International Reading Association.

Lamme, L. L. (1987). Children's literature: The natural way to learn to read. In Cullinan, B. E. (Ed.), *Children's literature in the reading program.* Newark, DE: International Reading Association.

Layton, K. (1986). Text adventures. *Media and Methods, 23*(4), 14-16.

Newman, J. M. (Ed.) (1985). *Whole language: Theory in use.* Portsmouth, NH: Heinemann, 1985.

Samuels, S. J. (1985). Automaticity and repeated reading. In J. Osborn, P. T. Wilson, & R. C. Anderson (Eds.), *Reading education: Foundations for a literate America.* Lexington, MA: Lexington Books, 215-230.

Schindel, M. (1981). Children's literature on film: Through the audiovisual era to the age of telecommunications. *Annual of the Language Association Division on Children's Literature and the Children's Literature Association, 9,* 1-13.

Schindel, M. (1968). The picture book projected. *School Library Journal.* (Reprint)

Starshine, D. (1990). An inexpensive alternative to word processing — FrEdWriter. *The Reading Teacher, 43*(8), 600-601.

Stoodt, B. D. (1988). *Teaching language arts.* New York: Harper & Row.

Wells, G. (1986). The meaning makers: Children learning language and using language to learn. London: Heinemann.

4

Promoting Recreational Reading

Timothy V. Rasinski

I t may be one of the great ironies of American reading instruction that during the course of successfully learning how to read a significant number of students lose the desire to read. First graders come to school with an intense interest in reading and an intense desire to learn how to read. Yet, by the time fifth and sixth grade comes along many of these same children will have burned out on reading. They will say that they no longer like to read and that they do not choose reading as one of their favorite pastimes.

The problem is called aliteracy — knowing how to read but choosing not to read. Evidence of the existence and development of aliteracy continues to mount. In a study of the leisure time activities of Irish primary students, for example, Greaney (1980) found that only 5.4 percent of students' available leisure time was devoted to reading. Nearly a quarter of his sample did not spend any time reading. Only 6.4 percent of the students gave at least an hour per day to book reading. When Walberg and Tsai (1984) asked children to indicate how much time they spent in the previous day reading for enjoyment, 44 percent responded that they had not read at all. Walberg and Tsai reported that students in their study reported reading only about one day in five. Anderson, Wilson, and Fielding (1988) found that reading books was the leisure time activity that was correlated most closely with proficiency in reading for elementary grade students. Yet, based upon their own results and the results of other studies, Anderson et. al. (1988) estimate that middle grade children in the United States read as little as eight to twelve minutes per day outside of school and only four to five minutes when just book reading is counted. While the reading behavior of school children is less than encouraging, the leisure reading habits of adults are equally distressing. Ley (1979), for example, cited evidence that 10 percent of the American population reads 80 percent of the printed material. Trelease (1985) reported on a study by the Book Industry Study

Group that found that 44 percent of the adults in the United States never read a book in the course of a year.

What is the reason for the drastic turn in attitudes and behaviors from the early elementary grades to the later school years and even adulthood? What is it that turns students off on reading? Certainly, a number of factors may be involved. Excessive television viewing takes time away from that which may be devoted to leisure reading. Boys, in particular, may learn to regard reading as a feminine activity, inappropriate for males. Lack of encouragement for children to read during their leisure hours may also work to minimize children's time devoted to reading.

What happens in school must also be considered a major factor in the diminishment of voluntary reading. The focus of most of the reading instruction that occurs in the United States is on learning how to read. Children are schooled in the skills of reading. Most of the time devoted to reading instruction is spent on becoming a good reader as measured by the standardized reading tests that are meant to determine progress in reading. Those tests do not measure students' attitude toward reading or leisure time reading behavior. Thus, despite the acknowledged importance of a positive attitude toward reading and of engaging in recreational reading both in and outside of school, because these variables are neither measured in school nor used to define excellence in reading instruction they are rarely a salient part of the school reading curriculum.

Nevertheless, aliteracy is a major obstacle in the quest to make all citizens literate. Developing positive reading attitudes and leisure reading habits in children can help to overcome adult aliteracy. Moreover, we know that leisure reading is associated with development of skilled reading. Thus, it makes great sense to work within the school reading curriculum to foster recreational or leisure reading in students.

For the purpose of this chapter recreational reading is defined as reading that is done by a person on his or her own volition and for his or her own purposes. Recreational reading assumes that people who engage in it enjoy a positive attitude toward reading and perceive reading as a meaningful and valuable tool to be used to accomplish their own goals.

ASSESSING READING PERCEPTIONS, ATTITUDES, INTERESTS, AND BEHAVIORS

If we are really interested in making recreational reading an important part of the school reading curriculum the place to begin is the place where the standardized reading tests leave off. We must assess students' perceptions of attitudes toward and interest in reading as well as their current and preferred reading behaviors. We do this to develop a baseline against which to measure progress and to get a sense for each child as a reader. Knowing whether students perceive reading as a process of obtaining meaning or simply getting the words right, whether they enjoy reading and what type of material they like most, and the preferences they have in their own reading can be invaluable in understanding the person as a reader and the reader as a person. The picture that one obtains from assessing these areas is considerably different than the picture that comes from reviewing a set of reading test scores. The information obtained should help in developing recreational reading programs and activities that match the needs, desires, and preferences of students.

The best way to assess students' perceptions, attitudes, interests, and behaviors in reading is to ask them. Either through personal interview or written survey, teachers can acquire a wealth of useful information about students. Figure 4-1 presents some typical questions that could be used to assess students' perceptions, attitudes, interests, and behaviors related to reading.

Perceptions of Reading

How would you describe reading to a person who doesn't know how to read?

Who is the best reader you know? Why do you think this person is a good reader?

When you come to a word you don't know in reading what do you do?

Attitudes Toward Reading

Do you like to read at home? School? why or why not?
Do you enjoy going to your local library? What do you usually do first when you go to the library?

Put the following list of things to do in order in which you would like to do them.

_____Play with friends
_____Watch television
_____Read a favorite book
_____Go out to eat at a fun restaurant
_____Have a good story read to you by your mom or dad
_____Play by yourself
_____Be on a sports team
_____Do your homework
_____Do your chores at home

(continues)

Figure 4-1
Questions for Assessing Students' Reading Perceptions, Attitudes, Interests, and Behaviors

Reading Interests

What are your favorite kinds of stories? Would you rather read books or magazines? If you could be a famous person for one day who would it be? Why?

Do you have any favorite books? Can you name them? If you were hired to create a new TV show what would it be about?

Do you have a favorite author? Who?

Reading Behaviors and Preferences

When you're at home how often do you read? (Circle one)
Everyday
A couple times a week
About one a week
Hardly ever

Do you have a special place at home where you like to read? Describe that place Do you have a special time when you're at home that you like to read? What time is that? Do you ever read to someone at home? Who? Do you like to read or hear stories more than once? Why? Ho do you choose books when you go to the library? When is the best time for you ro read at school? If you could pick any place to read in school where would it be? Why?

Figure 4–1 Continued

It is important to note that there is no one set of questions that is appropriate for all circumstances. The best questions are those that reflect the background and perceive needs of students. Unless attempting to get thorough understanding of one child, the number of questions in an interview or survey should be limited so as to be manageable for both students and teachers.

DEVELOPING A RECREATIONAL READING PROGRAM

The purpose of a recreational reading program (RRP) is to improve students' attitude and behavior related to reading. Essentially we want students to learn to value and enjoy reading and to read regularly for enjoyment.

Recreational reading programs should be tailored to the needs and interests of students as well as teachers' own style of classroom interaction. There are a variety of activities that can be put together to create a recreational reading program that fits the unique personality of any classroom. There is no set formula for fostering recreational reading.

It is important to understand the types of motivation that underline the various activities in an RRP. Activities that have an external motivation lead students to reading by offering a reward that is separate from the reading itself. Earning a prize for reading a certain number of books is an example of external motivation. The promise of a prize is at least partly responsible for motivating students to read. Internal motivation, on the other hand, refers to one's desire to read because of the self-satisfaction and enjoyment one finds in reading itself. Reading is its own motivation.

It should be rather obvious that the goal of a good RRP is to develop in readers an internal motivation for reading. That is not to say that external motivators should be avoided. On the contrary, for some children, especially those who have been thoroughly turned off on reading, external motivators may be the only way to get them back into books. Some children have experienced so much failure and frustration in learning to read and have had so few positive reading experiences that they actively, even aggressively, avoid reading. It is difficult for these children to understand that reading can satisfy many needs and desires. In cases such as these it may be futile for the teacher to try to interest these youngsters in reading by appealing to the satisfaction and enjoyment that can be found in reading. They won't buy it.

For these children teachers needs to try external motivators, payoffs for reading. The strategy behind external motivators is that if the reading experiences are planned carefully with the students' interests in mind after several reading experiences in which students read in order to obtain rewards, they will begin to develop an internal system for valuing and enjoying literacy. That internal system will eventually direct the student to read without the enticement of an external reward. Teachers who choose to employ external motivators need to be continually sensitive to the need to help their students develop a positive internal attitude toward and motivation for reading.

RECREATIONAL READING PROGRAMS BASED ON EXTERNAL MOTIVATION

Perhaps the most successful and wide ranging RRP that involves external motivation is the Pizza Hut "Book It" program. In the program students earn coupons for a free pizza and a decorative badge for reading a teacher-specified number of books per month. Through the program, millions of youngsters have been motivated to read books they may have otherwise passed up. The program makes the assumption, as do most eternal motivation programs, that internal motivation for reading will naturally develop as a consequence of the increased reading sparked by the external motivator. A key factor in the program is the criteria established by the teacher. The teacher needs to be sensitive to the abilities and interests of the students and set a criterion amount of reading that will stretch their reading without causing frustration or failure that can occur with a criterion that is too difficult or unobtainable. Beyond the Pizza Hut program teachers or schools can work with community businesses or civic groups to establish similar programs that have more of a local flavor.

Other examples of external RRPs abound. In one first-grade classroom a teacher established a book club that operated during the second half of the school term. To become a member students had to read ten books. Then, with each successive ten books read, students received some reward, from a little wall hanging to a book and even having lunch at a restaurant with the teacher! The book report form that students completed was quite simple. Students wrote the name and title and gave a one sentence reaction to the book. Parents signed the form to validate that the book was read.

A fourth-grade teacher connected recreational reading with the token economy used as part of his behavioral management program. Depending on the length and difficulty of the book, students were awarded "classroom dollars" that could be redeemed for prizes, parties, or free time at the biweekly classroom auction. Students also received "dollars" for other types of positive behavior.

For some children report card grades can be a powerful motivator. However, unless there is a specific grade for recreational reading, the reading grade normally assigned reflects student performance on reading tests and assignments and not on reading behavior.

Competition between classrooms or schools over who can read the most books can also motivate some reluctant readers. Some schools have devised and elaborate Olympic-like competition with "events" for different grade levels or for reading different kinds of books. Teachers need to be very careful, however, in the use of competition, especially when it occurs between individuals. Considerable research has shown that competition can have negative social and emotional consequences for children and leads to smaller academic gains than activities that require cooperation between students [see Kohn, (1986) for a detailed critique of the use of competition in the classroom and workplace].

Summer library reading programs have traditionally relied on external motivators. For reading a specified number of books children can receive stickers or other small prizes and may have their names placed in the library's "reading honor roll."

Parents, too, are aware of the power of external motivation. Paying their children to read, for example, from a penny a page to a dollar a book, can be sufficient inducement for many youngsters to read. The external motivation does little good, however, if the child has not developed an internal desire to read along the way. Other problems might occur as well. One parent reported using the penny a page motivation with his second-grade daughter and fifth-grade son over a recent summer. For the daughter the external motivation wasn't necessary; she was already an avid, self-motivated reader. For the son the payoff wasn't big enough. The external motivator did not have sufficient attraction to get him reading.

RECREATIONAL READING PROGRAMS BASED ON INTERNAL MOTIVATION

The goal is an RRP based upon internal motivation is to heighten students' interest in and desire to read directly throughout the activities present in the program. Programs that work to activate readers' internal motivation for reading avoid the difficulty of transfer of motivation that is inherent in programs based on external motivation. RRPs based on internal motivation present reading and books in such a way that students are lead to reading because of the potential usefulness and enjoyment that is entails.

Read-aloud

The one activity that is perhaps without equal in developing students' love of reading is being read to by a significant adult. I often ask students in the classes I teach to name one activity they can remember that positively affected their development as a reader. An overwhelming majority of students report being read to by a parent, grandparent, or teacher as the most memorable and positive event of their reading lives.

Reading aloud not only has a positive effect on students' attitude toward reading; it also has a positive impact on their development as readers. Durkin (1966), for example, found that one major home characteristic of children who learned to read before beginning school was having someone at home read aloud to them. Similarly, Cohen (1968) found that children in a classroom in which the teacher read aloud regularly throughout the year had greater improvements in vocabulary and comprehension than children in a classroom where reading aloud did not occur.

Reading aloud to children should be a key part of the reading curriculum at all elementary grade levels and beyond. Teachers should reserve a special time of the school day for reading to their class daily. Indeed, teachers may wish to consider several times each day for reading aloud.

Central to the read-aloud experience is the choosing of good books. Teachers should choose the very best literature that's available for reading aloud. This means that being familiar with many books and knowing how to find good books are critical. Familiarity with the various award winning books or access to annotated bibliographies of good books such as those found in *The Read-aloud Handbook* (Trelease, 1985) or in every issue of *The Reading Teacher* or *Language Arts* are excellent aids to choosing the most appropriate books to share. Word of mouth can also be helpful. Teachers (and students) will often share with others titles of books that worked well in their classrooms. The school media specialist should also be counted on to make recommendations for "can't miss" books.

Read-aloud can also extend beyond books. If the purpose of reading aloud is to activate and extend the students' interest in reading then articles from newspapers and magazines are entirely appropriate. One teacher who was assigned to a classroom of middle grade students who neither read nor liked to read found that the students' initial response to book reading was negative. He turned to the short, action-filled "Drama in Real Life" pieces that are found in nearly every issue of *Reader's Digest*. Sharing these articles became the bridge from not reading to hearing books read by the teacher and reading books on their own.

Teachers should not be afraid to share favorite books more than once with a class. Beaver (1982) found that students like hearing certain books repeatedly and felt that they came to greater levels of appreciation and comprehension as stories were presented more than once.

Reading aloud can be particularly effective when teachers connect books they read with other books by the same author. As the teacher shares a book with the class he or she should point out other books written by the same author and place a sampling of those books on the chalkboard ledge for students to choose on their own. If the book the teacher shares captures students' interest it won't be long before the other books on display will be taken.

Storytelling is a wonderful variation of read-aloud. In storytelling teachers tell stories from memory rather than read them aloud from a text. The stories told, however, can come from children's trade books. These stories are learned through the simple process of reading a story several times through and practice telling it alone until the storyteller feels comfortable. Storytelling adds a new dimension to read-aloud that most students thoroughly enjoy. Taught the process of learning to tell stories, most students can become storytellers themselves.

To maximize the enjoyment in read-aloud, teachers need to pay attention to the environment for reading aloud. It should occur regularly and at the same time each day so children can anticipate it and prepare themselves accordingly. Whether students sit at their desks or are invited to sit on the floor near the reader, they should be encouraged to relax and listen. Some teachers set the mood for read-aloud by dimming the classroom lights and turning on one desk or table lamp by which to read. The use of a comfortable "reading chair" can also set the stage for reading aloud.

There is no doubt that read-aloud can get students into books. Any teacher who has read aloud to children can tell stories of students who have found inspiration for reading. As school started this past year my fifth-grade son's teacher began the term by reading *Trumpet of the Swans* (19   ) by E. B. White. Mike, who had read at best only moderately over the previous summer, was captured by the story after only two read-aloud sessions. On the Friday before an early September weekend he checked the book out from the school library and finished it before the next Monday's read-aloud.

Free Reading During School

Whether it's called Sustained Silent Reading (SSR), Super Quiet Uninterrupted Reading Time (SQUIRT), Drop Everything and Read (DEAR), or whatever other imaginative acronym can be dreamed up, the need for students to have an opportunity during the school day to read must be a reality. If we want students to read on their own time, some school time must be given over to encouraging such behavior.

Sustained Silent Reading is a regular time during the school day devoted to free reading. Depending on the grade level it can range from ten to thirty minutes, although in beginning SSR many teachers find it best to start with a shorter period of time and gradually extend it as students become familiar with the routine.

The procedure for SSR is simple. Everyone reads, including the teacher and any visitor to the classroom, during SSR. Students should have a book or other reading material ready before SSR begins. Within limitations set by the teacher, students should be free to choose their own reading for SSR, from books to magazines and newspapers. Many teachers find that recreational reading is more nearly approximated when students are permitted to find a favorite "spot" in the room for free reading and to read with a friend if they wish.

Students should be encouraged to take the material read during SSR home so that they can develop SSR habits at home. Having SSR follow a read-aloud session gets students thinking about books and, if the teacher provides the class with other books by the same author, gives students a chance to try related books as well. Although many classrooms do SSR on their own, when it is made a schoolwide activity, students are made more aware that recreational reading is important and that is extends across grade levels.

SSR provides students with the tacit message that reading is a valued activity. It gives students an opportunity that they may not receive at home to develop recreational reading habits. And, it provides students with first-hand proof that reading can be enjoyable.

Teacher Encouragement of Reading

In addition to modeling literate behavior for students through read-aloud and Sustained Silent Reading, teachers need to excite and encourage students about reading. Hickman (1983) notes that teachers develop interest in reading by enthusiastically promoting reading, introducing children to exceptional books, and talking about books with students.

Students need to see that their teachers value literacy. Teachers can do this by sharing with the class what they themselves are reading, recreationally and professionally. They can share with the class their reasons for choosing a particular book, their level of enjoyment of the selection, and how they may respond to it when finished. Teachers can also occasionally introduce the class to good books without actually reading the books aloud. A teacher's testimonial can be sufficiently influential to get many children to give a book a try.

Perhaps the most powerful way a teacher can create excitement about reading is by talking with the students about what they are reading. Frequent and informal book chats communicate to students that the teacher cares about them and about reading. Questions such as "What are you reading?", "How do you like it?", "How does it compare with

_____?" or "What do you think you'll try next?" demonstrate to students that their teacher is genuinely interested in what they are reading. Reading becomes the vehicle for fellowship, and the chat itself becomes the model for how students can discuss books with one another.

Excitement about books and reading can be contagious. When teachers share their own personal excitement about and enthusiasm for reading students are likely to respond in ways that make reading an important part of their own lives.

Connect Reading to Other Areas of the Curriculum

A key to developing in students positive attitudes toward reading is to create an atmosphere in which reading and good books abound. Certainly, one way to do this is to take reading and trade books into curriculum areas such as social studies and science.

One recent criticism of textbooks used in the schools is that they are dull, trivialized, and can discourage independent reading. Bringing trade books into these curriculum areas can help contextualize the teaching of these subjects. Students learn that different perspectives can exist for historical, social, or scientific events. Moreover, students appreciate that the study of these areas is more than the learning of a set of isolated facts. Learning in the social studies and science can be made interesting and enjoyable and can lead to further reading and subject exploration by students.

The Revolutionary War, for example, is commonly taught in the schools. Teachers who read *Johnny Tremain* (1946) by Esther Forbes and *My Brother Sam is Dead* (1974) by James and Lincoln Collier show their students that there are many sides to war. War can be exciting and adventuresome; it can also mean death and tragedy. Historic events impact on the lives of individual people. The sharing of good literature is one way to demonstrate the personal meanings of the events studied in social studies.

Science can be contextualized by sharing biographies of famous scientists or the stories of great discoveries. Even picture storybooks can be made a part of a science curriculum. One first-grade teacher concluded the study of rocks with her class by reading William Steig's *Sylvester and the Magic Pebble* (1969). It was a fitting and fun end to the class investigation.

For many adults recreational reading means continued learning about things in which they have an interest. By bringing books and reading into the various curricular areas, teachers demonstrate to students that valuable and interesting learning can occur outside of textbooks, in books usually associated with independent reading.

Creating the Right Environment

So far, the activities that have been described for developing an internal motivation for reading make the assumption that students have easy access to a large number of trade books. Indeed, having an adequate classroom library is just one part of a classroom environment that encourages independent, recreational reading.

Even as adults, most readers have a favorite place and time for reading. Some may prefer to read at home right after dinner in a favorite easy chair. Others may prefer reading in bed just before turning out the lights. Still others may find reading during the lunch hour at a park bench to be immensely relaxing.

Although the physical dimensions and layout of a classroom may limit one's ability to create the most satisfying atmosphere for reading, teachers still need to work to make the classroom a place where good books are easily accessible and pleasurable reading can occur. The right environment can encourage voluntary reading. Studies on the subject by Morrow and Weinstein (1982; 1986) have found that literature-based reading combined with well planned reading/library centers resulted in increased numbers of children voluntarily engaging in literacy activities.

The first concern in creating an environment conducive to recreational reading is making the classroom rich in print. That is, the classroom should be filled with reading materials that attract the attention and interest of students. The library/reading area is the center for voluntary reading in the classroom. At a minimum, it should contain books that children can check out, housed in appropriate bookshelves, and comfortable places where children can sit or lay down and read.

Huck (1977) recommends that there be at least ten books per child in the classroom library. While this may seem to be an overwhelming number, especially for the beginning teacher, Morrow (1989) points out that it is not difficult to accumulate a classroom collection. Children's trade books can be purchased inexpensively at garage sales, flea markets, and through classroom book clubs. Some teachers have even conducted book drives in which parents of children in the room donate books. Some schools and community libraries allow teachers to check out many books for extended periods of time.

The books should be housed on shelves that border the reading/library center, and students should be taught the appropriate way to reshelve books returned to the center. Teachers who are exploring special topics or themes in the class can collect books related to the topic and place those books on a special shelf within the center. Colored strips of tape or stickers placed on the spines of the books can be used to organize the books according to topic and shelf. Multiple copies of favorite books should be shelved separately for groups of students who wish to read a book together.

Provisions should be made for displaying new books or special books to which the teacher might want to call students' attention. The top of the book shelf or a part of the chalkboard ledge could be used to display "Books of the Week."

The library/reading center should also be a place where students can read at their leisure. The strategic placement of a bookshelf cabinet, or other type of portable divider can separate the center from the rest of the classroom. The center itself can be furnished with an inexpensive throw rug and pillows that allow students to relax on the floor as they read. A worn couch or chair or a couple of bean bag chairs would also make the center more home-like and inviting for students. A small table with chairs and headsets would allow groups of students to listen to taped stories while reading or to talk quietly about a certain book.

The center should also be decorated with posters and slogans that extol reading, illustrations from books, and book covers. Although attractive posters are available commercially, students should be encouraged to decorate the corner with their own art work and slogans. This helps to give them a feeling of ownership over the center and adds to its specialness.

The positive connection between reading and writing is undeniable. Reading inspires children to write and writing helps students to appreciate the work of authors. A writing/bookmaking center is an integral part of a classroom environment that fosters recreational reading. The writing/bookmaking enter should be located near the library/reading center. The center should contain sufficient area for students to write and make books. One large or two smaller tables should be available.

The center should contain supplies for writing and bookmaking. Paper, pencils, pens, markers, construction paper, envelopes, a stapler, scissors, magazines for cutting out pictures, and other related supplies should be organized and available to the children. Writing folders for each child should also be at hand. Teachers of younger children may wish to have a tape recorder and blank tapes available so that students can dictate stories for later transcription. In addition to publishing students' writing in book form, teachers should also use classroom bulletin boards to display and publicize students' written accomplishments.

Mailboxes for each child (and teacher) in the classroom encourage the use of writing and reading as a means of functional communication. Empty oatmeal boxes or potato chip cans can be fastened together to form the mail center.

Morrow (1989) notes that other centers in the classroom, such as the science, music, art, or dramatic play centers, can be planned so that reading is an important and enjoyable component. In one dramatic play center made into a classroom restaurant, for example, students eagerly wrote and read menus, recipes, notes to the chef, advertisements and other documents that were integral parts of their restaurant.

Teachers who take the time to design classroom environments that encourage voluntary reading send the message to students that reading is important and something to be valued. There is no doubt that recreational reading will increase when classrooms contain a wealth of books and other materials for reading and when classrooms become a place where students learn that reading is special and to be enjoyed.

Vary Response to Reading

One of the major hindrances to recreational reading is the traditional book report. Many students have reported to me that knowing that a long written summary awaited their completion of a book acted as a deterrent to their recreational reading. The completion of a good reading experience should be satisfying. Forcing students to write summaries in some standard format for the sole purpose of verifying that the book was read runs counter to the goal of encouraging voluntary reading.

While not denying the need for allowing students the opportunity to engage in post-reading activity, Huck (1977) argues that great variety should be permitted in students' response to books. The purpose of the response activity should be to make the reading experience more memorable and to interest other students in reading the story. Verification that the book was read should, at most, be a secondary purpose.

Response to books should be an opportunity for students to interpret what they got out of the book and to use their creativity to express that interpretation. The variety of ways to respond to a reading experience is limitless. Some youngsters may draw an illustration of a favorite scene from a book while others might create a diorama. Still others might dramatize or pantomime a critical event in a story. Students familiar with readers' theater may wish to write a script for an important part of a book and then perform the script for the class.

Students can informally conference with the teacher or a group of classmates about a book. Booktalks are opportunities for student to summarize orally a book for their classmates, answer questions, and give recommendations. Students at the upper elementary grades are strongly influenced by what their peers are reading and what they recommend.

In one classroom, groups of students who read the same book and were familiar with video taping equipment created "advertisements" in which they summarized and made recommendations for their books. The students were able to employ the propaganda techniques that they had studied earlier. The "advertisements" were played for the entire class of Fridays and then kept for later use by students who might be looking for a good book to read. Another classroom took this response idea a bit further by creating a take-off on the movie review television programs. Pairs of students would read a book and then, as a pair, would review the book in front of the camera. In some cases one student like the book while the other panned it.

The use of jackdaws allows for variety in responding to books. A jackdaw is simply a collection of artifacts, real or facsimile, related to a particular book (Rasinski, 1985). Teachers have been known to put jackdaws together and share them with the class before reading as a way to build background for the reading. After students have learned what a jackdaw is all about they can be encouraged to make jackdaws or to add to existing ones.

One teacher included the Great Depression as a unit within his social studies curriculum. Besides having students read the textbook he read Irene Hunt's Depression era story *No Promises in the Wind* (1970). After reading the story and sharing some artifacts he had collected from the Depression, he invited students to ask their parents and grandparents for similar items to bring and share with the class. The number of items brought in exceeded the teacher's expectations. Old magazines, newspapers, phonograph records, preserved clothing, household tools and appliances, photographs and even a well-worn camera were among the treasures that students brought in. The experience demonstrated students' enjoyment of the story and contextualized their study of the Depression. The items were kept on display and lead to further reading about that time in history.

Whether it's simply drawing an illustration of a scene or putting together a dramatization or jackdaw, these types of responses invite the reader to think critically about the book, to search for deeper levels of meaning, and to interpret the book in a personal way. This not only means better comprehension for the reader it also generates interest in books for students who view these responses. Certainly, students will want to see how their peers have responded to and enjoyed books they are considering reading.

Rather than diminish students' motivation to read, varied response activities tend to be satisfying end to reading experiences and to create interest in further reading. Students, however, should not be expected to respond to every book read.

Reading with Others

Research in cooperative learning reports that students who engage in cooperative group learning tend to learn more, both academically and socially, than students who work alone or in competition with others (Johnson, Johnson, Johnson, & Anderson, 1976). Researchers into classroom reading have found that reading is more of a social process than originally thought. Hepler and Hickman (1982) used the term "community readers" to describe the group reading activities in classrooms in which literature plays a central part.

Children enjoy the opportunity to work with one another, and having students read together heightens the interest and satisfaction that comes from reading.

Some students may like to read in pairs during Sustained Silent Reading, or teachers may have groups of students read one book together. In both cases students have the opportunity to talk about the book with others, to share interpretations, and compare favorite episodes. Such talk permits students to enjoy stories and companionship at the same time. Moreover, it makes the responsibility for reading a book a shared one and thus less weighty.

Making communities of readers can also extend beyond the classroom. Students in upper grades, for example, can read to or with younger children. Parents and other adult members of the community can read favorite stories to small groups of students. Even the school principal can share books with students at all grade levels.

Enlisting Parent Support

Recreational reading at school is an empty vessel if it does not also occur in the home. Enlisting the support of parents in encouraging voluntary reading is one of the most important moves a teacher can make in developing a recreational reading program. In her review of research related to parental involvement in the academic and school related activities of their children, Henderson (1988) reported that parents have a decidedly positive impact on their children's education when they are encouraged to be involved. However, despite the research evidence and the general agreement among educators about the importance of parents, Henderson notes that professional educators tend to involve parents in tangential and less substantive ways such as bake sales, attendance at class plays, and school open houses.

A strong recreational reading program demands the involvement of parents. The question then becomes how can parental support and involvement be secured? Rasinski and Fredericks (1989) suggest a graduated model of parental involvement. That is, teachers first work to involve parents in low level, nonthreatening ways and then work to promote greater levels of parental involvement.

In terms of recreational reading a first step might be informational. Teachers (and schools) could provide parents with periodic information about the benefits of encouraging voluntary reading at home. Informational fliers sent home, articles in the school newsletter, posters displayed throughout the school during open house, and teacher comments made during parent-teacher conferences can point to the importance of recreational reading and ideas on how to promote it in the home.

Later, parents can be asked to be involved in more active ways. During a special week or month devoted to literacy, parents could be asked to monitor their children's reading and report the number of pages read or time spent reading over a specified time period. Parents could also be asked to "contract" with the school and their children to read to their children on certain evenings for a month or to engage in a family SSR activity three or four nights a week.

Even parents who have limited reading skills can get involved in their children's literacy development. Teachers can send their beginning readers home with predictable or patterned books. These books have recurrent phrase or sentence patterns that make them easy enough for even parents of limited reading proficiency to share with their children (sharing such books has the benefit of improving the adults' reading skills and attitudes as well). Talking books, texts that are accompanied by taped oral renditions, can also be sent home. Parents and children can share in listening to a text while following the printed version at the same time. Even parents who are unable to read can be encouraged to take their children to the library regularly, to ensure that there are plenty of reading materials in the home, to provide a regular reading time for their children at home, and to encourage and praise their children's efforts to become readers and writers.

Several schools have set up home reading contests in which children report the number of pages read (or amount of time spent reading) over a period of time. The pages are then added to a team total, and classroom teams vie for a school or grade level championship. Parents are informed of the contest and asked to encourage and verify their children's reading.

Once parental activity in recreational reading is established, schools can form parental advisory groups that give direction in coordinating school-home recreational reading and plan special events such as book fairs and visits by authors that promote further voluntary reading at home and school.

Involving the Community

Reading belongs outside the school. It is an activity for which the function lies in the community. Thus, schools should attempt to make connections with the community to promote recreational reading.

Many schools have formed alliances with retirement homes. Residents of the homes visit the schools to read to and with students and students visit the home to perform such reading related activities as plays and readers' theater for the residents. Pen pals can easily develop between students and home residents. In one middle school, students were given social studies and English credit for teaming up with individuals from a local retirement community (Rasinski, 1988). The textbook on recent American history was replaced with the stories about the 1930s and '40s told by the residents. The stories were transcribed into reports and lead to other reading and writing activities. Many students kept up correspondence with their partners long after the program ended.

Other community connections can be made in less obvious ways. Banks, supermarkets, and doctor's offices can be decorated with student-make posters that promote recreational reading. Similarly, schools can encourage medical offices and the like to stock their waiting rooms with good reading materials for children and sound advice to parents for promoting recreational reading. In Athens, Georgia, the local council of the International Reading Association developed advertisements on reading that were broadcast over the local public radio station. Many IRA councils, in conjunction with the local schools, have created their own "Reading Day" at the local mall. This is a day in which reading is celebrated and encouraged in a shopping area where there are sure to be lots of people. Local businesses can be encouraged to support all these activities and help supplement school and classroom book collections.

Schools should also make strong connections with local libraries. Library personnel can visit the schools to ensure that all students have a card and that they know about the benefits of the library. Schools can advertise special reading events in the library, and schools and libraries can coordinate their activities so that librarians can reinforce the reading at school by focusing their programs on similar themes and topics.

It is difficult to measure the exact impact of community connections on recreational reading. There is no doubt, however, that constant encourgement of and support for recreational reading will have a positive effect on many students' reading habits.

Special Activities for and Deterrents to Recreational Reading

Most of the approaches shared up to this point are viewed as long-term approaches to reading motivation and recreational reading. In addition to ongoing efforts to promote voluntary reading, however, schools can provide special activities that contribute to the overall effort. The possible kinds of activities that can be devised border on the infinite, but a few will be described here.

A "Read-in" is an overnight social event held at the school in which reading is the main activity. Students and parents bring their sleeping bags and reading material to the school gym. After sharing an informal potluck dinner, parents and children alternate reading for twenty to thirty minutes with some other activity such as aerobic exercising, a game, a snack, or some other group activity. Storytelling, read-aloud (ghost stories work very well in October), short writing tasks such as writing a limerick describing yourself or family, and plenty of discussion about what has been read or written also find their way into the "Read-in." On this one night students see their parents reading, enjoy the companionship of family and friends, and share the fun of reading.

A more common school activity that promotes recreational reading is the Book Fair. The school or a parent organization contracts with a book distributor to bring in books to sell to students. Usually over the course of one to two nights, parents and students are invited to view the book displays and purchase their choices. Schools need to ensure that the books put on sale are the very best in children's literature. There should be a wide variety of books and of such quality that children who read them will want to come back for more. Book Fairs are great opportunities for schools to promote reading. Student-made posters about reading can hang throughout the school. Students can also put on reading performances during the fair such as readers' theater, oral reading of poetry or famous speeches, storytelling, or read-aloud to younger children.

The International Reading Association sponsors a program called Children's Choices in which elementary school children from around the country read and rate recently published trade books. While not all schools can participate in the IRA program, any school can devise its own Children's Choices program. Teachers at a grade level select a set of recently written exemplary books appropriate for that grade level. Students are then asked to read the set or a subset of books over a specified period of time and rate them. The ratings can be based simply upon how well the book was liked or upon a set of criteria established by the children prior to reading. After all the reading and rating is finished students can be involved in the tallying and winners announced at a school or grade level assembly.

Many schools with funds for special events or with parent organizations that can provide financial support (the proceeds from the Book Fair could be one source of funds) can invite a children's book author to spend a day at the school. An appropriate connection would be to invite an author who won the school's Children's Choices competition.

One school recently had Tomie DePaola spend a day visiting classrooms, talking to children, teachers, and parents, and giving drawing demonstrations. In preparation for DePaola's visit children throughout the school read his books and had his books read to them. The school was then decorated with artifacts from the books. Strega Nona's pasta pot was strategically placed at the entrance to the school. Many children wore magic rings. Pictures of Strega Nona, Bambolona, and other DePaola characters were hung around the school, and in a skit based on one of DePaola's books, the school principal played the role of big Anthony!

In addition to considering special events for promoting recreational reading, teachers need to consider activities that can deter students from getting into books. Overuse of the traditional book report, for example, can be deadly for some students. When students know that a formal, lengthy, written report awaits them at the end of the books they read, they may learn to associate voluntary reading with an unpleasant task and do only the minimum amount of reading required y the teacher. While there may be occasion to have students report on books read in a formal written format, such occasion should be limited. Other, more enjoyable forms of response to books are available.

Many students find oral reading in front of a group to be a task that creates much anxiety toward and fear of reading. Again, teachers should not overuse oral reading in the classroom, and when students are asked to read for others they should, at a minimum, have the opportunity to practice the text beforehand. Radio reading (Greene, 1979; Searfoss, 1975) is one example of an oral reading instructional activity that allows for prereading practice and attempts to minimize the potential for embarrassment that is often associated with it.

The overuse of worksheet and workbook activities tend to take students' focus away from the functionality and enjoyment associated with reading. Although such activities are at the center of traditional reading approaches, teachers should be careful, cautious, and parsimonious consumers of such materials. It is easy for students to lose sight of what reading is all about. If a major purpose of activity sheets is to keep students busy, certainly getting students into books and book related activities would be more appropriate.

PUTTING IT ALL TOGETHER

What has been described in this chapter are important components and considerations in a school-based recreational reading program. One would not expect to find all these components in any one program. Similarly, some excellent programs may contain elements that have not been described here.

I make the assumption that teachers are knowledgeable about themselves as teachers, their children as students, and the school and community conditions in which they teach. Given that all three of these factors can vary, the kind of recreational reading program will vary from classroom to classroom and from school to school. It is the informed and empowered teacher who can best decide the design of a recreational reading program.

If a teacher has not consciously developed a recreational reading program, I suggest that he or she start slowly and gradually build a program, keeping things that work, dropping those that do not, and adding elements as needed. At the heart of any recreational reading program should be reading aloud. This is a good starting place for any voluntary reading program. Teachers should read aloud to the class daily, even more than once if possible. This means that teachers must be practiced readers and that they know books, especially those that appeal to their particular children.

Close behind reading aloud in any recreational program for reading would be implementing Sustained Silent Reading and creating a classroom environment that promotes reading. Teachers need to create opportunities, environments, and incentives for students to read on their own.

As a recreational reading program begins to gain momentum, teachers may wish to add to the program. They could work to involve parents in recreational reading at home as well as teachers in other grade levels. Recreational reading can also be integrated, through the use of children's literature, into all areas of the school curriculum. The goal is to make recreational reading something that is actively promoted in the major areas of a student's life, both in and out of school, and throughout the school years.

The key to any recreational reading program is the teacher. Teachers need to see recreational reading as an important goal of the overall reading curriculum. Once they recognize the importance of recreational reading they need to become knowledgeable in how to implement and sustain an RRP, based upon their perception of themselves as teachers, their students, and the learning environment. School administrators would go through much the same process, only on a larger scale.

Recreational reading can no longer be the stepchild of the reading curriculum. If we believe that children learn to read by reading, the promotion of recreational reading must be at the center of reading instruction. Commitment, time, and good ideas are much of what is needed to make recreational reading programs that really work to foster proficient and lifelong readers.

REFERENCES

Anderson, R. C., Wilson, P. T., & Fielding, L. (1988). Growth in reading and how children spend their time outside of school. *Reading Research Quarterly, 23*(3), 285-303.

Berglund, R. L., & Johns, J. L. (1983). A primer on uninterreupted sustained silent reading. *The Reading Teacher, 36*(6), 534-539.

Beaver, J. (1982). Say it! Over and over. *Language Arts, 59*(2), 143-148.

Cohen, D. N. (1968). The effect of literature on vocabulary and reading achievement. *Elementary English, 45*(2), 209-217.

Collier, J. & Collier, L. (1974). My brother Sam is dead. New York: Four Winds Press.

Durkin, D. (1966). *Children who read early.* New York: Teachers College Press.

Forbes, E. (1946). *Johnny Tremain.* Boston: Houghton Mifflin.

Greaney, V. (1980). Factors related to amount and type of leisure time reading. *Reading Research Quarterly, 15*(3), 337-357.

Greene, F. (1979). Radio reading. In C. Pennock (Ed.), *Reading comprehension at four linguistic levels.* Newark, DE: International Reading Association.

Henderson, A. T. (1988). Parents are a school's best friends. *Phi Delta Kappan, 70*(3), 148-153.

Hepler, S. I., & Hickman, J. (1982). "The book was okay. I love you" — Social aspects of response to literature. *Theory into Practice, 21*(4), 278-283.

Hickman, J. (1983). Classroms that help children like books. In N. Roser & M. Frith (Eds.), *Children's choices: Teaching with books children like.* Newark, DE: International Reading Association.

Huck, C. (1977). Literature as the content of reading. *Theory into Practice, 16*(5), 363-371.

Hunt, I. (1970). *No promises in the wind.* Chicago: Follett Publishing Co.

Johnson, D., Johnson, R., Johnson, J., & Anderson, D. (1976). Effects of cooperative vs. individual instruction on student prosocial behavior, attitudes toward learning, and achievement. *Journal of Educational Psychology, 68*(4), 446-452.

Kohn, A. (1986). *No contest: The case against competition.* Boston: Houghton Mifflin.

Levine, S. G. (1984). USSR — A necessary component in teaching reading. *Journal of Reading, 27*(5), 394-400.

Ley, T. (1979). Getting kids into books. *Media and Methods, 15*(4), 22-26.

Morrow, L. M. (1989). Designing the classroom to promote literacy development. In D. S. Strickland & L. M. Morrow (Eds.), *Emerging literacy: Young children learn to read and write.* Newark, DE: International Reading Association.

Morrow, L. M., & Weinstein, C. S. (1986). Encouraging voluntary reading: The impact of a literature program on children's use of library centers. *Reading Research Quarterly, 21*(3) 330-346.

Morrow, L. M., & Weinstein, C. S. (1982). Increasing children's use of literature through programs and physical design changes. *Elementary School Journal, 83*(2), 131-137.

Rasinski, T. V. (1988). Bridging the gap: Intergenerational collaboration. *The Educational Forum, 53*(1), 77-88.

Rasinski, T. V. (1985). Jackdaws: Bridging the gap between reading and the real world. *New England Reading Association Journal, 20,* 4-8.

Rasinski, T. V., & Fredericks, A. (1989). Dimensions of parental involvement. *The Reading Teacher, 43* 180-182.

Searfoss, L. W. (1975). Radio reading. *The Reading Teacher, 29*(3), 295-296.

Steig, W. (1969). *Sylvester and the magic pebble.* New York: Simon & Schuster.

Trelease, J. (1985). *The Read-aloud handbook.* New York: Penguin.

Walberg, H. J., & Tsai, S. (1984). Reading achievement and diminishing returns to time. *Journal of Educational Psychology, 76*(3), 442-451.

White, E. B. (1970). *Trumpet of the swans.* New York: Harper & Row.

A Response-based View of Writing with Literature

Karen D'Angelo Bromley

This chapter explores the reading-writing connection and the importance of the reader's response to literature as a catalyst for writing. It describes the use of literature as a basic ingredient and model for engaging students in meaningful writing activities that span the curriculum. Included are suggestions for classroom application and examples of student work.

THE READING-WRITING RELATIONSHIP

Both theory and research evidence support the notion that there is a relationship between reading and writing. Recent theories of the reading process explain reading and writing as essentially similar processes of meaning construction (Tierney & Pearson, 1983). In both, meaning is composed using the reader's or writer's background of experience; the author's cues or considerations about audience, form, and message; and the context within which the reading or writing occurs. The transaction that occurs between reader and text requires cognitive and linguistic processes that are similar to the transaction that occurs between the writer and the text he or she creates.

Many aspects of writing can only be learned through wide reading (Smith, 1984). Reviews of the literature (Hamill & McNutt, 1980; Shanahan, 1980; Stotsky, 1983) indicate that better writers display superior reading ability, better writers read more than poorer writers, and better readers produce the most complex sentence structures in their writing.

Several correlational studies report relationships between reading and writing. Loban (1963 found significant positive interrelationships between reading and writing that more become pronounced as grade level increases. A significant positive relationship was found between reading ability and the syntactic complexity of writing by Zeman (1969), at the primary level, and Evanechko, Ollila, and Armstrong (1974) at the intermediate level. Shanahan (1984) reported that at both the second and fifth-grade levels, reading ability measured by standardized tests accounted for 43 percent of differences in writing scores, and vice versa. Shanahan and Lomax (1986) provide evidence for an interactive model of the reading-writing relationship in second and fifth grade in which the components of reading (word analysis, vocabulary, and comprehension) correlate and interact with the components of writing (spelling, vocabulary diversity, syntax, and story structure).

This brief overview of some of the research on the reading-writing relationship confirms for us the existence of this important connection. Let us examine now the beliefs of several respected experts in the field of education to see how they view specific aspects of the relationship.

- "The reading-writing connections that matter most belong to the quiet moments when a writer is snuggled up, reading a book. (Calkins, 1986; p. 232).

- "... studies show almost consistently that ... better writers tend to read more than poorer writers." (Stotsky, 1983; p. 636).

- "All children need literature. Children who are authors need it even more." (Graves, 1983; p. 67).

These brief quotes help us see more clearly the vital link between reading and writing. We know that something special happens when a reader interacts with a book, and that interaction affects what a reader writes. We know that often the student who does not enjoy reading and reads little is the student who does not like to write and does not write well. We also know that the student who loves to read and devours books is often an eager and effective writer. Why is this so? How does the reading of literature help a student in his development as a writer? Perhaps two other quotes will help answer this question.

- "Students draw upon what they read as a source of knowledge when they write." (Cullinan, 1987; p. 13).

- "Writing is learned by writing, by reading, and by perceiving oneself as a writer." (Smith, 1988; p. 199).

When students read they learn about how writing looks and feels, as they gain information and ideas about content, form, and technique that they can use later in their own writing. Students who read as if they were writers, asking questions about why authors do this or that, become aware of a writer's craft and can begin to translate this into their own writing. We also know how important it is for students to see themselves as writers and authors in order to become one. We are aware of the important connection between reading and writing.

PERSONAL RESPONSE TO LITERATURE

Does becoming a writer require reading a lot of literature, learning from what is read, perceiving oneself as a writer, and writing? While these are important behaviors and attitudes for a writer to possess, there is a catalyst necessary to the process of using literature as a basic ingredient in writing that is often overlooked. A final quote contains a hint as to what that catalyst is.

- "One of the ways we can facilitate student learning from other writers is by introducing well-crafted pieces they will care enough about to internalize as models." (Atwell, 1987; p. 246).

The catalyst in connecting reading and literature with writing in the classroom may well be the student's personal response to that literature. Atwell implies that students must "care" about a story in order for it to have an impact on their writing. She says that it is necessary to expose kids to good writing, but it is crucial that the writing be on topics of importance to them if they are to be touched by it and become "literary borrowers."

Atwell (1987) found that as her eighth graders read, they borrowed genres, topics, themes, and techniques from their reading to use in their own writing. She found that they internalized the conventions and structures of the literary forms they read. Indeed, they reported to her that the most important influence on their writing was the professional writers whose work they read in their reading workshop.

How did Atwell's students respond personally to what they read? They most often connected stories about others' lives to their own feelings and experiences. They also connected literature and real life by responding to the specific information authors presented, and they learned something about the real world from their reading. She notes that students also commented on their own reading abilities and on the processes and styles authors used to write.

A personal response or connection between the student and what the student reads or hears is the necessary catalyst that sparks an interest and desire to write. The writing done by a student who has been touched by something in the piece of literature and is eager to explore the experience will be quite different from the writing done by a student who did not make a personal connection with the author or story and writes only to complete an assignment or satisfy a teacher. Literature is most successfully and effectively used as a model in writing when students connect personally with it first.

What does response to literature mean? Rosenblatt (1985) identifies two kinds of response that result from the transaction a reader has with print. One is an efferent or objective response in which the reader focuses on the information to be acquired in the reading. The other is an aesthetic or emotional response in which the reader draws on personal background knowledge and lives through the experience read about, identifying with it and finding inner meaning for it. The student who reads *Bridge To Terabithia* (1977), by Katherine Paterson, may have an efferent response, identifying Jess and Leslie as the two main characters, realizing that the story is set in the country outside Washington, D.C., and observing that Terabithia is a fantasy hideaway. The reader may also have an aesthetic response. Recognizing personal loneliness and longing for a special friend, the reader may feel the events in the story and the loss of Leslie in such a way that he or she experiences or lives through the story and is touched by it emotionally. In responding to *Bridge . . . ,* the literature became real for the reader, who experiences it in a unique way. Responding to literature has to do with how we personalize what we read, how it becomes real for us, and how it makes us feel.

Response to literature is influenced by many factors and has many forms. Personal style, reading preferences, cognitive development, and other factors contribute to a reader's response to text (Galda, 1988). Each student brings his or her own individual background of experiences, values, beliefs, and knowledge to the reading of literature. Each story or text possesses unique elements, such as genre, style, structure, and characterization, to name a few, that influence response. The context within which literature is read can also impact response, with teacher expectation and behavior, classroom atmosphere, and peers also contributing to that response. Thus, it should be clear that each student will have a different literary transaction and response to a story.

THE TEACHER'S ROLE IN ELICITING RESPONSE

For some students, making the jump from reading good literature to writing good prose comes easily. For other students, however, one does not necessarily follow the other; they may need help making the connection between reading and writing.

As a teacher you can help students write effectively using literature as an ingredient in their writing by nudging them first toward a personal response to what they have read. One way to increase the likelihood that literature will become real for students is to give them a voice in choosing what they will read, since they often choose according to their interests and this is critical to response. Another way is to select good literature to which you believe your students can relate. For example, a sixth-grade student who is an adopted child may have special reason to enjoy *Anne of Green Gables* (1988), by L. M. Montgomery, since it is about an orphaned child; or a second-grade student who lives on a farm may relate easily to *Charlotte's Web* (1952), by E. B. White, because the setting is familiar.

When there is no obvious link between your students and what they will read, you can establish that link with them in a number of ways. In general you can do this by being an explicit model (Gambrell, 1989). You can share with students specific passages from the books you read and show them how and why the passages are real for you. You can share a visual or sensory image that a passage evokes, your repulsion by a certain description, or your wonder at the extraordinary message you feel from a piece. By continually modelling for students the kinds of unique experiences you have with the literature you read, you provide a model for them and help them learn how to respond personally to what they read.

By preparing students for the piece they will read before they read it, you prepare them for a personal response. We know that the more information one brings to print, the easier will be the reading of it and the more one will take away from it. It is therefore important to spend time before reading to establish background for the text to be read. Whether it is sharing information about the author as a real person, establishing the setting on a map or timeline, creating a semantic web or map of things the students already know about the story, role playing a main character, introducing special vocabulary, or sharing a concrete object that is related to the story, you make the story more real for students by taking time to do this. While this kind of link is enough for some students, a more intense introduction to literature that involves students even more personally will benefit others.

When students know something about what they are to read you can encourage their further involvement by helping them make predictions. Discussion before reading that establishes background or actually reading the first chapter or section to students are two ways you can build the involvement that precedes response. Whether students predict what will happen to a character or how the author will handle a problem, they are in effect setting their own personal purpose for reading and will read with real interest. The literature therefore has a better chance of becoming real for them, and you increase the likelihood that they will have a personal response on which the quality of their writing will depend.

Discussion during and after reading can also have an effect on response. As students talk about the story, sharing their observations, revelations, opinions, and questions with each other and you, each one learns that a story is open for many interpretations. They discover that they are able to answer each other's questions and that their opinions are valid when they can be supported with information from their reading. Students learn that they can supply new endings to stories, as five-year-old Jeff did when he drew the picture in Figure 5-1 after hearing and discussing the fable about the tortoise and the hare. His scribbles mark the beginning of writing. As students share and talk they learn from each other and also gain confidence in their own interpretations and response to literature.

Through careful selection of material, teacher modelling, prereading discussion that includes background building, predicting, and purpose setting, as well as sharing that can occur during and after reading, you can develop response to literature. A personal response links reading and writing, and without it as a catalyst student writing may be halting, unwilling, and uninspired.

EXPLORING RESPONSE THROUGH WRITING

The preparation, sharing, and discussions in which students participate as part of the reading experience can help shape response. These activities also become part of the planning and rehearsal that often precedes good writing. There are other avenues for developing response as preparation for writing. Art, creative dramatics, music, and movement are all ways to respond and rehearse for writing as well.

Writing that uses literature as a basic ingredient and model serves many functions for students (Atwell, 1987; Bromley, 1991; Purves, Rogers, &

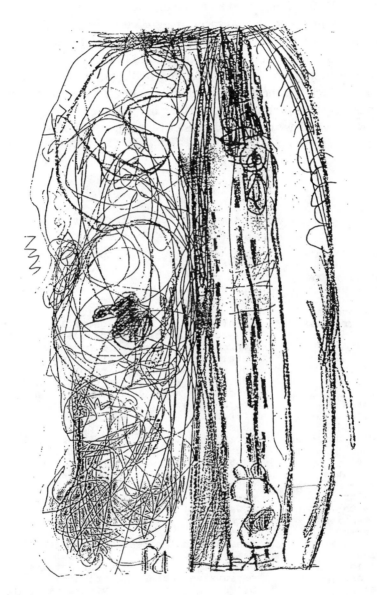

Figure 5-1
Five year-old Jeff responds to the fable about the tortoise and the hare with a
new conclusion, explaining that "Rabbit had a harder road, but tortoise stopped
at a friend's house so rabbit finished first."

Soter, 1990). Writing in response to literature allows students to express feelings, imagine, explain, interpret, analyze, evaluate, convince, and, most important, learn. When students hear or read a story or poem that is real in some way for them and then write in relation to that literature, they learn from what they write. Their writing may be literal or creative, but in the process of writing, the students read, connect, think, and extend their response and thus their learning. Writing in response to literature can take many forms and have different audiences. One hundred possible composition forms (Bromley, 1988) appear in Figure 5-2. Giving your students

Spoken and Written Composition Forms

acknowledgments	fables	product descriptions
addresses	folktales	puppet shows
advertisements	game rules	puzzles
allegories	graffiti	questionnaires
analogies	good news-bad news	questions
announcements	grocery lists	quizzes
autobiographies	headlines	quotations
awards	how-to-do-it speeches	real estate notices
billboards	impromptu speeches	recipes
biographies	interviews	remedies
book jackets	job applications	reports
book reviews	journals	requests
books	laboratory notes	requisitions
brochures	letters	resumes
bulletins	lists	reviews
bumper stickers	logs	riddles
campaign speeches	lyrics	sales pitches
captions	magazines	schedules
cartoons	menus	self-descriptions
certificates	mysteries	sequels
character sketches	myths	skits
comic strips	newscasts	stories
contracts	newspapers	slogans
conversations	notes	speeches
critiques	obituaries	summaries
definitions	observational notes	TV commercials
diaries	pamphlets	telegrams
directions	parodies	travel folders
directories	persuasive letters	tributes
dramas	plays	vignettes
editorials	poems	want ads
epitaphs	posters	wanted posters
encyclopedia entries	propaganda	wills
essays		

Figure 5-2
Writing in response to literature can take many forms.

opportunities to write in a variety of forms for real purposes and real audiences may stimulate their interest in the writing you ask them to do. Some of what students write in response to literature can be private writing done only for themselves, such as a diary or learning log. Some of it can be written for a peer or you to read, as in a buddy journal, literary journal, letter, essay, and the like. Some of the writing can be done for a wider audience, perhaps the class, another class, the school, or a publication beyond the school; for example stories, book reviews, posters, poems, and so forth. Writing in any of these forms, though, ought to grow first from a personal response to what is read so that the writing students do has meaning for them. Their writing can be formal or informal, impromptu and spontaneous, or planned and published.

Remember, too, that reading a variety of genres (folktales, realistic fiction, historical fiction, biography, poetry, fantasy, and nonfiction) and forms of writing is one of the best preparations for writing those forms. Students use literature in both conscious and unconscious ways as a model in their writing. Familiarity with literary elements and knowledge of story grammar enhances comprehension and gives students an understanding of organizational structure that they can follow in their own writing (Bromley, 1991). Besides exposure to models, however, keep in mind that students need practice in writing that spans the curriculum and is done for real purposes and real audiences.

The remainder of this chapter explores four kinds of writing — writing that is done to convey feelings, narrate, explain, and persuade. Suggestions for classroom application and examples of student work are also included.

As you help students learn each kind of writing you can use literature as a basic ingredient and model for engaging them in meaningful writing. These four kinds of writing overlap in many cases and are not mutually exclusive. For example, students may write a journal entry to explain what they learned from reading, and their entries may include their feelings of disgust and anger at the way a character acts or is treated. This kind of writing is only one way of grouping writing students do.

Writing to Convey Feelings

Writing to convey feelings or express inner thoughts and the self is one type of writing in response to literature. This kind of writing can take many forms, one of which for young children is drawing.

Young children often need to draw first in response to what they have read or heard and their drawing can then become a stimulus for talk and writing. In Figure 5-3, Karen drew a picture of a cat "strat" (stretching) after she heard the predictable and repetitive story *Have You Seen My Cat?* (1988), by Eric Carle. She explained that she loves cats and when a cat wakes up it stretches first. At age six she is interested enough in print to write the title of the book as well. Note the difference between the copied "a" from the book's cover and her printed "a" in "cat" and "strat." As she talked about her picture, Karen conveyed feelings the story had triggered for her, and she connected something she knew — how a cat looks when it stretches and extends its claws — with the story.

Another way to convey feelings in writing is through a response journal or log in which the student is encouraged to write a personal response to what he reads (Atwell, 1987; Fulwiler, 1987). Some teachers keep a dialogue journal (Kreeft, 1984) with a student by writing in response to what a student has written, as in Figure 5-4, and some teachers have students write back and forth to each other in buddy journals (Bromley, 1989). Of course students can convey feelings and express the self by writing in a variety of other formats. Taking the part of a character about whom they have read is one way. In Figure 5-5, as she responds to a book she is reading about the exploration of the Northwest, a fifth grader takes on the role of Sacagawea and keeps a journal that this person might have written.

After reading *Knots On A Counting Rope* (1989), by Bill Martin Jr. and John Archambault, and discussing the beauty and darkness in the characters lives, one sixth grader was moved to write the poem in Figure 5-6 about her grandfather. She undoubtedly had connected with this story of the American Indian girl who was blind and her grandfather.

Many of the 100 possible forms of writing allow students to express their personal feelings, values, reactions, and attitudes in one way or another. Letters, poems, first person accounts, and essays are a few that come to mind immediately.

Writing to Narrate

Writing to narrate is a second type of writing in response to literature. In this kind of writing, students give a fictional account of events or tell a story. This kind of writing may mean retelling in a student's own words a story just read or heard, or it may mean creating a new version of a story or a sequel. Knowledge of the story elements of setting, characters, problem, goal, action (events), and resolution is helpful as students create new stories.

Several examples show some of the possibilities for writing to narrate.

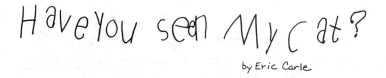

Figure 5-3
The beginning of writing is evident in Karen's drawing and one word label
which show her response to a story.

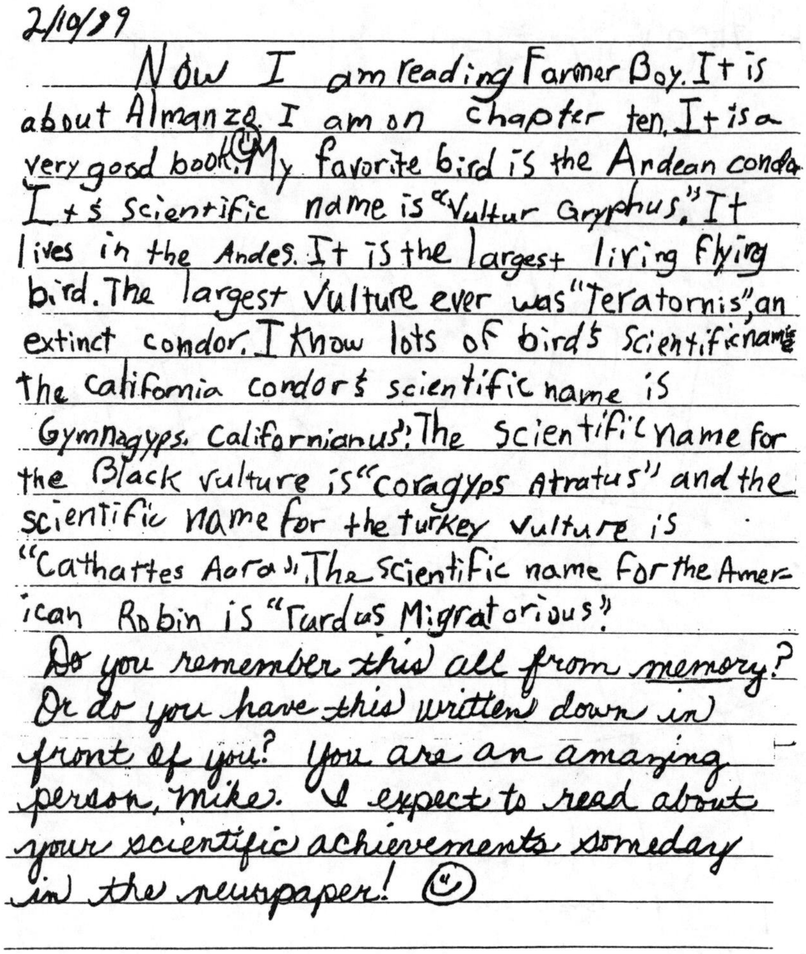

2/10/99

Now I am reading Farmer Boy. It is about Almanzo. I am on chapter ten. It is a very good book. My favorite bird is the Andean condor. Its scientific name is "Vultur Gryphus." It lives in the Andes. It is the largest living flying bird. The largest vulture ever was "Teratornis," an extinct condor. I know lots of bird's scientific names. the California condor's scientific name is Gymnogyps Californianus. The scientific name for the Black vulture is "Coragyps Atratus" and the scientific name for the turkey vulture is "Cathartes Aora." The scientific name for the American Robin is "Turdus Migratorious."

Do you remember this all from memory? Or do you have this written down in front of you? You are an amazing person, Mike. I expect to read about your scientific achievements someday in the newspaper! ☺

Figure 5-4

A third grader's response journal in which his teacher dialogues with him about his reading.

In writing to narrate, students should be able to write an introduction and conclusion and maintain an appropriate sequence of events. Cami, a sixth-grade resource room student, wrote the Black folktale in Figure 5-7 after reading and listening to Virginia Hamilton's stories *The People Could Fly* (1985). Cami's teacher used that collection of black folktales in conjunction with a social studies unit on the Civil War, and Cami was personally moved

Sacagawea's Journal

April 7, 1805: I think Lewis and Clark are nice men. I will go even though I'm scared. My husband really wants to go too. I am taking Jean Baptiste too.

May 15, 1805: We explored a river. Lewis and Clark named it after me.

June 15, 1805: I feel bad. I have stomach pains and a fever. Jean Baptiste is having teeth problems. Captain Lewis gave us both medicine. That was nice.

July 22, 1805: I rechognize the mountains we are coming to. I was captured here as a little girl. They are the Rocky Mountains.

August 17, 1805: We have found the Shoshoni tribe. A lot of my old friends were there. My long lost brother is also chief! That was a red suprize.

October 16, 1805: We had our first bite of salmon. We will follow this river to reach the Pacific Ocean.

November 7, 1805: We are very exited! We have finally reached the Pacific Ocean

Figure 5-5

A fifth grader becomes Sacagawea in this journal.

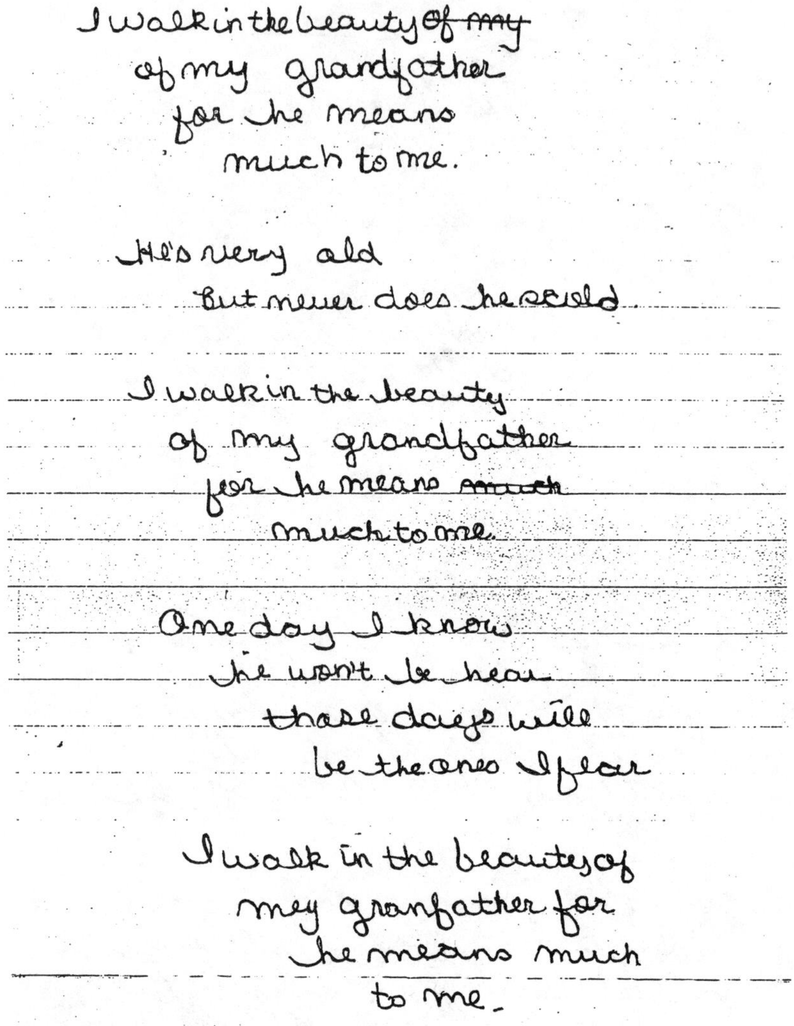

I walk in the beauty of my
of my grandfather
for he means
much to me.

He's very old
But never does he scold

I walk in the beauty
of my grandfather
for he means much
much to me.

One day I know
he won't be here
those days will
be the ones I fear

I walk in the beauty of
my granfather for
he means much
to me.

Figure 5-6
A sixth grader's feelings after reading *Knots On A Counting Rope*.

by them. As students write to narrate they may use personification by giving
animals human characteristics and using dialogue, as in the fable in Figure
5-8, or they may read historical accounts and write their own narrative
story, as in Figure 5-9. They may even write a skit, based on their narrative
account.

There once was a man by the name of Harry and he was a slave
owner. He owned fifty slaves and was recievin more

One day Harry was ridin on his favorite horse and saw Mr.
Wilson (another slave owner) whippin one of his slaves
The blood was pourin off of him. Harry felt so bad.

He said to himself, " This isn't right to'be whippin the
dickens out of that black slave. "

From then on Harry was a part of the Underground Railroad.
He was one of the biggest conductors of the whole Underground
Railroad system. He freed over one thousand slaves.

We will always remember Harry for opening up his eyes to the
big problem of slavery.

NOTE: This tale was told by all the village slaves
       throughout the county to show that someday the slave
       would flip to the other side. Tales like this
       gave hope that someday freedom would be theirs.

Figure 5-7
Black folktale created in response to *The People Could Fly.*

Again, many of the 100 possible forms of writing use narrative writing. Newscasts, obituaries, biographies, short stories, or sequels are some of the other forms students can use as they write in response to the literature they read.

Writing To Explain

Writing to explain or make factual information clear and understandable is a third kind of writing in response to literature. Sometimes this type of writing is aided when students create illustrative material such as a simple drawing, semantic web, or concept map. A graphic representation of ideas can often serve as a foundation for writing by providing organization and structure.

                    HOW THE KANGROO GOT ITS POUCH

ONCE UPON A TIME THERE WAS A KANGROO NAMED KANGA. SHE LIVED IN

A FIELD. ONE DAY A FROG CAME ALONG. HE SIAD. WILL YOU CARRY

THIS WORM FOR ME? HOW WILL ɪ CARRY IT ASKED THE KANGROO. BUT

THE FROG DIDN'T ANWSER HE JUST HOPPED AWAY. THEN ALONG CAME A

BUG. HE SAID WILL YOU CARRY THIS GRASSHOPPER FOR ME? HOW WILL

ɪ CARRY IT. ASKED THE KANGAROO. BUT THE BUG DIDN'T ANSWER HE

JUST CRAWLED AWAY.

ONE DAY THE KANGROO HAD ABABY THE BABY SAID. WILL YOU CARRY ME?

HOW WILL ɪ CARRY YOU? ASKED KANGROO THEN A WIZ ARD POPPED OUT

GO GET SOME CLOTH AND ɪ WILL SEW IT ON. THEY FOUND SOME CLOTH

AND THE WIZARD SEWED IT ON. AND THEN THE KANGROO HELPED EVERONE

AND CARRIED EVERTHING IN HER POUCH AND SHE LIVED HAPPILY EVER

AFTER.

Figure 5–8
A second grade student's first draft of a fable.

Abbey Karen Emily

Mrs Belva Lockwood

Mrs Belva A. Lockwood was born in Royalton Ny. June 1857. She started teaching when she was fourteen. She was married a few times, her madin name was McNoll. She was head of a school called The Owego Seminary she come in the fall of 1863 because she was head of that school. She left Owego in 1865. She got refused from a law school because the head of the school thought she would distract act the men and they wouldn't do there studying. She finaly got admited into the National Univarse. of Law. She was fanos because she was the first woman to practise for the seurpreme court. She ran for president of the U.S.A. in 1884 as the womens rights canadet. She was important person to the community.

Figure 5-9

The skit written from the narrative "Mrs. Belva Lockwood."

Two examples of nonfiction writing follow. In Figure 5-10, a seven-year-old draws a picture of "diploducus" in his journal and writes about what he has learned from reading a book about dinosaurs. In Figure 5-11, a fourth grader has read a "how-to" book about creating things using everyday objects. He writes the directions for making a paratrooper in his own words and accompanies them with drawings. A peer reads his directions and asks two questions — "What part?" and "Where?" — that are meant to help Brian revise for clarity.

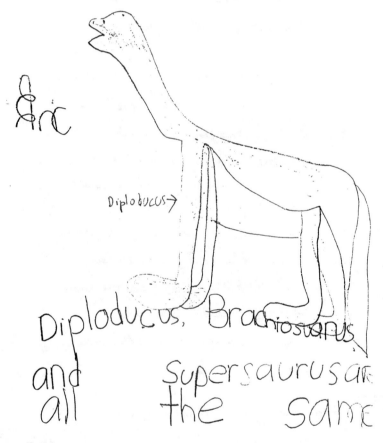

Figure 5-10
Eric explains what he has learned about three dinosaurs from his reading.

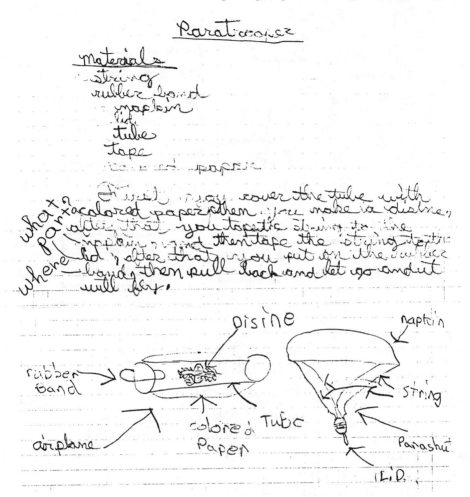

Figure 5-11
Brian's directions to explain how to make a paratrooper.

Two semantic maps created by third grade students and their teachers show you how webbing or mapping can be the basis for clearer explanatory writing in the form of character sketches and book comparisons. In Figure 5-12, character traits of the daughters in *Mufaro's Beautiful Daughters* (1987), by John Steptoe, are depicted. Ways in which Manyara and Nyasha are the same are shown in the boxes directly between their names. Words to describe how they are different appear in circles above Manyara and below Nyasha. Using this map, the writing of the three paragraph account to

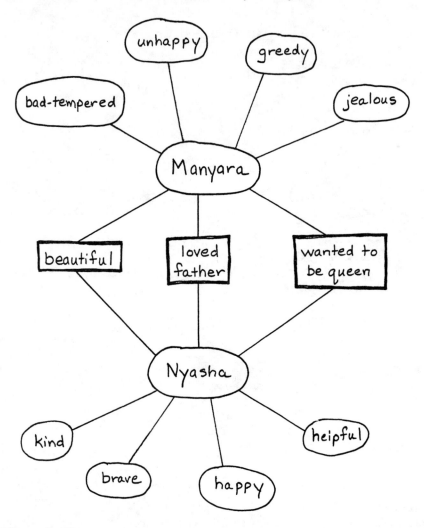

Figure 5-12
Semantic map created by third graders showing character traits of *Mufaro's Beautiful Daughters.*

explain how the story ends, in Figure 5-13, is made easier. The first paragraph describes Manyara's individual traits, the second Nyasha's, the third relates their common traits, and the fourth shows how the differences in their personalities result in the story's conclusion. In Figure 5-14, a group of third-grade students created a map to compare and contrast a story

Manyara and Nyasha

Manyara and Nyasha were the same in many ways. They were sisters, they were both beautiful girls, and they loved their father, Mufaro. Both of them wanted to be queen. They were both called before the king who was choosing a wife.

Manyara was not like Nyasha. Manyara was bad-tempered, unhappy, greedy, and jealous of her sister. Manyara snuck out to see the king first so he would choose her and not Nyasha.

Nyasha was different than Manyara. Nyasha was kind, brave, happy, and helpful. She helped some travelers on her way to see the king. Because she was kind and good she was chosen to be queen.

Figure 5-13
Character sketches written from the semantic map in Fig. 5-12.

whose pictures they especially liked, *Two Bad Ants* (1988), by Chris Van Allsburg, with the tale of Peter Rabbit, by Beatrix Potter, which they had heard and loved since kindergarten. Writing the report in Figure 5-15 about these two stories was much easier with the help of the map.

Student writing to explain or clarify can take many other forms that are also related to the literature they have read. Students can write letters of invitation, complaint, or inquiry or to inform. They can write reports, news articles, telegrams, interviews and sketches, learning logs, such as the one in Figure 5-16, and poetic song lyrics, such as those in Figure 5-17.

Writing To Persuade

A fourth type of writing done in response to literature is writing to persuade or convince. In this kind of writing, students try to change the opinion of others or influence the actions of the audience. Typically, students in grades three and beyond enjoy this kind of writing and do it with good success.

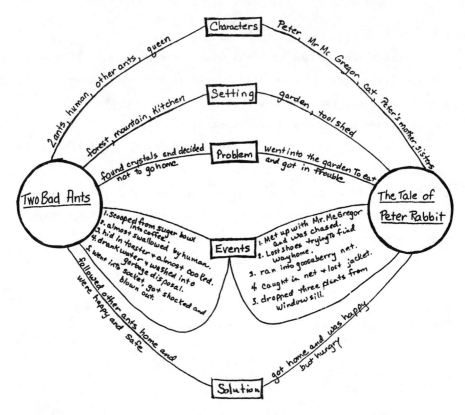

Figure 5–14
Semantic map made by third graders comparing the story *Two Bad Ants* and
The Tale of Peter Rabbit.

These two stories have the same problem. In both stories the main characters, Peter and the bad ants, go out to find food and get into trouble. Both stories end the same when Peter and the bad ants go back home where they are safe and happy. The setting for <u>Two Bad Ants</u> is a forest (grass in the lawn), a mountain (the brick house), and the kitchen of a house. The setting for <u>Peter Rabbit</u> is Mr. MacGregor's garden and the tool shed.

There are many events in both stories to show how the main characters get into trouble. In the story, <u>Two Bad Ants</u>, the ants get scooped from the sugar bowl and get thrown into hot coffee where they are almost swallowed by a human. Then, the two ants hide in a toaster where they almost get cooked. They become hot, they try and get a drink from the faucet. Accidentally, they get pulled into the garbage disposal. Finally, the two ants hide in a socket, only to find they are shocked and blown right out of the wall like "two bullets."

Peter Rabbit also gets into lots of trouble in his story. First, Peter meets up with Mr. MacGregor in the garden and Mr. MacGregor chased Peter. Peter gets away, but now he's lost. While Peter tries to find his way home, he loses both of his shoes. Then Peter ran into a gooseberry net and his jacket got caught. Mr. MacGregor sees Peter in the net. Peter frantically tries to escape. Peter escapes, only he loses his jacket in the process. Once again, Mr. MacGregor finds Peter in the tool shed. Peter jumped out of the window to get away. As he did this, three plants fell from the windowsill.

Both stories also have similar solutions. The bad ants found the other ants and followed them home. The ants were safe and happy. Peter Rabbit found the fence that would lead him home. Peter was safe and happy, too.

Figure 5-15
A book comparison written from the semantic map in Fig. 5-14.

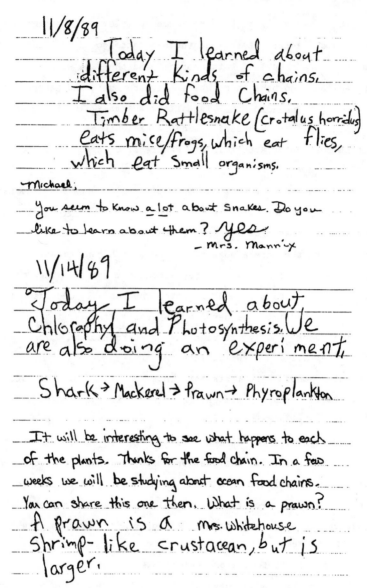

11/8/89

Today I learned about different kinds of chains. I also did food Chains.

Timber Rattlesnake (Crotalus horridus) eats mice/frogs, which eat flies, which eat small organisms.

Michael;

You seem to know a lot about Snakes. Do you like to learn about them? yes

— Mrs. Mannix

11/14/89

Today I learned about Chlorophyll and Photosynthesis. We are also doing an experiment.

Shark → Mackerel → Prawn → Phyroplankton

It will be interesting to see what happens to each of the plants. Thanks for the food chain. In a few weeks we will be studying about ocean food chains. You can share this one then. What is a prawn?

A prawn is a shrimp-like crustacean, but is larger.   Mrs. Whitehouse

Figure 5–16
Learning log of third grade student, with his teacher's responses.

Listen to the song

    we sing,

        Come and follow us

                Come and follow us

                   to the Underground

Come with us

Come with us,

    we're leavin' tonight

                We're comin'   we're

                  to ride the

                     train to freedom

We'll be leavin'

    tonight and we

        ain't coming back

                Listen to the

                 song we sing

                  and follow us

                    to freedom

                by Maxxe

Figure 5–17
A sixth grader connects with *If You Lived on the Underground Railroad* and explains its allure for slaves in these song lyrics.

In writing that persuades, students often need to state an opinion and support it with evidence, use vivid and specific vocabulary, and employ language and tone appropriate for a specific audience.

Here are two examples of this kind of writing. In Figure 5-18, the letter is an outgrowth of a social studies unit on the Civil War. The four students

East Middle School
167 East Frederick Street
Binghamton, New York 13904
October 2, 1989

Binghamton Press co.
Vestal Parkway East
Binghamton, New York 13902

Dear Editor:

Recently there was an issue before the Supreme Court about flag burning that we feel was resolved in an upsetting manner. We think it is important that we speak out on this manner as we feel it is unpatriotic to burn the flag in protest. Though it allows our freedoms as a democratic society to prevail it promotes trampling versus cherishing. The flag was flown for years over schoolhouses and public buildings as a symbol of the unity of our nation. Are we now going to allow someone the freedom to damage something that they teach us, as students, to pledge our lives and allegiance to everyday? We feel there should be an amendment to the Constitution that would protect our flag from such disfigurement. This amendment is needed to make the particular act flag burning punishable by law and to ensure the freedom of our flag to stand in its proper place. May our flag always remind us of the love and lives that allow us our freedoms today. Join us in writing to our Congress people for an amendment.

Sincerely,

Sincerely,

Gabe Guy
Gabe Guy

Marcia Hayes
Marcia Hayes

Robert Oakley
Robert Oakley

Melissa Rollins
Melissa Rollins

Figure 5-18
A persuasive letter written by sixth graders.

who wrote the letter had read their social studies text and several stories about the war, and they felt strongly that the flag represents freedom and democracy. They supported an amendment to the Constitution that would protect the flag and wanted to convince the readers of their local paper to write to their "Congress people" for an amendment. In Figure 5-19, the

THE INDIAN IN THE
Donald   a
CUPBOARD
by LynnE Reid Banks

The Indian in the Cupboard is about a plastic Indian given to Omri as a present. When he puts it in a medicine cabinet and locks it with an old key it becomes real. Omri has many adventures with his Indian. But then his friend makes a cowboy. This could only spell trouble with two 5 inch people involved.

Figure 5-19

A persuasive book review written by a sixth grade student.

book review of *The Indian In The Cupboard* (1981), by Lynn Reid Banks, was written by a sixth-grade student to convince her peers to read that book. Her class compiled a booklet called "Summertime Reading" of reviews of books they had read and particularly liked and thought their classmates might enjoy reading over the summer.

Advertisements, product descriptions, sales pitches, letters, tributes, and travel folders are a few of the many other forms that writing to persuade can take.

FINAL THOUGHTS

Whatever the form, type, or genre of writing in which you engage your students, remember that the link between reading and writing is critical because reading provides writers with connections that make writing more real and exciting for them. Remember, too, the importance of personal response to literature as a catalyst for writing. With these two thoughts firmly in place, you can more effectively engage your students in meaningful writing activities that use literature as a basic ingredient and span the curriculum.

REFERENCES

Atwell, N. (1987). *In the middle: Writing, reading, and learning with adolescents.* Portsmouth, NH: Heinemann.

Bromley, K. (1991). *Webbing with literature: Creating story maps with children's books.* Boston: Allyn & Bacon.

Bromley, K. (1989). Buddy journals make the reading-writing connection. *The Reading Teacher, 43*(2), 122-29.

Bromley, K. (1988). *Language arts: Exploring connections.* Boston: Allyn & Bacon.

Calkins, L. M. (1986). *The art of teaching writing.* Portsmouth, NH: Heinemann.

Cullinan, B. E. (1987). (Ed.) *Children's literature in the reading program.* Newark, DE: International Reading Association.

Evanechko, P., Ollila, L., & Armstrong, R. (1974). An investigation of the relationship between children's performance in written language and their reading ability. *Research in the Teaching of English, 8*(3), 315-326.

Fulwiler, T. (1987). *The journal book.* Portsmouth, NH: Heinemann.

Galda, L. (1988). Readers, texts, and contexts: A response-based view of literature in the classroom. *The New Advocate, I*(1), 84-91.

Gambrell, L. (1989). Developing motivated and strategic readers. Presentation to Binghamton Area Reading Council, Binghamton, NY, October 19, 1989.

Graves, D. (1983). *Writing: Teachers and children at work.* Portsmouth, NH: Heinemann.

Hammill, M. C., McNutt, G. (1980). Language abilities and reading: A review of the literature of their relationship. *Elementary School Journal, 80*(5), 269-277.

Kreeft, J. (1984). Dialogue writing: Bridge from talk to essay writing. *Language Arts, 61*(2), 141-150.

Loban, W. D. (1963). *The Language of Elementary School Children.* NCTE Research Report No. 1. Urbana, IL: National Council of Teachers of English.

Purves, A. C., Rogers, T., & Soter, A. O. (1990). *How porcupines make love II: Teaching a response-centered literature curriculum.* New York: Longman.

Rosenblatt, E. M. (1985). The transactional theory of the literary work: Implications for research. In *Researching response to literature and the teaching of literature: Points of departure.* Ed. C. R. Cooper. Norwood, NJ: Ablex, (pp. 33-53).

Shanahan, T. (1980). The impact of writing instruction on learning to read. *Reading World, 19*(4), 357-368.

Shanahan, T. (1984). Nature of the reading-writing relation: An exploratory multivariate analysis. *Journal of Educational Psychology, 76*(3), 466-477.

Shanahan, T., & Lomax, R. G. (1986). An analysis and comparison of theoretical models of the reading-writing relationship. *Journal of Educational Psychology, 78*(2), 116-123.

Smith, F. (1984). Reading Like A Writer. In J. M. Jensen (Ed.) *Composing and Comprehending.* Urbana, IL: National Council of Teachers of English, 47-56.

Smith, F. (1988). *Understanding reading, 4th ed.* New York: Holt.

Stotsky, S. (1984). Research on Reading/Writing Relationships: A synthesis and suggested directions. In J. M. Jensen (Ed.) *Composing and Comprehending.* Urbana, IL: National Council of Teachers of English, 7-22.

Tierney, R., & Pearson, P. D. (1983). Toward a composing model of reading. *Language Arts, 60*(5), 568-580.

Zeman, S. S. (1969). Reading comprehension and the writing of 2nd and 3rd graders. *The Reading Teacher, 23*(2), 144-150.

CHILDREN'S BOOK REFERENCES

Carle, E. (1988). *Have you seen my cat?* New York: Philomel.

Banks, L. R. (1981). *The Indian in the cupboard.* New York: Doubleday.

Hamilton, V. (1985). *The people could fly.* New York: Alfred Knopf.

Levine, E. (1988). *If you travelled on the underground railroad.* New York: Scholastic.

Martin, B., & Archambault, J. (1989). *Knots on a counting rope.* New York: Scholastic.

Montgomery, L. M. (1988). *Anne of green gables.* New York: Grossett & Dunlap.

Paterson, K. (1977). *Bridge to Terabithia.* New York: Crowell.

Potter, B. (1978). *A treasury of Peter Rabbit and other stories.* New York: Avenel.

Steptoe, J. (1987). *Mufaro's beautiful daughters.* New York: Lothrop, Lee & Shepard.

Van Allsburg, C. (1988). *Two bad ants.* Boston: Houghton Mifflin.

White, E. B. (1952). *Charlotte's web.* New York: Harper & Row.

6

"More Than Meets the Eye": Transformation Tales and the Integrated Curriculum

Jay Jacoby and Phyllis Allen

> "Change is our essence. We do not revere stasis or worship that which is stagnant. Whatever sacred quality there is to our lives is to a great extent dependent upon the powers of change.... It is a supreme mystery that the ever-changing should be ever so good and ever so enjoyable."
>
> J. McKim Malville, *The Fermenting Universe: Myths of Eternal Change*

Ours is a culture obsessed with change. To confirm this notion, we need look no further than our nearest Toys "R" Us. We discover there a world where, according to the people at Hasbro Toys, makers of the popular *Transformers,* there is "more than meets the eye." In that world, a truck is not just a truck but also "Autobot Leader Optimus Prime." Also, a crab is not just a crab but also "Deception Octopunch." Bringing about such multiple identities is child's play: A twist of the wrist can transform any object into something quite different from what it first appeared to be.

Hasbro is not alone in capitalizing upon children's fascination with toys that change. Galoob has marketed *Teenage Mutant Ninja Turtles,* lovable turtle pets turned into fighting turtle teens by way of a substance known as "Retromutagen Ooze" (a term that trips lightly from the lips of any aware second-grader). Mattel's *Popple* dolls can transform from pompons to cheerleaders and from flowers to cuddly playmates. Galoob's *Sweet Secrets* line offers baby dolls that become purses and lockets that become baby dolls ("There's always something new hiding inside for you").

Langdon Winner (1988) has observed that children's "playthings not only mirror current social obsessions but also nurture and sustain them" (p. 78). Our social obsessions are reflected not only in toys and games but also in what children see on television and at the movies. Saturday morning TV programs promote several transforming toys; for instance, *The Trans-formers: Dinobots S.O.S.* was a feature-length film. Many recent box office successes relate directly to the popular obsession with change: *Gremlins* (cuddly critters turn malevolent when allowed to eat after midnight); *Teen Wolf* (Michael J. Fox as adolescent werewolf); *Like Father, Like Son* (surgeon father and teenage son switch identities as a result of magic potion); *Batman* (millionaire Bruce Wayne becomes the Caped Crusader); *Honey, I Shrunk the Kids* (children reduced to micro-tots by dad's invention); *Big* (an eleven-year-old grows up overnight); and *Willow* (countless transformations, including men into swine).

At one time, it was considered sound educational practice to divert children's attention away from what were perceived to be the obsessions of popular culture, obsessions reflected in toys and films, as well as in folk and fantasy literature. Writing in *Education* (1921), Gilbert Brown saw little reason for using myths, folklore, and fairy stories as basal reading for children because "the contemporary child has nothing in common with ancient civilizations" (cited in Shannon, p. 48). In that same year, Lucy Sprague Mitchell likened folk literature to the circus, an empty stimulation unrelated to the present times (*Here and Now Story Book,* p. 21).

We think it fortunate that times have changed since Brown and Mitchell counseled elementary school instructors. Now, at all levels, it is acceptable classroom practice to acknowledge, encourage, develop, and critically examine the interests of folk and popular culture. What follows is an exploration of how teachers can cultivate one such interest — the fascination with change, especially as it is treated in ancient and modern stories of transformation.

We agree with J. McKim Malville that the ever-changing is "ever so good and ever so enjoyable." We would add to those qualities "ever so teachable." Because all children experience change daily, it is a subject that speaks directly to them. The theme of transformation has inspired many excellent children's stories. What is more, it is a theme that readily lends itself to integration into all aspects of the elementary school curriculum. Before focusing upon a specific sequence of activities for using transformation stories in the classroom, we offer the following classification and history of those stories along with a rationale for their use.

In tales of transformation, humans, mythical figures, animals, and even inanimate objects change their natural bodily form. At times those physical changes are total: animals change species or become human; humans become wolves, trees, machines, or other humans. Mary Rodgers's *Freaky*

Friday (1972) offers a fine example of this last kind of transformation. The book opens with thirteen-year-old Annabel Andrews announcing, "When I woke up this morning, I found I turned into my mother." In Rodgers's *Summer Switch* (1982) it is a boy and his father who exchange identities. In some stories, characters undergo multiple changes of form. *Once a Mouse* (1961), Marcia Brown's richly illustrated retelling of a fable from ancient India, describes how a hermit transforms a wretched little mouse into a stout cat, a big dog, a fierce tiger, and then back to humble mouse again.

Sometimes, transformations are only partial: humans become centaurs, mermaids, and so forth. Such is the case in David Small's *Imogene's Antlers* (1985), where a little girl awakens one morning to discover that she has sprouted a full head of antlers (all of which makes dressing for school quite difficult!). Similarly, nine-year-old Allen Brewster of John Reynolds Gardiner's *Top Secret* (1984) develops green skin and root nodules as a result of his science project on human photosynthesis.

In other stories, physical transformations involve just one aspect of anatomical change. In *Alice's Adventures in Wonderland,* for example, the title character remains human but undergoes several traumatic transformations in size. So does the young Vicky in William Sleator's *Among the Dolls* (1975). On the other hand, Irv Irving of Arthur Yorinks's *It Happened in Pinsk* (1983) transforms in neither size nor species but still experiences a remarkable change: "One morning, March 19, at breakfast, Irv was just about to eat a roll when he realized his head was missing." Any child who has been repeatedly told that "You'd probably lose your head if it weren't attached to your body" is likely to identify with poor Irv and with the exasperated response of Irv's wife: "Every day you lose something. Your keys. Your glasses. Now this."

The Transformer craze notwithstanding, these tales of change are not a recent phenomenon; nor are they bound to any one culture. According to folklorists, they are among the oldest and most widely distributed of all stories. At their simplest level, such stories reflect nothing more, and at the same time nothing more miraculous, than metamorphosis — the substitution of forms in nature — or development: an egg becomes a caterpillar, chrysalis, and butterfly; an ugly duckling changes into a beautiful swan. Metamorphosis is the subject of several wonderful works of nonfiction for children: Alvin and Virginia Silverstein's *Metamorphosis: The Magic Change* (1972), Gladys Conklin's *How Insects Grow* (1969), Barrie Watt's *Butterfly and Caterpillar* (1986), William White's *A Frog is Born* (1974), and Bronson's *Pollywiggle's Progress* (1942). Though transformation stories often focus on growth and development, they may also image decline. Shel Silverstein's *The Giving Tree* (19   ) provides an example of the latter.

When transformation is achieved voluntarily, without the action of another, it is referred to as *shape-shifting.* Proteus, a Greek god of the sea from whom we derive the word *protean,* meaning "changeable," assumed the shape of many fierce creatures to avoid having to tell the truth to a questioner; if the questioner was able to hold on to Proteus during this ordeal, the truth would be told. To carry out his various love affairs, Zeus appeared in the form of a white bull, a swan, and a shower of gold.

Many transformations of classical myth are treated in Ovid's *Metamorphosis,* which some regard as the forerunner of more recent tales of change. An excellent collection of such modern stories is Jane Yolen's *Shape Shifters: Fantasy and Science Fiction Tales about Humans Who Can Change Their Shapes* (1978). Yolen gathers stories of less traditional transformations such as human into bird (Dinesen's "The Sailor-Boy's Tale"), into insect (Kafka's "The Metamorphosis"), and into squid (Scortia's "The Judas Fish"), and accompanies them with introductory material that demonstrates the worldwide diffusion of tales of shape-shifting.

In addition to voluntary shape-shifting, transformation can be the result of magic, of the actions of supernatural powers. Several North American Indian creation legends have at their center the figure of Transformer, a trickster-hero who roamed the world changing animals and the physical environment into their current forms. It is not surprising that the theme of transformation figures so heavily in the culture of Native Americans, where kinship between man and animal is of vital importance. Paul Goble offers the following introduction to *Buffalo Woman* (1984), a retelling of the Indian legend of a buffalo that appears as a beautiful maiden in order to marry a young hunter: "It was felt that retelling the story had power to bring about a change within each of us; that in listening we might all be a little more worthy of our Buffalo relatives." For other Native American tales of transformation suitable for elementary readers, see Goble's *The Girl Who Loved Wild Horses* (1986), Elizabeth Cleaver's *The Enchanted Caribou* (1985), and Hettie Jones's *Longhouse Winter: Iroquois Transformation Tales* (1972).

In many folk and fairy tales, spells are cast upon the hero who then turns into an animal, an object, or a person. In *Beauty and the Beast,* a prince is transformed into a loathesome creature. The fair-haired heroine of Jane Yolen's *Dove Isabeau* (1989) is turned into a fire-breathing dragon by her evil stepmother. In Collodi's *Pinocchio,* the Blue Fairy changes a marionnette into a real live boy. Sometimes, as in the latter story, transformation occurs as a reward. Pinocchio's physical transformation occurs only after an inner transformation, which John Cech has characterized as "the process of growing up, of moving . . . from that egocentric, undisciplined inexperienced world of childhood into an adolescence or young adulthood that is self-sacrificing, responsible, knowing" (p. 172).

Sometimes transformation occurs as punishment. Lot's wife violates God's orders and is turned into a pillar of salt. Because she rivaled Athena in spinning, Arachne becomes a spider. Pinocchio's nose increases in size as a result of not telling the truth. Because he watches too much television, Shel Silverstein's "Jimmy Jet" becomes a TV set (*Where the Sidewalk Ends,* p. 29).

A special variation on the transformation tale is the story involving "transformation combat," wherein two individuals assume various shapes in an effort to defeat one another. The film, *Willow,* concludes with such a battle. The "Second Kalandar's Tale" of the *Arabian Nights* has the princess and the genie compete through many transformation: lion and sword, scorpion and serpent, cat and wolf, and so forth.

Frequently, transformation combat involves a competition between a master and an apprentice magician, with the pupil defeating his teacher (an event many children often dream about). Such a battle is described in Joanna Cole's wonderful *Doctor Change* (1986) where a poor boy named Tom is held against his will by an evil sorcerer. Tom manages to escape but is pursued by Doctor Change. He is then aided by Kate, a young woman whose coin he had retrieved from a well by transforming himself into a frog. Tom ultimately outwits his master through a series of marvellous transformations — bucket, saddle, ring, rice, and, finally, fox who eats Doctor Change, who had transformed himself into a rooster. Tom and Kate marry, and Tom is "so happy to be himself that he forgot all about changing into anyone or anything else." On the final page of the book, however, we see Tom in the form of a jack-in-the-box: "But sometimes he did [change] to make the baby laugh."

A story like *Doctor Change* should need no justification for telling in an elementary school classroom. It should be told and retold for its own sake, for the simple reason that, as Jane Yolen says, it's a "whopping good" tale ("Shape Shifters," p. 701). The same might be said for all the transformation stories addressed in this essay. Nonetheless, for those seeking a rationale for such stories or for making such stories the hub around which units will be developed — for when the principal, or parent, or supervisor asks — we offer the following observations.

Because they treat change and because the essence of life is change, transformation stories seem a natural choice upon which to center an elementary curriculum. Studying change in literature prepares readers to deal with changes they will encounter in life. Furthermore, transformation stories can easily stimulate learning and discussion activities that would fulfill curricular objectives in a variety of areas: science, social studies, health, math, and so forth.

Though this may provide a *practical* explanation for planning an integrated curriculum around transformation stories, it is perhaps the least important component of our rationale. Such stories should not be thought of peripherally — as means to the more pragmatic ends of, say, developing computational or word attack skills or learning about China's geography. At the heart of our plan is the idea that stories should be read, first and foremost, for their own sake, for the pleasure they provide.

At one level, the use of stories in the classroom, regardless of whether they deal with transformation or not, serves to advance children's aesthetic literacy. In addition to developing language skills, stories get back to the basics of our literary culture; they open doors for the rest of a child's literary experiences and perceptions. This is especially true of transformation stories since the content of such tales is central to nearly all literature. In a sense, all human stories are tales of transformation and growth: The hero ventures out, undergoes certain trials, and returns home, sometimes stronger, wiser, or broader of heart.

Perhaps the most basic questions for any literary study are: "Are the characters different at the end of the story from what they were at its beginning?" "How have they changed?" "Why?" A familiarity with the more visible changes that occur in basic transformation stories (Pinocchio's growth from wooden puppet to flesh-and-blood child) prepares young readers for the more complex, inner transformations they are likely to encounter in later literature (Pip's development from egocentric prig to a more morally aware individual in *Great Expectations*).

Readers who have been given a foundation of transformation tales upon which to base their later reading may be better prepared for the profoundly changeable nature of the people they will meet in modern literature, where characters are neither unitary nor internally consistent but complex and divided (see McCormick, Waller, and Flower, pp. 185–186). We would suppose, for example, that Nathan Zuckerman, the changeable anti-hero of Philip Roth's *The Counterlife,* would meet with less resistance from readers familiar with the myth of Proteus or *Doctor Change.*

In addition to enriching children's literary perceptions, frequent contact with stories extends children's perception of the world. Stories help children come to know a wide range of cultures and social patterns in terms of both time and space. Especially when studying variations on a theme — studying, for example, versions of "The Frog Prince" from Germany, Africa, and South America, or classic and modern versions of "The Ugly Duckling" — students can, while developing skills in classification and analysis, also develop greater tolerance and understanding of others.

A closely related reason for developing story-awareness in children is its moral value. A study of story serves to educate a child's imagination, which is, as Stefan Kanfer points out, "the foundation of the moral sense" (p. 68). A child who is able to imagine how a tormented classmate feels is less likely to torment that classmate, and perhaps more likely to stop others from their teasing.

Finally, stories are psychologically therapeutic. They are a means for developing inner resources with which we can think and feel. Finally, stories are psychologically therapeutic. They are a means for developing inner resources with which we can think and feel. In an excellent argument for "restorying the adult" in order to promote the primacy of the imagination, James Hillman observes that adults are far better able to cope with life if they experienced a childhood built with stories. He notes, "One integrates life as story because one has stories in the back of the mind (unconscious) as containers for organizing events into meaningful experiences. The stories are means of finding oneself in events that might not otherwise make psychological sense at all" (p. 43).

Nowhere is the therapeutic value of story more evident than in the tale of transformation. In accounting for why such tales have fascinated readers for so long, Jane Yolen eloquently notes (*Shape Shifters,* pp. 181-182):

> . . . we are all shape shifters. Only, instead of changing in a moment of agonizing alteration under the hollow-eyed moon, we have changed molecule by molecule, cell by cell, scale by scale, bone by bone, over eons of unrecorded time.
>
> . . . we are still changing. Scientists tell us so. They point out how mutations occur every day, brought on by both known and unknown sources: the food we eat, the air we breathe, the water we drink are all changing as the chemicals in the earth and sea and sky change. And they, in turn change us.
>
> . . . So we are not the end of creation but only a way-stop somewhere along the line. We are changing and being changed. None of us knows, really knows, what will be the next step, or can say with any certainty what humans *will turn into.*

Tales of transformation may remain popular because they prepare us to imagine the future. But, Yolen suggests, such tales also take us to our primal past; they return us "each to our animal beginnings when we ran on all fours and chittered at the moon" ("Shape Shifters," p. 699). It is this latter quality that is specially appealing to children, because "all children are born feral. And the memory of the beast is still within us" ("Shape Shifters," p. 700). For this reason, folklore — especially the transformation tale — provides what Yolen describes as a "perfect second skin," one that children can put on and take off at will. Moreover, she suggests that the vision conferred upon young readers by donning such a second skin has applications beyond animal and human duality. Such a vision, as stimulated by folklore, also takes in the world of both adult and child: "We need to be both child *and* adult, adult *and* child; to be able to change our emotional shapes enough so that in the end we can come back into our real skins and look both inward and outward with eyes that are clear" ("Shape Shifters," p. 703).

Children's absorption in transformation tales, wherein they may vicariously play dual roles (child and adult, duckling and swan, frog and prince), can lead them to make discoveries about themselves since sometimes the self can be known only when it is temporarily dissociated from the body, as something other than the self, or even opposite to the self (see Massey, p. 3). This form of dissociation, carried out through literary experience, can be viewed as a coping mechanism. As Yolen points out, "All shapeshifting might be viewed as a desire — or fear — of humans who feel unable to cope with their real lives" (*Shape Shifters,* p. 175).

Exposure to literary characters who change may help readers cope more with fluctuations in their own identities. They may come to value more the protean nature of the self, and they may be less predisposed to expect absolute consistency in human behavior. It is for holding such an ideal of consistency that D. H. Lawrence took that quintessential American, Benjamin Franklin, to task (*Studies,* p. 9): "I am many men. Which of them are you going to perfect? I am not a mechanical contrivance. . . . When every man as long as he remains alive is in himself a multitude of conflicting men. Which of these do you choose to perfect, at the expense of every other?"

Young readers, too, are many men and women. In a sense, the dual identities of characters a child encounters in transformation tales correspond with and somehow tacitly condone how that child will project on to someone else, often some imaginary being, all those aspects of behavior that are too negative to be recognized as part of him or herself. Such a projection mechanism can also apply to others. Thus, Bruno Bettelheim notes that the transformation of Little Red Riding Hood's Grandma into a wolf may appear silly on the surface (p. 66)

But when viewed in terms of a child's way of experiencing, is it really any more scary than the sudden transformation of his own kindly grandma into a figure who threatens his very sense of self when she humiliates him for a pants-wetting accident? To the child, Grandma is no longer the same person she was just a moment before; she has become an ogre.

Perhaps most importantly, exposure to transformation tales leads children to accept change as something natural, necessary, and positive. Bettelheim observes that "the child intuitively comprehends that . . . fairy tales depict in imaginary and symbolic form the essential steps in growing up and achieving an independent existence" (p. 73). Transformation tales reassure young readers that change is possible. Such reassurance, Bettelheim notes, is perhaps the greatest contribution folk and fairy tales make to a child's development (p. 179):

> If there is a central theme to the wide variety of fairy tales, it is that of rebirth to a higher plane. Children (and adults, too) must be able to believe that reaching a higher form of existence is possible if they master the developmental steps this requires. Stories which tell that this is not only possible but likely have a tremendous appeal to children, because such tales combat the ever-present fear that they won't be able to make this transition, or that they'll lose too much in the process.

The appeals of the transformation tales that Bettelheim describes here, along with those of Yolen, provide excellent reasons for using such tales in elementary classrooms. Such stories as *The Girl Who Loved Wild Horses* and *Beauty and the Beast* carry implicit messages that often cannot — and perhaps should not — be taught explicitly. Ursula Le Guin offers cogent commentary on such stories (p. 141):

> . . . they speak *from* the unconscious *to* the unconscious, in the *language* of the unconscious — symbol and archetype. Though they use words, they work the way music does: they short-circuit verbal reasoning, and go straight to the thoughts that lie too deep to utter. . . . They are profoundly meaningful, and usable — practical — in terms of ethics; of insight; of growth.

Vital as they are, the messages of those tales are the *by-products* of the readings we select and sequence for our students and the multiple activities we develop that relate to those readings. Needless to say, the process of selecting, sequencing, and integrating stories of transformation into the curriculum requires resourcefulness, creativity, and thoughtful planning.

There are two ways to begin planning for a literature-based integrated curriculum: 1) selecting a central theme, or 2) identifying a single story (or cluster of stories) that will link to instructional objectives and offer rich possibilities for activities. Regardless of how one begins, we suggest *webbing* to assist in planning (see Norton). Webbing is a way of generating, sorting, and displaying information; of subdividing a complex subject into more manageable subtopics.

Suppose that a teacher opts to develop a unit around the general topic of *transformation*. He might start with a web like the one reproduced in Figure 6-1.

Once the initial web is drawn, the teacher could, depending upon his purposes, select a subtopic and create an additional web as is illustrated in Figure 6-2 on page 156.

This web might have been created by a sixth-grade teacher who, after introducing the many wonders and advantages of transformation, wants to raise the students' consciousnesses about some possible disadvantages. That teacher may be heeding the warning of Langdon Winner, who laments the messages that toys such as Transformers send to "a generation that will face important ethical decisions about the possibilities offered by gene splicing and other forms of biotechnology" (p. 78). To call into question any uncritical acceptance of man-made change, students in this sixth-grade class will finish out their year's exploration of transformation with a study of the ethical dimensions of ecology and biotechnology.

In preparing webs, teachers can work alone, with colleagues, or with their students. To introduce a unit on transformation to fourth graders, a teacher might share with her students Arthur Yorinks's *Louis the Fish* (1980), a splendidly illustrated tale that begins "One day last spring, Louis, a butcher, turned into a fish. Silvery scales. Big lips. A tail. A salmon." Following a discussion of the book and the concept of transformation, the teacher might ask the class to identify various categories of transformations, recording their work in a web such as the one that appears in Figure 6-3.

For the next step, students and teacher can begin identifying stories that relate to each of the categories they have identified: the myth of Narcissus for "Human into Flower"; *The Fly* for "Human into Insect"; Steig's *Sylvester and the Magic Pebble* (wherein a donkey is changed into a rock) for "Animal into Object"; the Biblical story of Aaron's Rod for "Object into Animal"; and so forth.

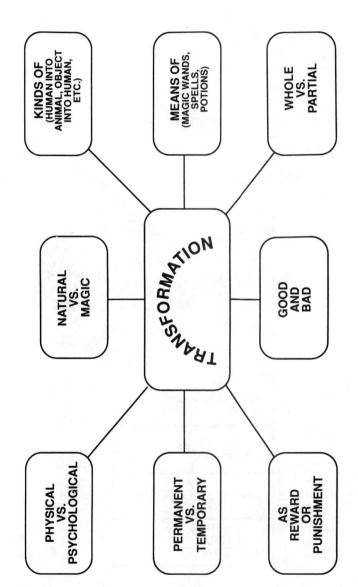

Figure 6–1
Types of Transformations

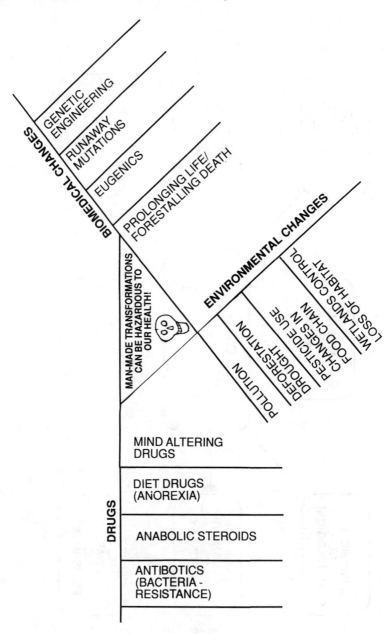

Figure 6-2
Transformation Chart of a Sixth-Grade Teacher

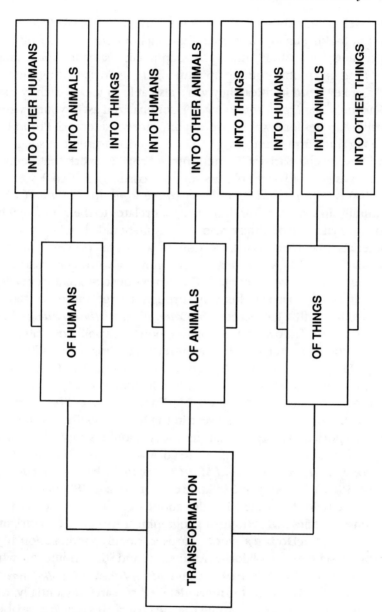

Figure 6-3
Categories of Transformation

To develop their library skills, students can discover books to add to the class list by looking up key words and reading book summaries from cards in the catalog. Under the "Human to Amphibian" category, for example, students had no trouble coming up with *The Frog Prince.* Using the word "Frog" as a key word in titles, they were also able to locate such works as Dale Carlson's *The Frog People* (1982), summarized as "A young woman frantically searches for a way to prevent any more residents of Proud Point from being transformed into frogs." They also discovered the song "One Day My Best Friend Barbara Turned Into A Frog" (a work that needs no summary!) as part of Barry Polisar's sound recording entitled *My Brother Thinks He's a Banana and Other Provocative Songs for Children* (1977).

Naturally, in searching for literature that relates to their unit, teachers should also make use of library resources. A first-grade teacher, searching for materials that treat transformation as a natural process and using "Caterpillar" as his key word, located the following works: Eric Carle's *The Very Hungry Caterpillar* (1981) (fiction: traces development from egg, to hungry caterpillar that eats his way through a large variety of food, to cocoon and butterfly); Jack Kent's *The Caterpillar and the Polliwog* (1982) (fiction: unaware of its own pattern of development, a polliwog watches the transformation of a caterpillar into a butterfly and hopes to do likewise); Caroline O'Hagen's *It's Easy to Have a Caterpillar Visit You* (1980) (non-fiction: the care and feeding of caterpillar, including what to do when it turns into a chrysalis); and Robert McClung's *Sphinx: The Story of a Caterpillar* (1981) (nonfiction: a year in the life of a sphinx moth).

One important resource that teachers should know about when searching for literature is Margaret Read MacDonald's *The Storyteller's Sourcebook: A Subject, Title, and Motif Index to Folklore Collections for Children* (1987). Indexing 556 folktale collections and 389 picture books, this resource helps to locate (1) tales about a given subject, (2) titles in collections, (3) tales from ethnic or geographical areas, and (4) variants of a specific tale. MacDonald's work is a user-friendly modification of the classification schemes of folklorists Antii Aarne and Stith Thompson, whose *The Types of the Folktale* (1961) and *Motif-Index of Folk-Literature* (1958) could be consulted for more detailed research. Essentially, these works categorize folklore according to type (narratives that are capable of maintaining an independent existence) and motif (an element of a narrative — a concept, phenomenon, happening, creature, object).

Read's *Sourcebook* lists no less than ten double-columned pages relating to the theme of transformation (motifs D. 8-D. 699). Subcategories include "Transformation: man to animal"; "animal to person"; "other forms" (flower to person, rice to gold); "means of transformation" (by putting on animal skin, by sticking magic pin into head, by eating,); and "miscellaneous transformation incidents" (escapes where small objects cast in pursuers' path change into massive obstacles: mirror becomes lake). Each of these listings will direct readers to a text containing a tale suitable for children. For example, a reader investigating animals who change into humans could look under "Transformation: rat to person" (Motif D315.1) and locate, in So-Un Kim's *The Story Bag: A Collection of Korean Folk Tales* (1955), a tale wherein a rat eats a student's nail clippings and assumes his identify (a perfect story to tie in with lessons on personal hygiene!).

Instead of looking under the broad category of transformation in Read's *Sourcebook,* we can also investigate narrower subjects, such as tales relating to a particular animal, and be rewarded with multiple references. For example, second graders who have encountered the motif of the snake who is really a prince in John Steptoe's *Mufaro's Beautiful Daughters: An African Folktale* (1987) might enjoy discovering worldwide variations on that theme. Read's index leads us to the following, to name but a few: Kermit Krueger's *The Serpent Prince: Folk Tales from Northeastern Thailand* (1969); John Hampden's *The Gypsy Fiddle and other Tales told by Gypsies* (1969); Ruth Bryan Owen's *The Castle in the Silver Wood and other Scandinavian Folk Tales* (1939); "Oda and the Snake," an Austrian tale collected in Ruth Manning-Sanders's *The Book of Sorcerers and Spells* (1973); and from Brittainy, "White Cat and the Green Snake," in *The Book of Princes and Princesses* (1969), also edited by Manning-Sanders.

Whether we identify similar transformation motifs through Read's *Sourcebook* or other research, arranging for comparative readings offers students at all levels the opportunity to discover that "All themes and characters and stories that you encounter in literature belong to one big interlocking family" (Frye, *The Educated Imagination,* cited in Moss and Stott, p. 1). In selecting and sequencing stories for children, we should reinforce this vital concept. Instead of basing story selection on vocabulary and skills taught, we should focus on meaning, encouraging literacy *through* the literature rather than as a prerequisite for it. Stories should be chosen and linked according to how they relate to the "family of stories" and yet retain their own individual, distinctive qualities. Students at all levels should be challenged to make connections between the stories they read or hear.

Consider, for example, the following sequence of picture books, chosen for a third-grade unit intended to help readers distinguish between natural and magical transformations:

—Eric Carle's *The Very Hungry Caterpillar* (1981): metamorphosis of a single species depicted realistically with the all-important exception of the food the caterpillar eats.

—Jack Kent's *The Caterpillar and the Pollywog* (1982): metamorphosis of *two* species contrasted in a whimsical but essentially factual manner.

—Alvin and Virginia Silverstein's *Metamorphosis: The Magic Change* (1972): a thoroughly realistic treatment of metamorphosis of several species, including, moths, frogs, dragonflies, and "The Sea Squirt: The Tadpole that Isn't." This text offers opportunities to check the accuracy of the more fanciful depictions and to address the figurative use of the word "magic" in the book's title.

—Steven Kellogg's *The Mysterious Tadpole* (1977): Louis's tadpole, a gift from his Scottish Uncle MacAllister, does not turn into a frog but rather into a loveable Loch Ness monster. A clear introduction to fantasy (talk about a "tadpole that isn't!").

—Leo Lionni's *Fish is Fish* (1970): a fanciful contrast of a species that undergoes metamorphosis (frog) with one that does not (fish), leading to the conclusion "Frogs are frogs and fish is fish and that's that!"

—Tomie dePaola's "The Frog Prince" (from his *Favorite Nursery Tales*) (1988): a classic challenge to the notion that "Frogs are frogs."

—Arthur Yorinks's *Louis the Fish* (1980): a challenge to the notion that those who are transformed are always unhappy. While the prince who was turned into a frog bewailed his fate and sought retransformation, Louis, an unhappy butcher who can't stand meat, is delighted to be a fish.

Once we have settled on a transformation theme to explore and a variety of texts to help in that exploration, we need to generate a list of activities that will actively involve students, activities that can stimulate, reinforce, and help assess student learning. It is here, especially, that we should make an effort to integrate our theme and the literature we have chosen with the objectives of various content areas of the curriculum. Once again, a web, such as the all-purpose one reproduced in Figure 6-4, can help get us started in the process:

In our planning, we think it important that activities be generated first, with an eye toward those that are based on the interests and needs of students and those that will excite student and teacher alike. Then we can link the activities with whatever specific learning objectives or competencies are specified by our curriculum guides, basic education plans, and so forth. Once this process has begun, we can ask whether we have adequately covered the content areas (we never feel compelled to cover them *all*) and

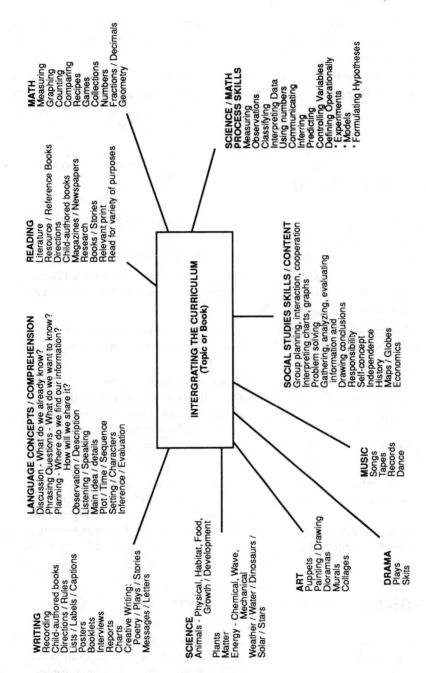

Figure 6-4
Integrating the Curriculum

whether our activities provide for different teaching strategies, learning modes, individual differences, and so forth. Then we can make any necessary adjustments.

What follows is a set of content area activities developed to correspond with the third-grade unit on "Transformations: Natural and Magical." Texts for this unit would include those listed on pp. 158-59, with special emphasis given to *The Frog Prince.*

SCIENCE/MATH

—Understanding physical vs. chemical change: Students will mold clay/carve soap into animal forms (physical change); they will combine egg, flour, shortening, and so forth to make cake (chemical change).

—Understanding life-cycles/interpreting charts: Students will read about and prepare charts showing various life cycles (seed-seedling-plant-seed; egg-tadpole-frog).

—Understanding transforming processes in nature: Students will learn about how plants convert sun, water and carbon dioxide into food, about human digestion, and so forth.

—Understanding human growth and development: Students will create a time line using photos of themselves to show changes from infant to toddler to nine-year-old; they will measure and chart their own growth (height, weight, lost teeth, time in mile run, physical fitness test results) at various times of the year; they will compare sizes (tracings of hands) with other family members.

—Performing experiments/generating hypotheses: Students will adopt a caterpillar, tadpole, seed, plot of school property, and observe and record changes that occur during the school year; students will generate hypotheses regarding growth and development, infer what changes would occur if variables change, and so forth.

GEOGRAPHY/SOCIAL STUDIES

—Students will understand how land masses are formed: They will study maps and globes showing how continents that are now separate were once connected; they will study volcanoes and earthquakes (fast changes) and weathering and erosion (slow changes) and their effects on the earth's crust.

—Students will understand basic concepts of ecology: They will learn how disturbances in food chains and other man-made changes such as pollution and deforestation have significant environmental consequences.

—Students will understand how stories are transmitted and transformed among various cultures: They will play a "Whispering Down the Lane" game, to demonstrate how a story changes each time it is retold; they will read transformation tales from several different cultures, locating those cultures on a map, reporting on their customs, discussing similarities and differences among stories; they will do likewise with several variants of *The Frog Prince* drawn from different countries, such as Norway (Mayer's *East of the Sun*), Germany (Segal's *The Juniper Tree*), Scotland ("The Well at the World's End" in Jacobs' *English Folk and Fairy Tales*), Russia (Isele's *The Frog Princess*), and South Africa (*The Bird Who Made Milk,* cited in Leach, p. 426).

—Students will understand how a story impacts on popular culture: They will locate in various magazines, newspapers, and the like allusions to "The Frog Prince." We found greeting cards, T-shirts, dolls (frog on one side/prince on other), bumperstickers ("You've Gotta Kiss Lots of Frogs before You Find a Prince"), ads for A. T. & T. (a toddler changes her baby sister into a frog) and photo stores ("Prints Charming"), comic books, cartoons by Gary Larson, Mike Thaler, and in *Mad Magazine* (the frog is transformed into rock star, Prince).

—Students will apply notion of multiple identities to their own self-concept.: They will create and discuss a "This is Me" collage, made up of pictures and phrases (gleaned from magazines, etc.) that represent the many parts that make up who they are.

ART/MUSIC/DRAMA/DANCE

—Students will develop visual literacy: They will compare written and filmed versions of *The Frog Prince* (several of the latter are available including a Muppet version and a Fairy Tale Theatre version starring Robin Williams and Terri Garr); they will compare various visual interpretations of *The Frog Prince* ranging from simple line drawings of Lenski (Hutchinson) and Gag, cartoon-like treatments of Marshall (Tarcov) and dePaola, more sophisticated pen-and-ink drawings of Rackham (Lucas) and Sendak (Segal), and full-scale color illustrations of Crane and Isadora.

—Students will create visual interpretations of a story: They will draw book covers, cartoons, illustrations of key scenes, dioramas for *The Frog Prince*; they will create masks and paper bag puppets (frog on one side, prince on the other) for the story.

—Students will create non-verbal and dramatic interpretations: They will engage in role-playing of parts from *The Frog Prince,* emphasizing especially physical movement (see Carr); students will do a puppet presentation of *The Frog Prince* (see Mahlmann); students will perform songs, dances, and other movement activities relating to transformation.

LANGUAGE ARTS/READING/WRITING

—Students will understand how words are transformed: They will review how silent "e" at the end of a word transforms preceding vowel from short sound to long, or how tense shift is signalled by changes (swim, swam, swum).

—Students will develop a sense of plot sequence: They will list events of a story and arrange them in their proper sequence.

—Students will discuss effects of changes in story elements: They will compare various ways in which frog was transformed into prince (a kiss, beheading, having skin burnt, being thrown against wall).

—Students will experiment in genre: They will translate the story of *The Frog Prince* into poems, limericks, haiku, rap, drama, and the like.

—Students will create their own transformation tales: They will write their own versions of a transformation myth, perhaps with the help of a story-starter: "When _____ woke up one morning, she discovered she was a _____." Here is an excerpt from one such story, written by third graders Jessica Tate and Shon Hampton, following a visit to their class from Jay Jacoby. The students decided to transform Jay into a pumpkin, the result of his not removing his jack-o-lantern costume after trick-or-treating. We pick up the action with Jay's mother trying to humor her pumpkin son:

"Okay, you *are* a jack-o-lantern so you can leave your costume on. Oops, I forgot, it's not a costume. I'm sorry."

So he kept it on for eight days. One day he came down for breakfast and his mother said, "Honey, you smell bad. Go take a shower."

Then she turned around and said, "Honey, what is that brown spot on you?" Then his sister Ellen walked in and said, "Hi, rot face!"

Shortly after this scene, sister Ellen convinces Jay that his mom is planning to bake him into a pie!.

—Students will write diaries and journals: They can keep a diary written from the point of view of a transformed character — "A Day in the Life of a Prince-turned-Frog"; students will record predictions for the future of transformed characters. Susan Mitchell's "From the Journals of the Frog Prince" (Mieder, pp. 38-39), though written for adults, offers a fine example: The frog, transformed back into prince, longs for his froggy days, "for wet leaves, the slap of water against rocks" and thinks "that trasnformations are not forever."

—Students will practice letter writing: They will write to "Dear Abby," explaining their transformation problems: "Dear Abby, Please help me! I woke up this morning with antlers on my head"; they will exchange letters, and write back from the standpoint of Abby: "Dear Antlers, The first thing you have to do is stay away from men wearing funny orange hats."

Our list of activities for integrating transformation stories into elementary content areas is by no means exhaustive. [For more suggestions, see Bette Bosma's excellent *Fairy Tales, Fables, Legends, and Myths: Using Folk Literature In Your Classroom* (1987).] We do hope to have shown that tales of transformation, like the toys they have inspired, can offer "more than meets the eye." In addition to being "whopping good tales," stories of transformation cannot help but promote exciting teaching and learning in several content areas. Keeping such stories alive for our children — in fact and in fiction — telling, hearing, reading, writing, drawing, and acting them, witnessing their many transformations through many cultures and generations, does have the power to bring about a change within each of us, an understanding, reverence, and hope for change that is our essence.

REFERENCES

Aarne, A. & Thompson, S. (1961). *The types of the folktale: A classification and bibliography* Helsinki: Suomalainen Tiedeakatemie.

Bettelheim, B. (1977). *The uses of enchantment: The meaning and importance of fairy tales.* New York: Vintage.

Bosma, B. (1987). *Fairy tales, fables, legends, and myths: Using folk literature in your classroom.* New York: Teachers College Press

Bronson, W. S. (1942). *Pollwiggle's Progress.* New York: Macmillan.

Brown, M. (1961). *Once a mouse.* New York: Scribners.

Carle, E. (1981). *The very hungry caterpillar.* New York: Putnam.

Carlson, D. (1982). *The frog people.* New York: Dutton.

Carr, R. (1973). *Be a frog, a bird, or a tree: Rachel Carr's creative yoga exercises for children.* New York: Doubleday.

Cech, J. (1986). The triumphant transformations of Pinocchio. In *Triumphs of the spirit in children's literature*. Butler, F. & Robert, R. (Eds.). Hamden, Ct.: Library Professional, pp. 171-177.

Cleaver, E. (1985). *The enchanted caribou*. New York: Atheneum.

Cole, J. (1986). *Doctor change*. New York: Morrow.

Conklin, G. (1969). *How insects grow*. New York: Holiday House.

Crane, W. (1980). *The frog prince and other stories*. New York: Mayflower.

dePaola, T. (1986). *Favorite nursery tales*. New York: Putnam.

Gag, W. (1936). *Tales from Grimm*. New York: Coward-McCann.

Gardiner, J. R. (1984). *Top secret*. Boston: Little, Brown.

Goble, P. (1984). *Buffalo woman*. Scarsdale, N.Y.: Bradbury.

Goble, P. (1986). *The girl who loved wild horses*. New York: Macmillan.

Hampden, J. (1969). *The gypsy fiddle and other tales told by gypsies*. New York: World.

Hillman, J. (1979). A note on story. *Parabola, 4*, 43-45.

Hutchinson, V. (1927). *Fireside stories*. New York: Minton, Balch.

Isadora, R. (1989). *The princess and the frog*. New York: Greenwillow.

Isele, E. (1984). *The frog princess*. New York: Crowell.

Jacobs, J. (n.d.). *English folk and fairy tales*. New York: Putnam.

Jones, H. (1972). *Longhouse winter: Iroquois transformation tales*. New York: Holt.

Kanfer, S. (1986, December 22). In all seasons, toys are us. *Time*, pp. 64-68.

Kellogg, S. (1977). *The mysterious tadpole*. New York: Dial.

Kent, J. (1982). *The caterpillar and the polliwog*. New York: Simon and Schuster.

Kim, S. (1955). *The story bag: A collection of Korean folk tales*. Rutland, Vt.: Tuttle.

Krueger, K. (1969). *The serpent prince: Folk tales from northeastern Thailand*. New York: World.

Lawrence, D. H. (1971). *Studies in classic American literature*. New York: Viking.

Leach, M. (Ed.). (1949). *Funk and Wagnall's standard dictionary of folklore, mythology, and legend*. New York: Funk and Wagnall.

LeGuin, U. (1975). The child and his shadow. *Quarterly Journal of the Library of Congress, 32*, 139-48.

Lionni, L. (1970). *Fish is fish*. New York: Knopf.

Lucas, E. (1980). Fairy tales of the brothers Grimm. London: Freemantle & Co.

McClung, R. M. (1981). *Sphinx: the story of a caterpillar*. New York: Morrow.

McCormick, K., Waller, G., & Flower, L. (1987). *Reading texts: reading, responding, writing*. Lexington, Ma.: Heath.

MacDonald, M. R. (1987). *The storyteller's sourcebook: A subject, title, and motif index to folklore collections for children*. Detroit: Neal-Schuman.

Mahlmann, L. & Jones, D. C. (1974). *Puppet plays for young players*. Boston: Plays, Inc.

Malville, J. M. (1981). *The fermenting universe: Myths of eternal change.* New York: Seabury.

Manning-Sanders, R. (1969). *The book of princes and princesses.* New York: Dutton.

Manning-Sanders, R. (1973). *The book of sorcerers and spells.* New York: Dutton.

Massey, I. (1976). *The gaping pig: Literature and metamorphosis.* Berkeley: Univ. of California Pr.

Mayer, M. (1980). *East of the sun and west of the moon.* New York: Macmillan.

Mieder, W. (1985). *Disenchantments: An anthology od modern fairy tale poetry.* Hanover, N. H.: Univ. Press of New England.

Mitchell, L. S. (1921; rpt. 1948). *Here and now story book.* New York: Dutton.

Moss, A. & Stott, J. (1986). *The family of stories: An anthology of children's literature.* New York: Holt.

Norton, D. (1982). Using a webbing process to develop children's literature units. *Language Arts, 59,* 348-356.

Norton, M. (1975). *Are all the giants dead?* New York: Harcourt Brace.

O'Hagan, C. (1989). *It's easy to have a caterpillar visit you.* New York: Lothrop, Lee & Shepard.

Owen, R. B. (1939). *The castle in the silver wood and other Scandinavian folk tales.* New York: Dodd.

Polisar, B. (1977). *My brother thinks he's a banana and other provocative songs for children* (Sound recording). Rainbow Music Alternatives.

Rodgers, M. (1972). *Freaky friday.* New York: Harper.

Rodgers, M. (1982). *Summer switch.* New York: Harper.

Segal, L. (1973). *The juniper tree and other tales from Grimm.* New York: Farrar, Strauss, and Giroux.

Shannon, G. W. B. (1981). *Folk literature and children: An annotated bibliography of secondary materials.* Westport, Ct.: Greenwood.

Silverstein, A. & V. (1972). *Metamorphosis: The magic change.* New York: Atheneum.

Silverstein, S. (1974). *Where the sidewalk ends.* New York: Harper.

Sleator, W. (1975). *Among the dolls.* New York: Dutton.

Small, D. (1985). *Imogene's antlers.* New York, Crown.

Steig, W. (1969). *Sylvester and the magic pebble.* New York: Simon and Schuster.

Steptoe, J. (1987). *Mufaro's Beautiful Daughters: An African Tale.* New York: Lothrop, Lee & Shepard.

Tarcov, E. (1987). *The frog prince.* New York: Scholastic.

Thaler, M. (1978). *The yellow brick toad: Funny frog cartoons, riddles, and silly stories.* New York: Archway.

Thompson, Stith, (1958). *Motif-index of folk-literature.* Bloomington: Indiana UP.

Viorst, J. (1981). *If I were in charge of the world and other worries: Poems for children and their parents.* New York: Macmillan.

Watts, B. (1986). *Butterfly and caterpillar.* Morristown, N.J.: Silver Burdett.

White, W. (1974). A frog is born. *London: Oak Tree.*

Winner, L. (*1988, November/December). The machine in the nursery.* Technology Review, pp. 19. 78.

Yolen, J. (1989). *Dove Isabeau.* New York: Harcourt Brace.

Yolen, J. (1978). Shape shifters: Every child's adventures in fairy tales. Language Arts, 55, 699-703.

Yolen, J. (1978). *Shape shifters: Fantasy and science fiction tales about humans who can change their shapes.* New York: Seabury.

Yorinks, A. (1983). *It happened in Pinsk.* New York: Farrar, Strauss, and Giroux.

Yorinks, A. (1980). *Louis the fish.* New York: Farrar, Strauss, and Giroux.

Zemach, H. & K. (1975). *The princess and froggie.* New York: Farrar, Strauss, and Giroux.

7

Multiethnic Children's Literature

Violet J. Harris

The term *multicultural literature* appears with increasing frequency in discussions about children's literature and literacy (Martinez & Nash, 1990). Multicultural literature refers to literature that focuses on people of color — African, Asian, Hispanic, and Native American; religious minorities, such as the Amish or Jewish; regional cultures, for example, Appalachian and Cajun; the disabled; and the aged. To some extent, the term encompasses literature that presents women and girls in a multitude of roles that are not gender stereotyped. The element common to each group member is its marginal status and its lack of full participation in "mainstream" institutions. In addition, each group's literature, with the exception of literature featuring women and girls, appears infrequently on recommended book lists, receives limited critical scrutiny, and remains in publication for relatively brief periods of time.

Multiculturalism entered into discussions about literature and the teaching of literature for a number of reasons. First, members of various groups categorized under the rubric multicultural literature demanded an end to their marginalization in literary canons and curricula. Second, educators, aware of the increasing ethnic diversity of schools, have sought ways to ensure that students' cultural heritages are included in schooling. Third, a group of writers appeared in the 1960s and '70s whose purposes for writing included the desire to challenge pervasive, stereotyped images. Fourth, the quality of the writing and the art produced by some members of these disparate groups captured the attention of critics, librarians, teachers, and members of awards committees.

This chapter addresses some of the issues relative to multicultural literature and its inclusion in elementary curricula. The purposes of the chapter are: 1) to provide rationales for examining one component of multicultural literature, multiethnic literature or the literature of people of color; 2) to identify the characteristics that distinguish multiethnic literature from other literature; 3) to delineate the benefits students might derive from its inclusion in elementary curricula; 4) to detail its current status; 5) to analyze the literature in terms of prevailing genres, authors, and themes; and 6) to discuss the availability of resources that offer guidance for the inclusion of multiethnic literature.

RATIONALES FOR THE INCLUSION OF MULTIETHNIC LITERATURE

Multiethnic literature as adopted in this discussion means the literature concerned with Africans, Asians, Hispanics, and Native Americans. These groups tend to be the most excluded from literary canons, recommended book lists, and elementary curricula (Bishop, 1990a, 1990b; Taxel, 1986; 1988). Some people are not convinced of the necessity for including multiethnic literature in basal readers, literature anthologies, textbooks, and on reading lists. The reason we should include multiethnic literature is because education should broaden students' knowledge and experiential bases and multiethnic literature does so. Some of the literature is excellent; many of the works contain universal truths developed through the specifics of a particular cultural heritage, and the literature is written in a variety of forms and in a variety of genres that can entertain, educate, socialize, and challenge.

More complex reasons why we should read or make available materials written by people in these groups are apparent in the poetry, fiction, and essays of some of the writers and critics. Their comments suggest the authors' intentions are not simply to provide an outlet for the expression of creative impulses but rather to engender the development of critical consciousness among readers; to provide readers with literature that challenges unauthentic and stereotyped portraits; to imbue readers with a sense of hopefulness and inspire them to challenge the caste status accorded to many of them; and to use literature as a way of understanding the human condition. For instance, Countee Cullen wrestled with his decision to become a poet and immortalized the contradictory feelings in a poem. His lamentations bespoke of the incongruity of being an African American and a poet. He penned "Yet Do I Marvel" (Emanuel, 1968) to convey his feelings about the paradox. The one-stanza poem captures the experienced by Cullen and other writers of color.

Cullen's lamentations are not meant to explain why all poets or writers of color engage in a craft shaped by the vagaries of taste, the economics of publishing, canons, and talent. Instead, his remarks provide some understanding of the complexities involved in the seemingly paradoxical status of being African American and a poet.

Some would argue that the experiences detailed by Cullen are peculiar to all writers and not just writers of color. Perhaps so, but the experiences of people of color have tended to converge and diverge from the experiences of others. Race and ethnicity create additional lenses through which one can interpret experiences. For example, compare the depictions of rural African Americans in *Roll of Thunder, Hear My Cry* (Taylor, 1976) and *Words By Heart* (Sebestyen, 1979). Sebestyen portrays family members who are willing to sacrifice some of its members so that a racist, white character can undergo a moral conversion. In contrast, Taylor presents a family with a strong sense of race consciousness committed to racial uplift and not sacrifice of its members.

MULTIETHNIC LITERATURE DEFINED

A specific type of multiethnic literature, "culturally conscious," is emphasized here. Sims (1982) who coined the termed, wrote specifically of African-American children's literature, but her comments apply to other groups as well. Culturally conscious literature is literature that reflects the social and cultural traditions of the group depicted. The literature contains characters who are African, Asian, Hispanic, or Native American; the story is told from the perspective of the group's members; and the reader is able to identify the characters as African, Asian, Hispanic, or Native American by physical descriptions, language, cultural traditions, and so forth (p.49).

Culturally conscious literature, with some exceptions, appeared in the 1970s as a result of several interrelated events (Sims, 1982, 1983; Nieto, 1982). The number of authors of color writing for children increased dramatically, with African-American authors constituting the largest segment. Publishers and booksellers displayed increased receptiveness to multiethnic literature (Muse, 1975). The infusion of federal dollars in literacy programs to serve minority children prompted a scramble for materials deemed relevant to these students. Parents and teachers requested the literature. These socio-cultural factors combined to create an ideal context for the emergence of culturally conscious literature.

Culturally conscious literature has an aura of authenticity, and the portrayals are not monolithic. In the past, people of color were presented in monolithic fashion or stereotyped: the happy slave, the gang banging Puerto Rican male, the cunning Chinese, or the savage Indian (Broderick, 1973; Nieto, 1982; Chin, 1981; Stensland, 1979; Palomino, 1988). Or, people of color were presented in grim hopeless stories that centered on the negative aspects of being a person of color in the United States. Grim, realistic stories serve a crucial function: They help keep historical memories alive, often correct deliberate historical distortions, and offer alternative interpretations of events. For example, *To Be a Slave* (Lester, 1968) utilized the memoirs of former slaves to contradict the stereotype of slavery as a benevolent institution. Unadorned, realistic stories are needed, but other experiences are equally important: stories of families that survive with love, grace, and solidarity such as *Felita* (Mohr, 1979) or stories about children unencumbered with notions of inferiority as in "Putting It On For Juanita," a short story in *Stories From El Barrio* (Thomas, 1978), or stories of the love shared between parents as in *M. C. Higgins, the Great* (Hamilton, 1974), and many more. Culturally conscious literature presents these multifaceted views.

Some of the authors who write culturally conscious literature are Nicholasa Mohr, Walter Dean Myers, Laurence Yep, and Virginia Driving Hawk Sneve. Noted author Virginia Hamilton (1987) captured the sentiments of many authors who write culturally conscious literature with this statement:

> Each one of my twenty books has presented aspects of story, style, and language from the perspective of a parallel American culture. It has been my desire to create for young people original and startling images of themselves and to celebrate who they are in unique and positive ways through story lines (p. 67).

A few authors, however, have chosen not to make their ethnicity an integral component of the stories they weave; or at least, a surface examination of their work reveals little about the ethnicity of the author or illustrator. For example, Donald Crews' excellent books *Carousel* (1982) and *School Bus (1984)* do not reflect the author's ethnicity; instead, his work presents universal experiences in multiracial settings.

Another issue relates to authors who are not members of the group about which they write. For example, Paul Goble is neither Native American nor American, and yet his interpretations of the myths and legends of Plains Indians are regarded as authentic. Similarly, Byrd Baylor captures the essence of the Southwest of the Navajo and Chicanos in her many stories. Some authors, according to critics, should not write about ethnic groups for whom they lack an empathetic or knowledgeable perspective (Seals, 1989; Sims, 1984; Chin, 1981; Nieto, 1982; Taxel, 1986). When authors lack an insider perspective or possess limited knowledge of a culture, stereotypes can result. Some typical stereotypes and inaccuracies include picture books that do not reflect the physical diversity of people of color or writers who portray all Puerto Ricans as living in New York City or all Asian Americans as adhering to Confucianism. Today, most publishing companies make concerted efforts to avoid publishing books with stereotypes; however, occasionally a book slips through, and many of the older books remain in circulation. Despite these concerns, a body of culturally conscious literature exists that is authentic and benefits students in a number of ways.

BENEFITS OF MULTIETHNIC LITERATURE

Multiethnic literature, like all literature, provides numerous benefits for all students. Two categories of benefits are identifiable: cognitive and social/affective. When students engage in reading literature on a consistent basis, their vocabularies increase; comprehension improves; their base of knowledge expands; they are exposed to several written forms of language that can serve as models for writing and speaking; they develop visual literacy; their general reading skills improve; they develop a sense of story; their imaginations are sparked; they are entertained; and their aesthetic sensibilities are evoked (Fielding, et al., 1984; Strickland & Taylor, 1989).

The social and affective benefits are numerous as well (Huck, et al., 1987; Larrick, 1965; Sims, 1990a, 1990b). For example, Huck, et al. considered the role of multiethnic literature in society in this manner:

In a true democracy it is essential that we learn to respect and appreciate the diversity of all cultures within our pluralistic society. Books can never substitute for first-hand contact with other people, but they can raise the consciousness level of all children and deepen their understanding for cultures that are different from theirs. Rather than falsely pretend that differences do not exist, children need to discover that which is unique to each group of persons and the universal to the experience of being human (pp. 501-502).

They consider literature essential to the creation of a tolerant society in which diversity is respected. We should heed the words of author Eloise Greenfield (1975), who notes that words cannot solve each complex social, cultural, linguistic, or racial problem confronting society:

> My attempts and those of other writers to offer sustenance will necessarily be largely ineffectual. Not only do we as human beings have limitation —so also does the written word. It cannot be eaten or worn; it cannot cure disease; it cannot dissipate pollution, defang a racist, cause a spoonful of heroin to disintegrate. But, at the right time, in the right circumstances, falling on the right mind, a word may take effect (p.624).

Others are concerned with the underlying messages readers can acquire from the omission of people of color from literature or the continuous exposure to stereotyped images. Larrick (1965), referring specifically to the lack of literature about African Americans, suggested that white children would develop an unwarranted sense of racial superiority from reading literature that only extolled the lifestyles, history, and perspectives of whites. She also contended that African American children would develop a sense of inferiority when reading the same books. Her conclusions are shared by others (Bishop, 1990a; 1990b). Multiethnic literature ameliorates some of these potential problems because it enables children of color to know and understand how their people and culture have contributed and continue to contribute to human life. They can begin to perceive themselves, their communities, and their cultures as valued elements of schooling. In a sense, their worth as human beings is affirmed, and they can become empowered through increased knowledge. White children can begin to understand some of the complex sociohistorical factors that shape interracial and cross ethnic relations.

Most important, children of color can derive pleasure and pride when reading and hearing stories about children who look and sound as they do. Purves and Beach (1972) found that children tend to have more positive responses to literature when the literature includes characters with whom they can identify or characters who resemble themselves; contained stories that sometimes parallel their personal experiences. They have a tendency to evaluate characters as favorable when they resembled themselves. In contrast, white children who interact with multiethnic literature can begin to perceive that certain values, actions, and customs are common to all people and that they, too, can receive pleasure from reading about those who share some beliefs and values.

The inclusion of multiethnic literature in elementary curricula is crucial because some of the literature presents themes, dilemmas, and experiences that enable children to discuss, think about, and write about issues of concern such as racial injustice, the quest for racial justice, and the role of the individual in both processes. Equally important, multiethnic literature, as all excellent literature, can touch the heart, mind, and souls of readers as well as entertain them; to do so, however, multiethnic literature must be made available.

CURRENT STATUS OF MULTIETHNIC LITERATURE

Any discussion of the status of multiethnic children's literature must note its precarious existence and the multiple functions it serves in addition to the traditional aesthetic ones The past twenty-five years have been quite tumultuous. The tumult results not only from the wildly fluctuating number of books published and the roles of publishers and booksellers but also from the quality, authenticity, and purposes of the books. Because of these issues and others, multiethnic literature has not simply existed as a literary product evaluated in terms of literary criteria; the ideological and social functions are integral as well (Taxel, 1986, 1988; Aitken, 1988).

The number of books available is one issue. A number of people — especially librarians, teachers, and parents — have long argued for more books with diverse portrayals of people of color (Baker, 1975; Rollins, 1948). The Civil Rights movement, the expansion of federal support for literacy education with an emphasis on literature, the emergence of authors, changes in publishing, and one timely article resulted in a surge of multiethnic literature in the 1970s. The article, "The All-White World of Children's Books" (Larrick, 1965), directed attention to the dearth of books about African Americans. Larrick queried publishers to determine the number of books published during 1962, 1963, and 1964 that contained illustrations of or included an African-American character. Larrick concentrated on African Americans because they were the most visible minority during the period. Larrick's results indicated that 6.7 percent of the 5,206 books published during the three-year period included

illustrations of or plots about African-American characters. Larrick concluded that the exclusion of African Americans had profound negative
consequences for both African-American and white children.

By the mid-1970s the percentage of African Americans in children's
books increased to 14.4 percent (Chall, et al., 1979). Interest in the number
of books with Asians, Hispanics, and Native Americans surfaced as well. The
Asian American Book Project (1981) found that approximately 1 1/2
percent of children's books published during the previous decade included
one or more characters who were Asian American. Further, they found that
an average of one book per year appeared between 1945 and 1964, and the
number in subsequent years rose slightly. The end of the 1980s and the
beginnings of the 1990s suggest that the 1 1/2 percent proportion of the
1970s has not and will not be surpassed (Bishop, 1990). Analyses
completed for Hispanics yielded similar results. Puerto Ricans and
Mexican-Americans (Chicanos) are the two Hispanic groups most often
depicted in childrens literature. Only fifty-six books were published about
Puerto Ricans in the ten years between 1972 and 1982 (Nieto, 1982).
Stories about Chicanos appeared in similar numbers (Schon, 1984; 1989.
Other Hispanics — for example, Guatemalans, Nicaraguans, and Hondurans
— began appearing in children's literature but not in substantial numbers.
Hispanics did not fare well as the 1980s ended; fewer than 20 books about
Hispanics were published, the majority being informational and folk tales
(Bishop, 1990a). Native Americans suffered a publishing fate comparable
to the other groups. Although quite pervasive in previous decades (usually
in stereotyped fashion), the Native American appears in fewer than 2
percent of children's books published (Bishop, 1990). When Native
Americans do appear, it is most often in folk tales or legends. One could
argue that specified numbers of books would subvert the purposes of
literature, the independence of publishers, result in mediocrity and
didacticism, and impose "literary quotas." However, the numbers are
revealing; they detail the limited publication and availability of multiethnic
literature.

A second consideration that shapes the existence and status of
multiethnic literature revolves around notions of stereotyping, authenticity,
and authorial expression (Taxel, 1986; 1988; Aitken, 1988; Mingle, 1984;
Bishop, 1984). A central question for some is whether authors can
accurately portray cultures that they only observe but do not necessarily
have interactions with (Sims, 1984; Hurmence, 1984; Rockwood, 1982).
Related to this concern is the issue of stereotyping. Stereotypes can result
when an author is unaware of the sociocultural conditions of a people, lacks

basic knowledge, or is insensitive. Two recent books, *Jakes and Honey-bunch Go to Heaven* (Zemach, 1982) and *The Indian in the Cupboard* (Banks, 1982), illustrate the unauthentic, stereotyped depictions that result when authors lack an "insider perspective" (Sims, 1982). A number of stereotypes exist in children's literature about each group. One should bear in mind that children's literature is one cultural artifact out of many that stereotypes people of color. Films, television, and advertisements for food products are but a few of the other cultural products that use stereotypes in one form or another.

Seven stereotypes of African Americans pervaded children's literature before the advent of culturally conscious literature (Brown, 1933; Broderick, 1973). These included the contented slave, the wretched freedman, the comic Negro, the brute Negro, the tragic mulatto, the local color Negro, and the exotic primitive. Asian-American stereotypes included the garden/houseboy, the geisha girl, the expert in martial arts, the excessively obsequious individual, the exotic foreigner, the "yellow peril," and the sly, sinister, cruel, individual (Asian American Book Project, 1981). One "positive stereotype," in that other groups are encouraged to emulate the behavior associated with the stereotype, is the Asian American as the "model minority." The model minority is assimilated and accepts the values associated with "mainstream" Americans, eschews political activism (at least progressive or radical activism), and achieves stable, middle-class status. Hispanics were generally pictured as docile, passive, childish incompetents who could not overcome the dreary and debilitating life of "el barrio" (Nieto, 1982; Moore & MacCann, 1987a, 1987b). Hispanic children were portrayed as "brown waifs" in many books. Adolescent males typically appeared as juvenile delinquents or gang members. Women and girls were portrayed as tempestuous spitfires, girl gang members, sheltered innocents, and rotund earth mothers. Two contradictory images of Native American males dominated children's literature, the noble Red Man and the heathen savage (Stensland, 1979; Seale, 1989; Moore & MacCann, 1988). Other stereotypes included the murderous thief, the idler, the drunkard, the vanishing race, and the faithful friend and servant. Native American women tended to appeared as the "woman of bravery" or the "beautiful Indian maiden" (Stensland, 1979).

Several people, including authors and critics, have argued that stereotyped literature should not be available as the only introduction to literature about people of color (Clifton, 1981; Sims, 1982; 1984). For them, it is not an issue of any book being better than none because the effects are potentially lifelong and devastating. Significantly, books with stereotypes accounted for a major portion of the total number of books related to people of color prior to 1970.

A third factor that colors discussion about multiethnic literature is the emergence of a cadre of writers who offer multilayered and complex stories of life within their communities. They write for a variety of purposes: Some write because they wish to express some creative impulse; others write to reshape the images of their group; a few write to capture some childhood experience; and many write to offer children hope or to motivate them. Some write for all of these reasons. Occasionally, their interpretations are disputed or censored. Evidence of the quality of their work is evident in the number of Newbery, Caldecott, Boston Globe-Horn Book, and Coretta Scott King awards accorded to some of the works. Books such as *Mufaro's Beautiful Daughters* (Steptoe, 1987), *Lon Po Po* (Young, 1989), and *Scorpions* (Myers, 1988) are exemplars of literary and aesthetic excellence.

Despite the literary excellence of the works and the need for the books as expressed by parents teachers, writers, and critics, their availability is limited. Many chain bookstores do not stock representative samples of multiethnic literature; some claim that there is little demand for the books. On the surface, this might appear to be true; however, one should note that many of the communities in which people of color reside lack bookstores. An additional complicating issue is that many of the works do not remain in publication for significant periods of time. Nonetheless, those who are interested in incorporating the literature in their curricula can begin the process of discovery, reading, and analysis that will enable them to share the literature in a sensitive and informed manner. The next segment details a beginning place of study and includes discussions of each group's literature with an emphasis on genres, authors, and themes.

ANALYSIS OF MULTIETHNIC LITERATURE

Acquisition of Historical Knowledge

An understanding of the histories of people of color, while not a prerequisite for sharing multiethnic literature for children, might prove helpful for teacher and student as they engage with multiethnic literature. Textbooks, like tradebooks, generally distorted omitted, or provided limited discussions of the history and contributions of people of color (Anderson, 1096; Elson, 1963, Nieto, 1982). For example, social studies textbooks generally include sections on African Americans that focus on slavery, the Civil War, Reconstruction, and the Civil Rights movement; few examine the role of African Americans in the Revolutionary War era, the status and experiences of free blacks, the participation of African Americans in the labor movement, racism, or the development of independent cultural institutions as a response to *de facto* and *de jure* segregation. Similarly, Hispanics tend to appear in the section on Texas history or in postwar sections on the problems of urban areas or immigration policies. In general, people of color appear in sections where minority concerns are discussed. The possibility exists, then, for the inaccurate belief to develop that national or international concerns do not relate to people of color or that they are less affected by the issues.

A number of histories and biographies exist that offer more complete discussion than what is typically found in textbooks. For instance, a number of biographies, such as *Rosa Parks* (Greenfield, 1973), have been published for primary age children. Intermediate students might find the Women of Our Time series informative. Upper elementary students might read the finely crafted histories and biographies of Milton Meltzer, such as *Bread and Roses* (1967). Imagine the discussions they will have after reading *The Chinese Americans* (Meltzer, 1980) and discovering that Asian Americans were responsible for a significant portion of the transcontinental railroad. Current controversies about Native American remains in museums and university laboratories might be viewed differently when one reads *Wounded Knee* (Brown, 1974).

Several trends are apparent in histories and biographies for children. Although still prevalent, biographies of "great men and women" no longer predominate; many more biographies of the "common man or woman" exist. Athletes and entertainers are popular subjects as well as current newsmakers. Biographies of controversial figures appear with increasing frequency. Some of these trends are evident in multiethnic literature. For example, *Dance in Black America* (Haskins, 1990), *Great Lives: Human Rights* (Jacobs, 1990), *Women Who Changed Things* (Peavy & Smith, 1983), *Rehema's Journey* (Margolies, 1990), *Malcolm X* (Adoff, 1970), and *The Mexican Americans* (Catalano, 1988) augment and enhance traditional offerings.

These books are important for another reason: They lessen the stereotype of the person of color who only achieves in athletics or entertainment or of groups dependent upon whites for political advancement. The number of biographies of Roberto Clemente demonstrates the overemphasis on athletes and entertainers. This is not to suggest that Clemente's achievements do not deserve honor; rather, it is to suggest that a balance needs to be maintained, and biographies of Clemente should emphasize his humanitarian work as well. Similarly, biographies of Jackie

Robinson highlight his involvement in baseball, but, until recently, few children's biographies mentioned the period in his life when he was court-martialled because he refused to abide by illegal segregation rules. When biographies de-emphasize or omit the political actions of individuals, they present the individual as unaffected by social and historical processes and limit knowledge of how direct political action affects institutions and individuals.

Milton Meltzer deserves special recognition for his biographies and histories that include people of color or focus upon them entirely. For example, *Bread and Roses* (Meltzer, 1967) is a balanced examination of the history of the labor movement with stories of the contributions of people of color woven throughout. The book is an example of engaging, well-written history that captures attention because of its inclusion of the excluded, its style — presentation and interpretation of fact intermingled with the memoirs of the famous and non-famous. In a comparable manner, Meltzer's histories of African Americans, Chinese-Americans, Hispanics, slavery, and the Ku Klux Klan are praised for the thoroughness of the research, the inclusion of the voices of the excluded, and the tone the author assumes.

One could easily integrate a number of these histories and biographies in elementary curricula and throughout the academic year, not just during Black History month, Hispanic American month or some or similarly designated month or week for ethnic observances. These histories and biographies are an integral component of the United States' development, and their inclusion enables students to understand more fully some of the complex issues that confront people of color.

The next section contains an examination of the genres, major authors, and themes found in each group's literature. Because the emphasis is on culturally conscious books, the exemplars were selected from among books published since 1970; these books are less likely to contain stereotypes or unauthentic details.

AFRICAN-AMERICAN CHILDREN'S LITERATURE

African Americans produced the majority of books under the category of multiethnic. African Americans began producing literature for children in the 1890s, but the literature did not flourish until the 1970s (Harris, 1990). Some of the factors that account for the early creation of the literature and the emergence of the authors include a strong literacy tradition that began in the 1700s; social, religious, and political organization that devoted considerable energies to acquiring literacy for African Americans; the development of African American publishing companies and the African American press; and the existence of a middle-class elite that sought to imbue children with notions of race consciousness, refinement, and political activism through literature and schooling (Harris, 1987;1990).

African-American authors draw upon a variety of cultures and cultural traditions: stories that depict life in the deep South, for example, *Mississippi Bridge* (Taylor, 1990) and *Mirandy and Brother Wind* (McKissack, 1988); life in the urban North, in all its facets such as *The Young Landlords* (Myers, 1979), *Scorpions* (Myers, 1988) or *The Enchanted Hair Tale* (De Veaux, 1987); the experiences of Caribbean immigrants as depicted in *The Friends* (Guy, 1974); and stories of growing up set in the Southwest such as *The Golden Pasture* (Thomas, 1986). The variety of cultural and historical conditions depicted belie the stereotype that all African Americans are alike or have had similar experiences.

The authors create literature in a variety of genres: biography, poetry, drama, fiction — contemporary realistic, historical, fantasy, and science —information books (nonfiction), and adaptations of folk tales, myths, and legends. Two writers, Virginia Hamilton and Walter Dean Myers, have each published in excess of twenty books in a variety of genres for a range of ages. Hamilton, who is considered one of the best writers for children today, was the first children's author to win the Newbery Medal, Boston Globe-Horn Book Magazine Award, and National Book Award for one single work — *M. C. Higgins, the Great* (Hamilton, 1974). She was also the first African American to win the Newbery Medal. Myers' work is notable not only for its quality and its appeal to children but also for its portrayal of youths in New York City who represent a range of classes, family structures, and states of contentment or happiness, and for stories with genuine humor and appeal for boys.

Other writers whose tenure parallels that of Hamilton and Myers are Lucille Clifton, Eloise Greenfield, Rosa Guy, Sharon Bell Mathis, the late John Steptoe, Mildred Taylor, and Brenda Wilkinson. Some of them have won numerous awards for the quality of their writing such as the Newbery Medal. Taylor's novels about Mississippi in the 1930s and 1940s have won the Newbery Medal and critical acclaim for their searing, honest, painful, and yet hopeful depictions. Illustrator John Steptoe garnered critical acclaim for his willingness to experiment with various art styles. Similarly, illustrator Tom Feelings captured attention for the beauty of his work and his technical proficiency. These authors form what might be considered the vanguard of culturally conscious literature. Many other writers form a second generation in terms of the length of time they been involved in children's literature and the number of books they have had published. Among this group are Jeanette Caines, Patricia McKissack, Mildred Pitts Walter, and Camille Yarbrough. They, too, present a variety of stories in a variety of genre. A third group of writers emerged in the early to late 1980s. Among this group are Joyce Carol Thomas, Emily Moore, Angela Johnson, Joyce Hansen, and Rita Garcia-Williams. The sheer number of writers suggests that the number of books about African Americans should increase or, at the least, remain constant.

A few of the writers explicated their literary philosophies and the goals they hoped to accomplish with their works. Greenfield (1975), for example, wrote that she desired to provide children with "words that take effect." Words that take effect for Greenfield are those that "generate a love of the arts and provoke creative thought and activity, develop positive attitudes, present ways to solve problems; cause children to cherish the contributions of their elders which make survival possible, provide knowledge of African-American experiences and heritage, bring to the fore African-American heroes and heroines; reflect positive aspects of children's lives; share the author's feelings; and which enable children to celebrate life" (pp. 624-626). Several other authors and illustrators expressed similar beliefs (Hamilton, 1983; Feelings; 1985; Clifton, 1981).

A number of themes appear in culturally conscious African American literature (Sims, 1982;1983). These include the importance of family and community for survival; the love African Americans possess for each other that has sustained them through innumerable hardships; the value of familial and cultural traditions and universal themes such as "coming of age"; the relationships that exist between friends and family members; the factors that shape an individual's personality; and the reactions to ordinary events such as a bedtime story.

This culturally conscious literature exhibits certain characteristics (Sims, 1982). The first characteristic is the varied use of language forms. According to Sims, the language of narrators and characters in some of the books is marked by distinctive grammar, lexicon, and style. Examples of the distinctive use of language may be found in picture books such as *Me and Neesie* (Greenfield, 1975) and *My Brother Fine With Me* (Clifton, 1975), or in novels such as *Ludell* (Wilkinson, 1975) and *The Mouse Rap* (Myers, 1989).

A second feature of culturally conscious fiction is the depiction of the relationship that exists between an older person and a very young person. Many examples of this characteristic abound in the literature: *Grandpa's Face* (Greenfield, 1989), *The Hundred Penny Box* (Mathis, 1975), *Song of the Trees* (Taylor, 1975), and *When I Grow Old With You* (Johnson, 1990).

A third feature of culturally conscious books is the constitution of families. Many of the books feature extended families. Sims (1982) concluded that such inclusions "speak to a tradition of respect for older people within Afro-American families and communities and a traditional awareness of the ties that bind disparate members of those families and communities together" (p. 20). *The Lucky Stone* (Clifton, 1979), *The Mouse Rap* (Myers, 1989), and *Willie Bea and the Time the Martians Landed* (Hamilton, 1983) each portray families that nurture and support its members.

The issue of intragroup differences in skin color is considered rather honestly in several books; these discussions extend far beyond a preference for "light-skinned" or "dark-skinned" individuals. Instead, a few authors have addressed the cultural, historical, and social factors central to the creation of intragroup color differences. Some examples of books that include this issue in a sensitive manner are *Thank You Dr. Martin Luther King, Jr.* (Tate, 1990), *The Shimmershine Queens* (Yarbrough, 1989), and *Blue Tights* (Garcia-Williams, 1987). In addition, heroines in many books are noticeably brown or dark skinned. One of the first books to focus on the beauty of dark-skinned African Americans was *Zeely* (Hamilton, 1967). The title character, Zeely, is described by the protagonist, Geeder, as being exceptionally beautiful with skin like ebony. The mere equation of dark skin with physical beauty and attractiveness is a major departure in children's literature. Picture books by illustrators such as Jerry Pinkney — *Mirandy and Brother Wind* (McKissack, 1988), *The Talking Eggs* (San Souci, 1989); Tom Feelings — *Daydreamers,* (Greenfield, 1981), *Now Sheba Sings the Song* (Angelou, 1987); and Leo and Diane Dillon — *The People Could Fly* (Hamilton, 1985), and *Aida* (Price, 1990) — convey the range of variation in hair texture and skin color found among African Americans.

Other characteristics center on the use of names and terms of address — Sookie, Toeboy, Big Momma, Sister, and Muh Dear; the depiction of African-American historical and cultural traditions such as comments about jazz, the blues, and historical figures such as Booker T. Washington, Paul Robeson, or W. E. B. DuBois; and references to religion, gospel music, and spirituals. These are the elements that would be most apparent in the writings of authors who possess an insider perspective, are African

American, or have extensive knowledge of the features that make a culture distinctive. Many books, such as *The Times They Used to Be* (Clifton, 1974), *Sweet Whispers, Brother Rush* (Hamilton, 1982), *The Golden Pasture* (Thomas, 1986), and *The Gold Cadillac* (Taylor, 1987), contain these characteristics.

African-American children's literature offers many outstanding examples of inventive use of language, fully developed characters, traditional and experimental forms, complex plots, and distinctive styles. Some difficulties arise when one recommends classic examples or books that exemplify the literary tradition. Nonetheless, some books should appear in elementary curricula such as *M. C. Higgins, the Great* (Hamilton, 1974), *Roll of Thunder, Hear My Cry* (Taylor, 1976), *Mufaro's Beautiful Daughters* (Steptoe, 1987), Clifton's Everett Anderson series, *Aida* (Price, 1990), *Paul Robeson: The Life and Times of a Free Black Man* (Hamilton, 1975), *Honey, I Love* (Greenfield, 1978), *The Hundred Penny Box* (Mathis, 1975), and *Scorpions* (Myers, 1988). Additional recommendations appear in the bibliography.

ASIAN-AMERICAN CHILDREN'S LITERATURE

Although considered to be the "model minority," Asian Americans have not fared well in literature. One book, *The Five Chinese Brothers* (Bishop & Wise, 1938), typified the image of Asian Americans in children's literature. Alternatives to this classic emerged in the 1970s when writers such as Taro Yashima, Laurence Yep, and Yoshiko Uchida created stories about what it means to be a person of Laotian, Cambodian, Chinese, Japanese, Korean, or Vietnamese descent. Palomino (1988) documents why this was so even though an independent Asian press and literary community existed. A few of the reasons are comparable to those for African Americans: The voices of the writers were not included in traditional literary curricula or canons, the authors were ignored by the critical community, and bookstores did not stock them. Many of the writers who were "undiscovered," such as Toshio Mori, Momoko Iko, and Milton Murayama, wrote fiction, poetry, drama, and essays that centered on the experiences of working class Asian Americans. Palomino cites the *Woman From Hiroshima* as an exemplar of the "lost works." Mori's *Woman From Hiroshima* depicts an Issei grandmother recounting to her grandchildren the journey from Japan in the early 1900s, the culture shock she endured, the racial prejudice she overcame, and her emergence through it all as a "sturdy earthy woman of the soil" (p. 128). According to Palomino, Iko and Murayama captured the working class conflicts and language of Nisei in Hawaii and California.

Some Asian American authors find themselves ensnared in the same double consciousness bond as African Americans. Yep (1984) discussed the cultural paradoxes he had to resolve in order to write his books with themes about Asian Americans:

> I had grown up as an American child of the 50s and 60s, but to write Dragonwings (Harper & Row, 1975), I had to grow up again but this time as a child of the 1900s. For example, if there was a picture on the wall, I had to be told it was a picture of the kitchen god. An American chessboard had to seem strange because it had no river running down its middle. As a result, writing Dragonwings from the viewpoint of an eight-year-old boy was more than a narrative device: it was close to the process of self-discovery which I myself was experiencing in exploring my Chinese American past (p. 11).

Yep was not alone in undergoing this process of self-discovery. Self-discovery stories and other types of stories written by Asian Americans appear in several genres including fiction — historical, fantasy, and contemporary realistic, some short stories, some drama, and many adaptations of folk tales. Yep and Yoshiko Uchida are responsible for a significant number of books published since the 1970s; other authors include Taro Yashima, Ed Young, Paul Yee and authors who are not Asian American but write about Asians or Asian Americans such as Katherine Paterson. Yep garnered favorable critical support as evidenced by his acceptance of the Newbery Medal. Other writers and illustrators have leaped to the fore as well with award-winning work. For example, illustrator Ed Young's retelling of a Chinese variant of Little Read Riding Hood, *Lon Po Po* (1989), was awarded the Caldecott Medal. Paul Yee's *Tales From Gold Mountain* (1990) signals the emergence of a writer whose ability to tell tales and recount history is unique. Although she now writes for adults, Bette Bao Lord's work, *In the Year of the Boar and Jackie Robinson* (1984), is of importance as well.

The Asian American Book Project — AABP — (1981) developed a list of characteristics that authentic books contained or should contain. First, the AABP wrote that the books should depict genuine Asian American cultures and not images of Asian Americans imitating whites. This means that the settings, speech, clothing, and behavior portrayed in the books were not of some generic Asian culture but specific to a group. For example, the following excerpt presents authentic, working-class language, a pidgin dialect, used by some in a plantation camp in Hawaii:

> "I sick and tired getting hit all the time," he (Tosh) muttered. "From nowon I goin'dish it out too. You doan know how much he been beat me up when I was a kid. He always called me a crybaby. I was no samurai, I had no gaman (patience), no enryo (holding back). But shit, thass the only way I can fight him. If I start holding back, I play right into his hands. Hard work, patience, holding back, waiting your turn, all that crap, they all fit together to keep you down." (p. 131)

This is not the typical language of Asian Americans in children's books.

Second, the books should transcend stereotyped about Asian Americans. All adults are not gardeners, houseboys, or workers in laundries and restaurants. The language should not resort to the use of misplaced R's and L's to indicate that an Asian American is speaking. Third, the books should help to rectify historical distortions and omissions. For example, *The Journey* (Hamanaka, 1989) presents the feelings of anger, pain, and hurt experienced by some Asian Americans placed in concentration camps in Utah and other states. Fourth, the books should not perpetuate the image of Asian Americans as the "model minority" or the "super-achieving" minority. While a seemingly positive stereotype, it does not allow for varying levels of achievement among Asian Americans or the variances in cultural and historical experiences that differentiate Asian Americans. Fifth, the roles of women should include more than the "China Doll" stereotype. Girls and women should be depicted in a multitude of roles that parallel the ones they assume in life. For example, the female protagonists in Uchida's books participate in jump rope games, worry about their appearances, observe traditional rituals, and are spunky. Finally, picture books should extend beyond the traditional portrayal of Asian Americans with bowl haircuts, buck teeth, myopic vision, kimonos, and putrid yellow skin.

The number of books that meet the criteria established by the AABP is quite small. For instance, the AABP reviewers could recommend, without reservation, only the works of two authors, Yep and Yashima. Since the evaluation was published, some other authors have appeared whose works would meet or surpass the groups criteria such as Ed Young and the authors published by the Children's Press; for example, *Aekyung's Dream* (Paek, 1989), *The Little Weaver of Thai-yen Village,* (Tuyet, 1987) and *Nine-In-One, Grr! Grr!* (Xiong, 1989).

A multiplicity of themes are found in works of Asian-American authors. For example, *Dragonwings* (Yep, 1977) chronicles the experiences of father and son as they attempted to participate in two cultures, immigrant Chinese American and Euro-American. They must walk gingerly between the two for they are not entirely understood of fully accepted by either. Uchida's books such as *The Jar of Dreams* (1981) present the universal story of growing up, with occasional inclusions about being Japanese American. Other themes include generational conflicts that pit elders against children who no longer adhere to traditional values, stories about festivals and rituals, folk tales that entertain and that impart traditional values, and stories about significant events in Asian American history.

HISPANIC-AMERICAN CHILDREN'S LITERATURE

Very few Hispanic authors for children are published. As a result, culturally conscious literature is limited. A large segment of the literature is imported from various Spanish speaking countries or includes translation into Spanish of traditional literature such as *A Snowy Day* (Keats, 1962) (Schon, 1982; 1989; 1990). The genres most often included are contemporary realistic fiction, some short stories, many adaptations of folk tales and legends, picture books, and collections of nursery rhymes and songs. Some of the major authors include Piri Thomas, Nicholasa Mohr, Pura Belpre, and Gary Soto. Most of the works reflect the experiences of Puerto Ricans and Chicanos.

Nieto (1982) examined the fifty-six titles about Puerto Ricans published between 1972 and 1982. She could only recommend, without reservations, eight books. Some of the recommended books included *Felita* (Mohr, 1979), *Fast Sam, Cool Clyde and Stuff* (Myers, 1975), *Stories From El Barrio* (Thomas, 1978), and *Juan Bobo and the Pig* (Chardiet, 1973). Schon (1990) also created a list of books about Hispanics and found that the list was limited to nineteen books, with the majority being folk tales.

The themes in some of the books emphasize life in el barrio in all its complexity. El barrio is not a bleak, horrific, ghetto but a community of individuals who share a common language and some historical experiences, values, and rituals. Other themes that emerge are ones which highlight the reconciliation of cultural differences without the loss of one's cultural identify, the strength of families, the clash between parents or older guardians who adhere to traditional values and their younger relatives who seem to abandon or ignore traditions, surviving oppression, living life in ways comparable to other cultures, and universal themes such as quests, coming of age, or decision about peer and family relations.

Nicholasa Mohr's work is notable because the protagonists are females. In *Felita* (Mohr, 1979) and its sequel, *Going Home* (Mohr, 1986), Mohr explores what it means to be a Puerto Rican girl in New York city. Felita, the title character, has a loving family; she is not alienated from her community or heritage; and she grows up undistorted or not made hopeless by prejudice. Similarly, Piri Thomas' *Stories From El Barrio* (1978) contains some humorous and bittersweet stories about Puerto Rican males in New York city who experience joys, disappointments, some failures and successes, and typical occurrences such as impressing a young lady. *Scorpions* (Myers, 1988), with its African-American and Puerto Rican protagonists, presents one modern coming of age story shaped by the negative influences of gangs, violence, and drugs; yet, the reader is left with a hopeful stance because Tito and Jamal have dreams that sustain them and familial support to guide them as they defy some conditions in their communities. Martel Cruz's *Yagua Days* (1976) is an excellent picture book that depicts a boy in a loving family who lives in a community with Puerto Rican professionals, service workers, retirees, and small business owners. The characters in *Yagua Days* represent the varieties of skin color and hair textures found among Puerto Ricans. The text is sprinkled with Puerto Rican Spanish and the foodstuffs eaten and rituals engaged in are those in which many Puerto Ricans find familiar. Byrd Baylor has a few books that depict some Chicano experiences in the Southwest. For example, *Amigo* (1963) has a universal theme; a young boy finds an animal in the wild and makes him a pet. Similarly, *Hawk I'm Your Brother* (1976), chronicles a young boys symbolic identification with a hawk. A number of folk tales, especially those about Coyote, capture the rich oral traditions of Hispanics. Although poetry is a valued literary form, few poetry books exist. *Flamboyan* (Adoff, 1988) utilizes a style that is poetic and that incorporates some elements of folk tales. The relative dearth of books signals a need for more authors and books to expand the cultures depicted and the experiences portrayed.

NATIVE AMERICAN CHILDREN'S LITERATURE

Native Americans and some aspects of Native American culture have been integral to children's literature for generations. Culturally conscious portrayals appeared in small quantities in the 1970s. The most prevalent genres are fiction — contemporary realistic, historic, and fantasy, folk tales, legends, and myths, and some poetry.

A number of authors have attracted critical attention: Virginia Driving Hawk Sneve, Jamake Highwater, Byrd Baylor, Paul Goble, Gerald McDermott, and John Bierhorst. Many of the authors have written essays about the portrayal of Native Americans or reasons why they choose to write about and interpret Native American culture and experiences. Sneve, for instance, wrote of her attempts to interpret Native American life in the manner in which she experienced it and felt was accurate:

> In my writing, both fiction and nonfiction, I try to present an accurate portrayal of American Indian life as I have known it. I also attempt to interpret history from the viewpoint of the American Indian and in so doing I hope to correct the many misconceptions and untruths which have been too long perpetrated by non-Indian authors who have written about us. (pp. 193-194)

Sneve's works demonstrate her attempts to incorporate these elements, although her work has met with mixed critical evaluation. Others, like Seals (1989), encouraged the creation of multifaceted stories that would not present Native Americans as hopeless outcasts who must assimilate or face certain doom or extinction.

Several themes are apparent when one examines the work of major authors. *Jimmy Yellow Hawk* (Sneve, 1972), a winner of the first prize offered by the children's Interracial Books Council, explored ideas such as which historical memories are bequeathed to future generations, the exploitation of Native Americans, the effects of assimilation and formal schooling that discouraged the use of Native American languages and customs and values, and the value of family and peer relations. The author manages to explore these themes without becoming overtly didactic. A mixture of character types are found in the novel, and the author crafts a story that entertains and informs readers. The following illustrates Sneve's weaving of an informative story:

> He liked the teacher, Miss Red Owl, the first Indian teacher the day school had ever had. She was one of the few Indians who had graduated from college and returned to the reservation to work with her people. Because she was Sioux she understood the children's shyness. She accepted, without trying to change, their Indian ways of not looking into an adult's eyes when speaking to them. The white teacher who was at the school before Miss Red Owl thought the children were rude and disrespectful when they wouldn't look at her when she spoke to them. She didn't understand that they believed it was rude to do so. (pp. 14-15)

Sneve has also written a number of books about the Lakota including contemporary realistic fiction and biographical anthology entitled *They Led a Nation* (1975), which provides biographies of twenty Lakota leaders.

Jamake Highwater is a critically acclaimed but controversial author. Considerable debate arose about his ethnicity; he has been accused of passing himself off as a Native American (Senich, 1989). Highwater addressed those critics who questioned the veracity of his biographical statement and his aesthetic philosophy. He argued that his was Native American and wrote of himself and his writing in a manner reminiscent of the dual identity many other writers examined:

> I am rooted in the natural world . . . There is a little of the legendary Anpao in me, but also a little of Mick Jagger. I stand in both those worlds, not between them. I'm very much a twentieth-century man, and yet I'm a traditional Northern Plains Indian . . . I talk and think as a poet, but I don't want to perpetuate the romantic notion of the Indian as watching chipmunks his entire life, waiting to see which side of the tree the moss grows on. For the Indian, art is not reserved for a leisure class, as it is in Anglo society. It is a part of our fundamental way of thinking. We are an aesthetic people. (Senich, 1989; pp. 19-21)

Despite the controversy, Highwater has managed to create what many consider to be authentic stories about Native Americans. He authored several books, among them the Newbery Honor book, *Anpao* (1977), an epic tale that incorporates traditional tales about the Great Plains and Southwest Indian. This excerpt demonstrates his knowledge of the folklore his talent as a writer:

> But Oapna had changed into some unimaginable thing. It was astonishing. Anpao lay helplessly on the ground, for roots had grown over his body while he had lain unconscious. In the silence he stared at his brother, who had changed into something he had never seen before. He turned golden and fibrous and hard — like a gigantic cocoon. He had become a blank, membranous gourd, inside of which Anpao could see Oapna's translucent body slowly pulsating. (p. 83)

Highwater received critical praise for his *Ghost Horse Cycle,* a three-generation saga set among Northern Plains Indians. Highwater's other works include anthologies, such as *Words in Blood* (1984); poetry — *Moonsong Lullaby* (1981); and several nonfiction works. Paul Gobles' work — for example, *The Girl Who Loved Wild Horses* (1978) and *Her Seven Brothers*

(1988) — capture the essence of Plains Indian tales and legends in a comprehensible manner; his works are also beautifully illustrated. The folk tales of Gerald McDermott — for example, *Arrow to the Sun* (1978) — are notable for the quality of the illustrations and the artistry of the writing. Scott O'Dell and Jean Craighead George have also received praise for their fiction with Native American characters. Although few in number, Native American authors or those who write about Native Americans in a culturally conscious fashion, have contributed greatly to the body of children's literature.

SOME CONSIDERATIONS

The preceding sections illustrate the similarities and differences in multiethnic literature as well as the multiple and complex issues which shape the literature. Some of these issues need to be considered before multiethnic literature is included in curricula. First, the decision to include the literature should emanate from the classroom teacher. She or he should not feel compelled to include the literature. A teacher must express genuine willingness to share the literature with children. Compulsory inclusion might result in resentment, grudging acceptance, or, worse, hostile inclusion that conveys to children a negative attitude toward the literature and the group's members. Ideally, teachers should want to include the literature because it is a part of world literature, many of the works are excellent, and children deserve to expand their knowledge of the world's cultures and histories.

Second, teachers will have to develop strategies for solving some of the problems that arise because of the controversial issues in some of the works. Consider, for example, books that do not fit under the rubric culturally conscious literature but have received critical praise or are popular with children such as *The Indian In the Cupboard* (Banks, 1982), *Sounder* (Armstrong, 1969), or *The Cay* (1969). Or what about those works that are historically accurate and well-written but depict acts of violence against people of color or include derogatory names for people of color such *Mississippi Bridge* (Taylor, 1990)? When is it appropriate for children to read these texts? Will children ascribe to the texts the meanings that adults do who criticize the works? Do these books offer golden opportunities for developing and enhancing students' critical abilities? These are but a few of the decisions teachers will make.

The use of multiethnic literature involves some instructional issues as well. A number of texts use the vernacular English of the particular group portrayed. It is quite likely that some teachers and parents will protest the use of text with explicit language or nonstandard forms. Further, the way in which some of the authors interpret their historical experiences contradicts commonly accepted versions in textbooks. For instance, some authors refer to the removal of Japanese Americans into camps as placement in concentration camps and not placement in internment camps (Hamanaka, 1990). How does a teacher reconcile these disparate views, or is it possible or desirable to do so? These controversial and difficult issues should not serve as impediments to sharing the literature; they should only result in informed use.

RECOMMENDED RESOURCES

Teachers can draw upon a number of resources once the decision has been made to include multiethnic literature in the curriculum. The guidance in selection and evaluation offered by these resources is helpful. A general guide for the selection of multiethnic and multicultural literature is *Children's Literature: An Issues Approach* (Rudman, 1984). Each group discussed in the chapter has available an annotated bibliography: African Americans — *Shadow and Substance* (Sims, 1982), Asian Americans — *Literature for Children About Asians and Asian Americans* (Jenkins & Austin, 1987); Hispanic Americans — *A Hispanic Heritage* (Schon, 1978, 1983); and Native Americans — *Literature by and About the American Indian* (Stensland, 1979). Teachers can supplement these guides with current articles from journals such as *Children's Literature Association Quarterly, Horn Book Magazine, Interracial Books for Children Bulletin, Language Arts, The Lion and the Unicorn, The New Advocate, Perspectives,* and *The Reading Teacher.*

The following lists should not be considered as exhaustive or complete. They represent a sample of the literature available and provide an introductory foundation to multiethnic literature. The books discussed in the text are ideal candidates for inclusion as well. Books listed with an asterisk are suitable for use with preschool and primary aged children. Full bibliographic citations appear in the bibliography.

African American

Barrett, J. (1989). *Willie's Not the Hugging Kind.*
*Bryan, A. (1989). *Turtle Knows Your Name.*

Boyd, C. (1988). *Circle of Gold.*
*Greenfield, E. (1988). *Nathaniel Talking.*
*(1989). *Grandpa's Face.*
Guy, R. (1983). *New Guys Around the Block.*
Hamilton, V. (1986). *The House of Dies Drear.*
(1988). *Anthony Burns.*
*Johnson, A. (1990). *When I am Old With You.*
*Lessac, F. (1989). *Caribbean Canvas.*
Myers, W. (1989). *The Mouse Rap.*
(1988). *Fallen Angels.*
*Steptoe, J. (1988). *Baby Says.*
Taylor, M. (1990). *The Road to Memphis.*

Asian American

*Boholm-Olsson, E. (1988). *Tuan.*
*Heyers, M. (1986). *The Weaving of a Dream.*
Houston, J. and Houston, J. (1973). *Farewell to Manzanar.*
Lord, B. (1984). *In the Year of the Boar and Jackie Robinson.*
Louie, A. (1982). *Yeh Shin.*
Paterson, K. (1988). *Park's Quest.*
*Surat, M. (1983). *Angel Child, Dragon Child.*
*Torre, B. (1990). *The Luminous Pearl.*
Uchida, Y. (1981). *The Best Bad Thing.*
Yep, L. (1989). *The Rainbow People.*

Hispanic American

*Adoff, A. (1988). *Flamboyan.*
*Baylor, B. (1963). *Amigo.*
Belpre, P. (1973). *Once in Puerto Rico.*
*Byers, R. (1990). *Mycca's Baby.*
Chardiet, B. (1973). *Juan Bobo and the Pig: A Puerto Rican Folktale Retold.*
*Cruz, M. (1976). *Yagua Days.*
*Delacre, L. (1989). *Arroz Con Leche.*
Mohr, N. (1973). *Nilda.*
(1975). *El Bronx Remembered.*
Soto, G. (1990). *Baseball in April and other stories.*

Native American

'Baylor, B. (1976). *Hawk, I'm your brother.*
Bierhorst, J. (1969). *The fire plume: Legends of the American Indians.*
'DePaola, T. (1987). *The Legend of the Indian paintbrush.*
Freedom, R. (1988). *Buffalo hunt.*

WORKS CITED

Aitken, J. (1988). Children's literature and the sociology of school knowledge: Can this marriage be saved? *Curriculum Inquiry, 18,* 195-216.

Anderson, J. (1986). Secondary school history textbooks and the treatment of Black History. In D. Hines (Ed.), *The State of Afro-American History: Past, present, and future* (pp. 253-274). Baton Rouge: Louisiana State University Press.

Asian American Book Project (1981). How children's books distort the Asian American Image. *Interracial Books for Children Bulletin, 7,* (2 & 3), 3-33.

Baker, A. (1975). The changing image of the Black in children's literature. *The Horn Book Magazine, 51,* 79-88.

Bishop, R. S. (1990a). Mirrors, Windows, and Sliding Glass Doors. *Perspectives, 6,* ix-xi. (1990b). Walk tall in the world: African American Literature for today's children. *Journal of Negro Education, 59,* 556-565.

Broderick, D. (1973). *Image of the Black in children's literature.* New York: R. R. Bowker.

Chall, J., Rashburn, E., French, V., & Hall, C. (1979). Blacks in the world of children's books. *The Reading Teacher, 32,* 527-533.

Clifton, L. (1981). Writing for Black children. *The Advocate, 1,* 32-37.

Chin, F. (1981). Where I'm coming from. *Interracial Books for Children Bulletin, 7* (2 & 3), 24-25.

Commire, A. (Ed.). (1976). Virginia Sneve. *Something About the Author, 8,* 193-196.

Elson, R. (1963). *Guardians of tradition.* Lincoln: University of Nebraska Press.

Fielding, L., Wilson, P., & Anderson, R. (1984). A new focus on free reading: The role of tradebooks in reading instruction. In T. Raphael (Ed.). *The contexts of school-based literacy* (pp. 149-162). New York: Random House.

Greenfield, E. (1975). Something to shout about. *The Horn Book Magazine, 51,* 624-626.

Hamilton, V. (1983). The mind of a novel: The heart of the book. *Children's Literature Association Quarterly, 8,* 10-14.

Hamilton, V. (1987). The known, the remembered, and the imagined: Celebrating Afro-American folktales. *Children's Literature in Education, 18,* 67-76.

Harris, V. (1987). Jessie Fauset's transference of the "New Negro" philosophy to children's literature. *Langston Hughes Review, 6,* 36-43.

Harris, V. (1990). African American children's literature: The first one hundred years. *Journal of Negro Education, 59,* 340-355.

Huck, C., Hepler, S., & Hickman, J. (1987). *Children's literature in the reading program.* (4th ed.). New York: Holt, Rinehart and Winston.

Hurmence, B. (1984). Point of view: A question of perspective II. *The Advocate, 3(4),* 20, 23.

Jenkins, E. & Austin, M. (1987). *Literature for children about Asians and Asian Americans.* New York: Greenwood Press.

Larrick, N. (1965). The all-white world of children's books. *Saturday Review, 48,* 63-65, 84-85.

Martinez, M. & Nash, M. (1990). Bookalogues: Talking about children's literature. *Language Arts, 67,* 599-601.

Mingle, P. (1984). Some thoughts on judging children's literature. *Top of the News, 40,* 423-426.

Moore, O. & MacCann, D. (1987a). Paternalism and assimilation in books about Hispanics: Part one of a two-part essay. *Children's Literature Association Quarterly, 12(2),* 99-102, 110.

Moore, O. & MacCann, D. (1987b). Paternalism and assimilation in books about Hispanics: Part two of a two-part essay. *Children's Literature Association Quarterly, 12(3),* 154-157.

Moore, O. & MacCann, D. (1988). The ignoble savage: Amerind images in the mainstream mind. *Children's Literature Association Quarterly, 13(1),* 26-30.

Muse, D. (1975). Black children's literature: Rebirth of a neglected genre. *Black Scholar, 7,* 11-15.

Nieto, S. (1982). Children's literature on Puerto Rican Themes-Part 1: The messages of fiction. *Interracial Books for Children Bulletin, 8,* (1 & 2), 6-9.

Purves, A. & Beach, R. (1972). *Literature and the reader.* Urbana, IL: NCTE.

Rockwood, J. (1982). "Can novelists portray other cultures fairly." *The Advocate, 2,* 1-5.

Rollins, C. (1948). *We build together.* (rev. ed.). Chicago: NCTE.

Rudman, M. (1984). *Children's literature: An issues approach.* (2nd ed.). New York: Longman.

Schon, I. (1978). *Books in Spanish for children and young adults.* Metuchen, NJ: Scarecrow Pres.

Schon, I. (1983). Noteworthy books in Spanish for children and young adults from Spanish-speaking countries. *The Reading Teacher, 36,* 138-142.

Schon, I. (1984). Recent outstanding and ordinary books about Mexico, Mexicans, and Mexican-Americans, *Top of the News, 41,* 60-64.

Schon, I. (1989). Recent children's books about Hispanics. *Youth Services in Libraries, 2,* 157-161.

Seals, D. (1989). Indians without hope, Indians without options — The problematic theme of Hatter Fox. *Interracial Books for Children Bulletin, 15(3),* 7-10, 22.

Senich, G. (Ed.). (1989). Jamake Highwater. *Children's Literature Review, 17,* 19-32.

Sims, R. (1982). *Shadow and Substance.* Urbana, IL: NCTE.

Sims, R. (1983). What has happened to the "all-White world of children's books. *Phi Delta Kappan, 65,* 650-653.

Sims, R. (1984). A question of perspective. *The Advocate, 3,* (3), 144-155.

Sims, R. (1985). Children's books about Blacks: A mid-eighties status report. *Children's Literature Review, 8,* 9-13.

Stensland, A. (1979). *Literature by and about the American Indian.* Urbana, IL: NCTE.

Strickland, D. & Taylor, D. (1989). Family story book reading. In Strickland, D. & L. Morrow (Eds.), *Emerging literacy: Young children learn to read and write* (pp. 27-34). Newark, DE: International Reading Association.

Taxel, J. (1986). The Black experience in children's fiction: Controversies surrounding award winning books. *Curriculum Inquiry, 16,* 217-281.

Taxel, J. (1988). Children's literature: Ideology and response. *Curriculum Inquiry, 18,* 217-230.

CHILDREN'S BOOKS CITED

Adoff, A. (1970). *Malcolm X.* New York: Thomas Crowell.

Adoff, A. (1988). *Flamboyan.* New York: Harcourt Brace Jovanovich.

Angelou, M. (1987). *Now Sheba sings the song.* New York: E. P. Dutton.

Armstrong, W. (1969). *Sounder.* New York: Harper.

Banks, L. (1982). *The Indian in the cupboard.* New York: Avon.

Barret, J. (1989). *Willie's not the hugging kind.* New York: Harper.

Baylor, B. (1963). *Amigo.* New York: Aladdin.

Baylor, B. (1976). *Hawk, I'm your brother.* New York: Scribner's Sons.

Belpre, P. (1973). *Once in Puerto Rico.* New York: Warne.

Bierhorst, J. (Ed.). (1969). *The fire plume.* New York: Dial.

Bishop, C. & Wise, K. (1938). *The five Chinese brothers.* New York: Coward-McCann, Inc.

Boholm-Olsson, E. (1988). *Tuan.* New York: R & S Books.

Boyd, C. (1988). *Circle of gold.* New York: Apple Paperbacks.

Brown, D. (1974). *Wounded Knee.* New York: Holt, Rinehart and Winston.

Bryan, A. (1989). *Turtle knows your name.* New York: Atheneum.

Catalono, J. (1988). *The Mexican Americans.* New York: Chelsea.

Chardiet, B. (1973). *Juan Bobo and the pig*. New York: Walker.

Clifton, L. (1974). *The times they used to be*. New York: Holt, Rinehart and Winston.

Clifton, L. (1975). *My brother fine with me*. New York: Holt, Rinehart and Winston.

Clifton, L. (1979). *The lucky stone*. New York: Delacorte.

Crews, D. (1982). *Carousel*. New York: Greenwillow.

Crews, D. (1984). *School bus*. New York: Greenwillow.

Cruz, M. (1976). *Yagua Days*. New York: The Dial Press.

Delacre, L. (1989). *Arroz con leche*. New York: Scholastic, Inc.

de Paola, T. (1987). *The legend of the Indian paintbrush*. New York: Putnam.

De Veaux, A. (1987). *Enchanted hair tale*. New York: Harper Junior.

Emanuel, J. (1968). *Dark symphony*. New York: Free Press.

Freedman, R. (1988). *Buffalo hunt*. New York: Holiday House.

Goble, P. (1978). *The girl who loved wild horses*. New York: Aladdin.

Goble, P. (1988). *Her seven brothers*. New York: Bradbury Press.

Greenfield, E. (1973). *Rosa Parks*. New York: Crowell.

Greenfield, E. (1975). *Me and Neesie*. New York: Harper Trophy.

Greenfield, E. (1978). *Honey, I love*. New York: Harper Trophy.

Greenfield, E. (1981). *Daydreamers*. New York: Dial Books.

Greenfield, E. (1988). *Grandpa's Face*. New York: Philomel.

Greenfield, E. (1988). *Nathaniel Talking*. New York: Black Butterfly Children's Books.

Guy, R. (1974). *The friends*. New York: Bantam.

Guy, R. (1983). *New guys around the block*. New York: Delacorte.

Hamilton, V. (1967). *Zeely*. New York: Macmillan.

Hamilton, V. (1968). *House of Dies Drear*. New York: Macmillan.

Hamilton, V. (1974). *M. C. Higgins, the great* New York:

Hamilton, V. (1975). *Paul Robeson: The life and times of a free Black man*. New York: Harper.

Hamilton, V. (1982). *Sweet whispers, Brother Rush*. New York: Philomel.

Hamilton, V. (1983). *Willie Bea and the time the Martians landed*. New York: Aladdin.

Hamilton, V. (1985). *The people could fly*. New York: Alfred A. Knopf.

Hamilton, V. (1988). *Anthony Burns*. New York: Alfred A. Knopf.

Haskins, J. (1990). *Dance in Black America*. New York: Crowell.

Heyer, M. (1986). *The weaving of a dream*. New York: Viking Kestral.

Highwater, J. (1977). *Anpao*. New York: J. B. Lippincott.

Highwater, J. (1981). *Moonsung lullaby*. New York: Lothrop, Lee & Shephard.

Highwater, J. (Ed.). (1984). *Words in blood*. New York: Meridian.

Houston, J. W. & Houston, J. (1973). *Farewell to Manzanar*. Boston: Houghton Mifflin.

Jacobs, W. (1990). *Great lives: Human rights*. New York: Scribners.

Johnson, A. (1990). *When I am old with you. New York: Orchard Books*.

Keats, E. (1962). A snowy day. New York: Viking.

Lester, J. (1968). *To be a slave*. New York: Scholastic.

Lessac, F. (1989). *Caribbean canvas*. New York: Lippincott.

Lord, B. (1984). *In the year of the boar and Jackie Robinson*. New York: Harper.

Louis, A. (1982). *Yeh Shin*. New York: Philomel.

Margolies. B. (1990). *Rehema's journey*. New York: Scholastic.

Mathis, S. (1975). *The hundred penny box*. New York: Viking.

McDermott, G. (1978). *Arrow to the sun*. New York: Viking.

McKissack, P. (1988). *Mirandy and Brother Wind*. New York: Knopf.

Meltzer, M. (1967). *Bread and roses*. New York: Signet.

Meltzer, M. (1980). *The Chinese Americans*. New York: Crowell.

Meltzer, M. (1982). *The Hispanic Americans*. New York: Crowell.

Mohr, N. (1973). *Nilda*. New York: Harper.

Mohr, N. (1975). *El Bronx remembered*. New York: Harper.

Mohr, N. (1979). *Felita*. New York: Dial Press.

Mohr, N. (1986). *Going Home* New York: Dial Press.

Myers, W. (1975). *Fast Sam, Cool Clyde and Stuff*. New York: Viking.

Myers, W. (1979; 1989). *The young landlords*. New York: Puffin.

Myers, W. (1988). *Fallen angels*. New York: Scholastic.

Myers, W. (1988). *Scorpions*. New York: Harper.

Myers, W. (1989). *Mouse rap*. New York: Harper.

Paek, Min. (1989). *Aekyung's dream*. San Francisco: Children's Book Press.

Paterson, K. (1988). *Park's quest*. New York: Lodestar Books.

Peavy, L. & Smith, U. (1983). *Women who changed things*. New York: Macmillan.

Price, L. (1990). *Aida*. New York: Harcourt Brace Jovanovich.

San Souci. R. (1989). *The talking eggs*. New York: Dial Books for Young Readers.

Sneve, V. (1972). *Jimmy Yellow Hawk*. New York: Holiday House.

Sneve, V. (1975). *They led a nation*. Sioux Falls, SD: Brevet Press, Inc.

Soto, G. (1990). *Baseball in April and other stories*. New York: Harcourt Brace Jovanovich.

Steptoe, J. (1980). *Daddy is a monster . . . sometimes*. New York: Lippincott.

Steptoe, J. (1987). *Mufaro's Beautiful Daughters*. New York: Lothrop, Lee & Shepard.

Steptoe, J. (1988). *Baby says*. New York: Lothrop, Lee & Shepard.

Surat, M. (1983). *Angel child, dragon child.* New York: Scholastic.

Tate, E. (1990). *Thank you Dr. Martin Luther King, Jr.* New York: Franklin Watts.

Taylor, M. (1975). *Song of the trees.* New York: Dial.

Taylor, M. (1976). *Roll of thunder, hear my cry.* New York: Dial.

Taylor, M. (1987). *The gold Cadillac.* New York: Dial.

Taylor, M. (1990). *Mississippi bridge.* New York: Dial Books.

Taylor, T. (1969). *The cay.* New York: Avon.

Thomas, J. (1986). *The golden pasture.* New York: Scholastic.

Thomas, P. (1978). *Stories from el barrio.* New York: Knopft.

Tuyet, T. (1987). *The little weaver of Thai-Yen village.* San Francisco: Children's Book Press.

Uchida, Y. (1981). *The jar of dreams.* New York: Atheneum.

Wilkinson, B. (1975). *Ludell.* New York: Bantam.

Williams-Garcia, R. (1987). *Blue tights.* New York: Lodestar Books.

Xiong, B. (teller). (1989). *Nine-in-one, GRR! GRR! San Francisco: Children's Book Press.*

Yarbrough, C. (1989). The shimmershine queens. New York: Putnam.

Yee, P. (1990). *Tales from Gold Mountain.* New York: Macmillan.

Yep, L. (1977). *Dragonwings.* New York: Harper.

Yep, L. (1989). *The rainbow people.* New York: Harper.

Young, E. (1989). *Lon Po P.* New York: Scholastic.

Zemach, M. (1982). *Jake and Honeybunch go to heaven.* New York: Farrar, Strauss, & Giroux.

8

Native Myths and Multicultural Awareness

Jon C. Stott

INTRODUCTION

A story is created from carefully selected details — characters, settings, and actions — arranged in an intentional structure — basically the introduction, development, and resolution of a conflict. Understanding occurs when, on at least one level, readers or listeners notice the details, perceive the patterns, and interpret the significance, often implied, of the details and patterns. Virtually all readers of stories are able to do this on at least a simple level. With greater skill, readers can see more in apparently simple stories and can better understand more complex ones.

Generally the stories people read come from within their own cultures. Thus the basic meanings of the details and structures are part of their cultural literacy. In the case of children's literature, most picture books, folk tales, short stories, and novels were, until the last two decades, created by and for members of the dominant Anglo-European culture and were about that culture. Stories about minority groups were frequently altered so that elements were familiar to readers from the majority culture. Of course, minority cultures had their own stories, but in their original forms they were seldom made available to outsiders. North America may have been a "melting pot," but too often, the intention was to make minority cultures invisible or as much like Anglo-European culture as possible.

We have now come to realize that multiculturalism involves difference and diversity and that the integrity of different racial and ethnic groups is to be understood, respected, and preserved. A people's cultural heritage is one of its most valuable possessions, and one of the essential elements of a heritage is the body of stories it includes. The stories a people knows and shares helps to define itself. By coming to know the stories of other groups, we can better understand them.

One way of becoming a healthy multicultural society is to make sure that the children we teach know their own and other people's stories. To do this we must be able to interpret the details and patterns of these stories in the manner of the members of the stories' culture. In developing literature curricula, we must select stories from the non-majority cultures and then of presentation that will get younger readers closer to their cultural content.

For teachers of Anglo-European background, this will require careful study of the literature and culture of other peoples. Only then can appropriate stories be selected and presentation strategies be devised. In this chapter, we shall provide suggestions for method of study and presentation, drawing on two recent and highly acclaimed picture books that retell Native American myths: Gerald McDermott's *Arrow to the Sun* (1974) and Paul Goble's *Buffalo Woman* (1984).

SPIRITUAL ELEMENTS OF NATIVE CULTURES

In part because of the dime novels of the late nineteenth century and Hollywood westerns of this century, a stereotyped notion of native peoples emerged. The image of the bloodthirsty, nearly naked savage, riding on horseback, brandishing a tomahawk, and emitting horrifying whoops as he swooped down on and massacred defenseless white settlers is familiar to nearly everyone. It is incorrect: Those specific native people who did attack white settlers were doing so in defense of lands that were often being treacherously and illegally taken from them. Moreover, not all native peoples rode horses or used tomahawks. The vicious heathen is an image created by non-native peoples, as are the images of the "Noble Savage," the "Vanished American," and the "First Ecologist."

The reality is that there is not a generic Indian; there are dozens of native cultural groups, each with its own distinct identity. These cultures have been in a state of constant change, as each group encountered other native groups and, later, European invaders. Members of modern native groups live in houses, drive cars and pickup trucks, often live in large cities, and watch television. In many ways, their lives are not much different from the lives of members of the dominant Anglo-European culture.

However, in a very significant way, the lives of Native Americans are very different. In recent years, more and more of them are rediscovering spiritual heritages that are unlike those of Anglo-Europeans. While traditional native customs and beliefs differed widely across the continent, there was one basic element that was found nearly everywhere. Human beings were felt to be a part of the universe in which they lived. They were equals with, brothers and sisters to, other living creatures. They had to show respect to the rest of the world. A fulfilled life was possible only when individuals existed in harmony with the natural and supernatural elements of their environments. This view differs widely from that of European peoples. Both the Christian and Greco-Roman traditions emphasized the superiority of human beings to the rest of creation, which was felt to exist for their benefit. The western world saw human beings as being apart from the rest of the creation rather than as a part of the entire universe.

The widespread native belief in the need to live in harmony with other beings, which possessed spirits and deserved respect, influenced every element of life, particularly the procurement of food. Both agricultural societies, such as the Pueblo people, and hunting societies, such as the various groups of the Northern Plains, possessed myths and developed important ceremonies relating to the growing of crops and hunting of game. It is believed that many of the myths were narratives explaining the original gifts of food and the various ceremonies, group rituals, and private prayers used to make the planter or hunter spiritually worthy of receiving these gifts. Successful horticulture and hunting were not merely the results of employing skills; they were the reward to those accomplished technicians who had proved themselves spiritually worthy, who had become integral parts of an harmoniously interrelated universe.

In retelling traditional native myths, Gerald McDermott, in *Arrow in the Sun,* and Paul Goble, in *Buffalo Woman,* carefully studied the physical and spiritual cultures of the Pueblo and Northern Plains peoples respectively. The adult who becomes familiar with the visual and verbal details of the two picture books and who then studies the traditional cultures of the two Native groups will quickly recognize the cultural significances of the two stories.

CULTURAL SIGNIFICANCE OF ARROW TO THE SUN

For many agricultural societies, food was the gift of a sky father god and earth mother god, whose union provided life sustenance for worthy people. The production of successful crops each year depended, in part, on the people's continued proof of their worthiness through the conduct of their lives and their commitment to sincere enactment of rituals. Only then would the life-giving rains enter the earth to nurture the seeds planted there. It is a popular misconception that native rain dances were deliberate attempts to force rain down, a kind of ceremonial seeding of the clouds to produce precipitation. In fact, they were actions designed to make them spiritually worthy for the gift of rain and to demonstrate that worthiness to the spirit powers.

An agricultural society, the Pueblo people's main crop is corn. The original corn was created in mythic time:

> When the earth was first created it was female, our Mother Earth. Its tutelary deity, Sotuknana, was instructed to create a substance to provide nourishment to mankind. Having no female partner, he gathered the moisture and fertilized the female earth with rain, bringing forth vegetation to supply with food all living creatures crawling upon her breast. Grass thus became as milk to the creatures of the animal kingdom, and corn became the milk for mankind. Corn . . . unites the two principles of Creation. It is a sacred entity embodying both the male and female elements. (Waters, 1963)

Traditional Pueblo religion, still observed by many today, involved a series of annual ceremonies related to the northerly and then southerly progress of the sun and to the planting, germination, growth, and harvesting of corn. These observances were designed to demonstrate the people's worthiness of receiving and to assist in the growth of a bountiful harvest.

The casual reader who brings to *Arrow to the Sun* a superficial knowledge of the Pueblo people quickly recognizes McDermott's use of designs and patterns of Pueblo art. The reader who takes time to examine the book's illustrations and narrative structures in relation to the people's spiritual beliefs will see how fully McDermott has embodied cultural concerns. Not only does the Boy, whose logo is a stylized cross-section of an ear of corn, bring the life giving rains symbolized by the rainbow, but also the stages of his quest for self-identify are deeply rooted in Pueblo belief. By achieving spiritual power, he finds self-worth and a central role in the life of his village.

As the child of a sky father and an earth mother, the Boy has the potential to be the mediator between the two forces on which depend the growth of the corn. However, as the early illustrations and text indicate, the people are not yet ready to receive him, and he has not yet achieved the maturity required for effective action. The people reveal their spiritual impoverishment by mocking his orphan status. Not surprisingly, orange, yellow, and brown colors dominate, symbolizing both the land's physical and the people's spiritual aridity. He is as yet untested, a child, as is symbolized by his drooping headdress, a symbol of newly sprouted corn. As Frank Waters has noted, "When the plant begins to grow, the leaf curves back to the ground like the arm of a child groping for its mother's breast" (Waters, 1963).

At the story's conclusion, the situation is reversed. The Boy is no longer driven from the circle of the villagers. Now he is at its center, surrounded by dancers representing the spiritual powers he encountered during his journey and corn in various stages of growth. He dances on a rainbow, symbol of the life-giving sun and rain, holding a small corn plant, while in the background large stalks of corn flourish. A direct line can be drawn between the sun, his mother, and himself. He has united the forces of sky and earth. His headdress is full, both like an arrow and the mature corn; his vestments are brightly colored. He has discovered and has taught the people the spiritual goodness that leads to a full crop.

To achieve his position of leadership, the Boy has had to travel on a solitary journey of initiation. His specific quest has been to find his father so that he might earn a place among the other boys. However, he is also searching for his own identity. To find it, he must pass through the four chambers of ceremony: the Kiva of Lions, the Kiva of Serpents, the Kiva of Bees, and the Kiva of Lightning.

Kivas were underground chambers in which were held Pueblo religious ceremonies, not the least of which involved the initiation of young males. These chambers were entered into by a ladder descending from a hole in the roof. "[A kiva] was sunk deep, like a womb, into the body of Mother Earth, from which a man is born with all that nourishes him" (Waters, 1963). Symbolically, the youth, having learned that spiritual basis of Pueblo life, emerged as an adult. This is parallel to what happens in *Arrow to the Sun,* except that the Boy encounters directly the spiritual powers that influence the growing of the crops.

Mountain lions represent warring societies. As the illustrations reveal, the Boy shrinks them and smoothes their ruffled fur. He has tamed them, or, symbolically, created the condition of peace without which agriculture cannot prosper. The second kiva contains rattlesnakes, which were used in the sacred rain ceremonies. After the ceremonies, they would be released at the edge of the village so that they could travel to the mountains there to report to the spirits that the people possessed the necessary reverence. The Boy's shaping them into circles, a universal symbol of harmony and unity, indicates that he possesses this reverence. In his third test, the Boy transforms the swarming bees into a functioning hive, a necessary condition for pollenization of the corn plants. His actions also indicate that cooperation among people is necessary in agriculture.

In the fourth and most important test, the Boy does not act but is acted upon. Lightning for a large majority of native cultures is the embodiment of supernatural or spirit power, in this case the power of the Boy's father, the Lord of the Sun. Having proved himself worthy in the first three kivas, he is struck with the lightning that embues him with this power. As he leaves the kiva, he trails a rainbow, product of the sun and rain, that he brings to his people. In his quest, he has established his identity as the emissary and son of a god, and to do that, he has undergone tests that fulfill the prime duty of a leader, social responsibility and leadership.

Read in the light of these culturally significant symbols, *Arrow to the Sun* can be seen as a myth of great significance for the Pueblo people. It provides an example of spiritual conduct that leads to a bountiful crop and a full life.

CULTURAL SIGNIFICANCE OF BUFFALO WOMAN

Just as in agricultural societies a right relationship must be achieved with the powers of earth and sky that provide the gift of food, so in hunting societies, a right relationship must be achieved between the hunter and the animal that gives its body so that the people may have meat. As mythographer Joseph Campbell has stated:

> The basic hunting myth is a kind of covenant between the animal world and the human world. The animal gives its life willingly, with the understanding that its life transcends its physical entity and will be returned to the soil or to the mother through some ritual of restoration. (1988)

At least an equal to the hunter, and, like the hunter, possessed of a soul, the animal willingly gives its body to the worthy hunter. In many societies, elaborate rituals of preparing for and conducting the hunt and for appeasing the souls of slain animals were developed. Scarcity of game and unsuccessful hunting were most frequently seen as indications of spiritual failure on the part of human beings.

The buffalo was the central animal in the lives of the Northern Plains people. When the great buffalo herds disappeared during the latter part of the nineteenth century, the traditional ways of life quickly sank into oblivion. The Sioux holy man Black Elk referred to the buffalo as "chief of all the four-leggeds upon our sacred mother," (1932) and with good reason. Virtually all parts of the buffalo were used. Hides were made into robes, tipi covers, shields, and containers, horns into ladles and spoons, bladders into water vessels.

Not surprisingly the buffalo possessed great spirit power and occupied a central position in the religious ceremonies of the people. The hunt itself, as Ruth Underhill has written, was "something like a religious pilgrimage. It was a mass contact with the Powers that kept them alive" (1965). Throughout the year, human beings studiously strove to avoid insulting the buffaloes, for if they did not show proper respect, hunting would be poor. The leader of the hunt was generally someone who had prepared himself through dreams and fasting.

The greatest gift the buffalo gave the people was knowledge of how to conduct the sacred ceremonies. Speaking of the mythical White Buffalo Cow Woman, Black Elk said, "It was the will of *Wakan-Tanka* . . . that an animal turn itself into a two-legged person in order to bring the most holy pipe to His people" (1953). Appearing to the human people one winter day, she prescribed the ceremonies they must perform and then left the village.

The story of a man who married a buffalo is found throughout the Northern Plains and is undoubtedly of ancient origin. In the mythologies of many tribes it is treated as an historical account of long-ago events. In addition to explaining the origin of certain ritual societies and such natural phenomena as buffaloes' tendency to run from people, the myth embodies the native belief in the interrelationship between all creatures. In his introduction to *Buffalo Woman,* Goble states the significance of the myth:

> The lives of both [human beings and buffaloes] were closely interwoven, and the story teaches that buffalo and people were related. . . . These stories were not simply for entertainment; they had the power to strengthen the bond with the herds, and to encourage the herds to continue to give themselves so that the people could live. It was felt that retelling the story had power to bring about a change within each of us; that in listening we might all be a little more worthy of our buffalo relatives.

Buffalo Woman may be divided into three sections, each one dealing with a phase of the movement toward the reestablishment of harmony between the young man and his buffalo wife. The opening part of the book traces the meeting and marriage of the hunter and the buffalo woman. In the illustrations for the half-title and title pages, the central characters are introduced. His skill as a hunter is demonstrated by the fact that, camouflaged in a wolf-hide, he has crept to within a few yards of an unsuspecting bull. Her relationship to the herd is seen as she stands calmly in front of it. The text states that the hunter "felt a wonderful harmony with the buffalo. . . . When they had hunted, the young man gave thanks that the buffalo had offered themselves." The double spread that follows portrays the young man on a knoll, raising a skull toward the sky. In a semi-circle around him several skulls are on clumps of sage. Four colored ribbons are tied to a small aspen, and a rawhide thong forms a second circle outside the skulls. The circles indicate his harmony with the universe; the placing of the skulls on the sage, a sacred plant, his respect for the animals he has slain. The colors of the ribbons — blue, white, red, and yellow — represent west, north, east and south, respectively, the four directions of the world (Neihardt, 1970). Clad in a buffalo robe, turned skin side out as was the custom for sacred ceremonies, he is standing on the earth and reaching to the sky. He is, in effect, in contact with all elements of his world.

When the buffalo cow he spots turns into a woman, she explains her mission: to create a relationship between her people and his. "My people wish that the love we have for each other will be an example to both our peoples to follow." The accompanying illustrations depict the peaceful natural setting that reflects the harmony they feel.

The second part of the story presents the destruction of the harmony. Although the young man loves his wife and son, the other people reject her; they do not wish to maintain the bond between the human and buffalo people. In spite of the warnings from his wife that her people will kill him, the hunter follows his family to the land of the buffalo nation. The earlier illustrations in this section reflect a sense of alienation. The wife and child are seen in the corner of one picture, separated from the other villagers by the tipi, which should represent unity and harmony between people. Walking alone across the prairie, the young man is similarly depicted in the corner of the illustrations. As his love and courage persist, he assumes a more central position. On the day of his arrival at the home of the buffalo, he sits in the middle of a clump of flowers, surrounded by a number of birds who tell him where his wife and child have gone. He is reestablishing his relationship with the nonhuman world.

In the third section, the young man must pass a test to become reunited with his family: he must recognize his wife and son, who have returned to their buffalo forms, by spotting them as they mingle with the great herd. To fail will mean instant death. Aided by his son, he passes the test and is himself transformed into a buffalo. "That was a wonderful day! The relationship was made between the People and the Buffalo Nation; it will last until the end of time." The important point to notice is the almost complete alienation of the man when he first reaches the herd. He is the only human being in the place. Goble emphasizes this alienation by picturing the smallness of the hunter surrounded by buffaloes. At first he is seen at the edge of the herd. The power of the buffalo chief is indicated by the size — he fills nearly half of a double spread — and by his anger — supernatural lightning flashes from his nostrils as he charges forward. Walking through the ranks of buffalo looking for his wife and son, the man is nearly lost. However, in the depiction of the buffalo transforming him into one of their number, he is difficult to spot. Thematically, his nature and that of the animals are becoming the same; he will soon be indistinguishable from them. *Mitakuye oyasin*. We are all related.

Unlike Gerald McDermott, Goble makes sparing use of the iconographic aspects of native art. There is little direct symbolism. However, through his portrayal of the central characters against the village and prairie landscapes, Goble subtly reinforces his major themes.

NATIVE MYTHS IN THE CLASSROOM

The analyses *Arrow to the Sun* and *Buffalo Woman* indicate how deeply the two myths embody the beliefs of specific agricultural and hunting societies respectively. Through their words and pictures, McDermott and Goble have implicitly communicated the spiritual meanings of the narratives, the backgrounds of which they have carefully researched. We must now consider how the two picture books can be presented in upper elementary and junior high school. The objects are not only to help students become aware of the specific meanings of these two myths but also to acquire techniques of reading stories from many diverse cultures. The end result of presenting the stories should be greater sensitivity to the multicultural dimensions of the world in which the students live.

Presenting Arrow to the Sun

Arrow to the Sun makes an excellent introduction to a unit of hero stories, tales in which the central character's journey involves a quest to discover his inner identity and his contributing role within his society. The nature of the hero's quest has been discussed by Joseph Campbell in *The Hero With a Thousand Faces* and is found in such diverse narratives as the ancient myth *Arrow to the Sun* and the modern motion picture *Star Wars*. Although the underlying pattern of "separation — initiation — return" (Campbell, 1949) is found all over the world, the specific events of the journey vary from culture to culture and are reflections of the values and beliefs of specific societies.

After a first reading of *Arrow to the Sun*, during which the students have ample time to look at the illustrations, the teacher can lead a general discussion of the Boy's character and his changed status after he has finished his journey. One way of facilitating awareness of the character growth is to have students fill out the "Obstacles Chart" (see figure 8-1). On the upward slope of each set of joining lines, the students should write the obstacle the Boy faces; on the downward slope, his solution. Then, on the line beneath each obstacle, students should write a word that best describes the quality of character the Boy exhibits in overcoming the obstacles. For example, for the first obstacle, they can write: rejected by boys, begins search, determination.

This initial reading, discussion, and activity has simply considered the book as a story with conflict, character growth, and resolution. A second day's presentation will introduce the cultural dimensions. The first step is to introduce the geographical location of the story, the Southwest desert area. Photographs of Pueblo villages and adjacent areas would be useful here. The second step is to ask students to examine a cross-section of an ear of corn to see if they can relate it to any of the visual elements of the story. Usually several will see that it resembled the logo the Boy has on his chest. What, they can then be asked, is the main crop of the Pueblo people? The answer, of course, is corn. Why then is the logo appropriate for the hero of a Pueblo myth?

Having established the agrarian basis of the story, students should look at the story's final illustration and consider, in sequence, the following questions. What has the Boy brought from the sun to the people? (A rainbow.) What do you need to form a rainbow? (Sun and rain.) Why are these two things so important to the Pueblo people? (They are needed to grow the corn. Rain, in such an arid country is especially important.) Why, then, is he a hero to the Pueblo people? (He brings the sun and rain they need for food to sustain life.)

Referring back to the "Obstacles Chart" completed in the previous class, explain to the students that to earn the right to help his people, the Boy had to overcome a series of obstacles, to pass a series of tests; only then

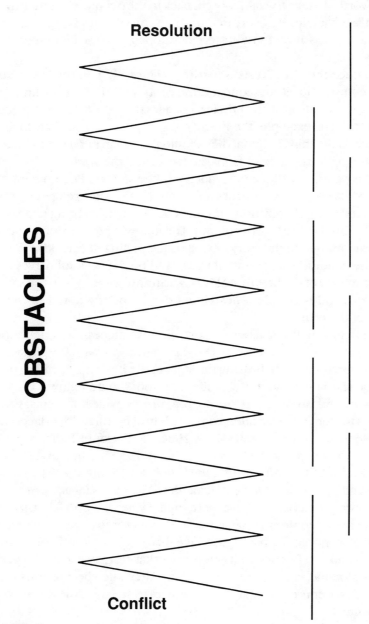

Figure 8–1
Obstacles

was he worthy to take the rainbow gift back to the people. Have them briefly review the obstacles he overcame both on the sun and before his arrival there and discuss how these tested, developed, or revealed inner heroic qualities.

Introduce the "Kiva Tests" chart (see figure 8-2). In the first column, the students should list, in sequence, the contents found in each kiva. In the second, they should note the physical changes that take place, as revealed in the pictures. For example, the lions (cougars) become smaller, their hair smoother. In the third column, they should note, in general terms, what the Boy has done. In the Kiva of Lions, he has tamed the animals.

At this point, introduce the students to the specific Pueblo symbolism associated with the occupants of each kiva (war, religious power, cooperation and pollenization, and spirit power that can bring rain). These should be listed in the fourth column. The following discussion can center on the importance to the story of what is happening in each kiva. The boy brings the conditions necessary if there is to be a successful harvest. Only after the actions of the first three kivas is he transformed, given the spiritual power to help his people. These ideas can be briefly noted in the final column of the chart.

In conclusion, the teacher can explain that successful agriculture for the Pueblo people depended on the right relationship with the physical and spiritual environment. In hearing the story of the Boy's heroism, the people would be learning about a way of life they, too, should follow.

This careful study of *Arrow to the Sun* provides students with an approach to studying hero tales from a variety of cultures. "Scarface: Origin of the Medicine Lodge" (Stott/Moss, 1986), a Blackfoot Indian myth; "Sir Gareth, or the Knight of the Kitchen" (Green, 1953), a medieval Arthurian romance from Britain; *Momotaro, the Peach Boy* (Shute, 1986), a Japanese legend; and *Taran Wanderer* (Alexander, 1967), a fantasy written by a contemporary American, all deal with unlikely heroes who find their roles and serve their people after passing tests encountered during their circular journeys from home and back again. Like *Arrow to the Sun*, each can first be studied without reference to its culture so that readers can have a general sense of plot and character development. After, the specific tests can be noted and students can research the cultures to see what these tests would have signified.

Arrow to the Sun also provides the starting point for a study of other picture books by McDermott. Recognizing that he incorporates artistic and well as thematic aspects of the specific culture of each myth or legend he adapts, students can research the art styles of each culture so that they can

KIVA TESTS

Kiva of	Physical Changes	General Meaning of Changes	Pueblo Meaning of Kiva	Pueblo Meaning of Changes

Figure 8-2
Kiva Tests

identify and then comment on the significance of the style of each book. For example, *Anansi the Spider* (McDermott, 1972) uses weaving designs of the Ashanti people of West Africa. Into the end papers he incorporates Ashanti weaving designs that also contain the logos of the various characters. The use of weaving patterns is appropriate for a story about spiders and family interrelationships. In *The Stonecutter* (McDermott, 1975), a Japanese legend, McDermott imitates the style of Japanese watercolors and banners and even includes patterns representing the Japanese script characters that signify important objects and characters in the story.

Presenting Buffalo Woman

Buffalo Woman provides an excellent introduction to the beliefs of the hunting societies of the Northern Plains, a contrast to many of the beliefs of agrarian societies such as that depicted in *Arrow to the Sun,* and a contrast to stories of human-animal marriage stories found in many cultures. As was the case in presenting *Arrow to the Sun,* detailed discussion should begin only after the student have enjoyed the narrative and had time to familiarize themselves with the illustrations.

Before beginning indepth analysis, write the words *mitakuye oyasin* on the board. In what sense do the values signified by this Sioux phrase, meaning "we are all related," resemble Pueblo attitudes to the relationship between human beings and the rest of the creation as seen in *Arrow to the Sun? Arrow to the Sun* focuses on the relationship between the human and supernatural worlds, while *Buffalo Woman* focuses on the human-animal relationships. Students should study and discuss the importance of the buffalo-human relationship for the people of the Northern Plains.

Study of *Buffalo Woman* should begin with a careful examination of the dust-jacket (or paperback) cover, the half-title page, and the title page. What types of beings are seen in each illustration and what is the relationship between them? They should notice that the human family on the dust-jacket cover does not seem frightened of the herd, that the buffalo seems aware of the hunter creeping toward him and still stands quietly, and that the girl seems almost to be a part of the herd. There is no sense of hostility or conflict.

The opening part of the narrative ends with the marriage of the hunter and the buffalo woman. It is important for students to discuss why this is an appropriate marriage and why, of all the human people, the hunter is most suited as husband. Two sentences in the opening paragraph should be noted: "He felt a wonderful harmony with the buffalo. . . . When they had hunted, the young man gave thanks that the buffalo had offered themselves." Why are the words "harmony" and "had offered themselves" important? What do they tell you about the values of this hunting society? Looking at the double spread in which the hunter thanks the buffalo, students should list all of the details that they think might be important. They can then be told how the various objects in the scene have spiritual significance and can discuss how this picture reinforces the idea of the goodness of the hunter.

Up to the point of the marriage, it could be said that there is no story, for there is no conflict. But when the people reject the woman and her son, the conflict begins. Unkindness to others is never good; but what is specifically wrong with the people's reasons for rejecting the buffalo woman and her son? They refer to her as an animal, which she is; but they don't wish to strengthen the human-animal relationship. Notice that they have rejected the truth of the phrase *mitakuye oyasin*. They don't seem to understand why the marriage occurred in the first place: "My people wish that the love we have for each other will be an example for both our peoples to follow."

The illustration depicting the rejection is significant. Explain to the students the importance of the tipi as an embodiment of interrelationship and harmony and then ask them to notice where the people are in relation to the tipi. They should see that it divides the figures on the page instead of uniting them.

Conflict requires resolution. Who is the character most suitable to see to repair the rift between the human and animal people? It is the hunter; however, he must prove himself worthy by passing a series of tests. Using the "Obstacles Chart" also used in *Arrow to the Sun* (see figure 8-1), list the obstacles, how he overcomes them, and the qualities of character that the hunter reveals at each stage of his journey. The students should notice that he leaves the village immediately after learning of their departure, continues his trek even though his wife warns him first of danger and then of death, and refuses to leave the vicinity of the buffalo tribe even when his son warns him back. Students should discuss why he receives assistance, first from the birds, later from his son. Their answers should focus on the worthiness he has revealed up to this point in his quest.

Students should also notice that the final tests, leading to the hunter's transformation into a buffalo, take place within a series of concentric radiating circles. After explaining to them that the circle was a symbol of unity and harmony among the Plains people and that the radiating circle design symbolized the spiritual aspects of this, ask them why it is an appropriate formation for the concluding tests. Not only is the hunter to be reunited with his family, he is reestablishing the physical and spiritual bonds between the buffalo and human peoples.

In reviewing the book, students can notice how Goble subtly reinforces the movement of his narrative through the patterns created by similar illustrations. Using the "Tipi-Home" chart (see figure 8-3), they can discuss the meanings of the tipis found in five of the illustrations. In the picture with the villagers, the tipi is shown, but not the buffalo designs. Both mother and son are outside of it. Away from the people, the buffalo designs are seen on the tipi, symbolic of movement toward the buffalo nation. On the plains, father and son are first seen outside the tipi, with the mother inside, and later with all three, still in human form, inside. There is a movement towards reestablishment of family unity. In the final two tipi pictures, no human beings are seen; the hunter in human form is, at first, hidden inside. Then the tipi, the human dwelling is destroyed, and the hunter, now almost completely transformed into a buffalo, is outside of it.

Having finished the study of the cultural meanings of the story, the students are now ready to discuss why it was so important a myth within the culture. Refer to Goble's statement that "These stories . . . had the power to strengthen the [people's] bond with the herds." Knowing about the relationship between people and buffalo, a young hunter might ask, "Is the buffalo I am about to kill a descendant of the marriage between my ancestor and the buffalo woman?" He would probably then realize that he, too, should strive to be as worthy as the hunter in the story. As in *Arrow to the Sun,* myth was not just a record of legendary history but an ongoing lesson to help individuals and societies achieve right relationships with their natural and supernatural environments.

Unlike Gerald McDermott, who has responded to cultures from around the world, Paul Goble has restricted his storytelling to the myths and historical narratives of the relatively homogenous cultural groups of the Northern Plains. Like *Buffalo Woman, The Friendly Wolf* (Goble, 1974), *The Girl Who Loved Wild Horses* (Goble, 1978), and *Her Seven Brothers* (Goble, 1988) also deal with the theme *Mitakuye oyasin,* discussing respectively the relationship between human beings and a wolf, a horse, and the stars. In each story, Goble carefully selects visual details that reenforce character and theme and incorporates native designs that have implicit cultural meaning. Several Goble books can be studied after detailed examination of *Buffalo Woman,* with readers discussing each as a variation of the relationship theme and noticing how and why Goble selects specific visual details. Such a unit will do much to overcome the often degrading

TIPI - HOME

	Where tipi located	What characters are in picture	Location of characters in relation to tipi	Significance of who is in picture, their location, tipi's location
1				
2				
3				
4				
5				

Figure 8–3
Tipi-Home

stereotypes still held by many people and will bring younger people closer to a way of life that can teach modern, industrialized, urbanized people a great deal.

Buffalo Woman can also be used to introduce a group of stories that portray marriages between human beings and animals. While this story type is found throughout the world, attitudes to the union differ. In "East o' the Sun, West o' the Moon" (Stott, Moss, 1986), a Scandinavian folktale, the human prince is cursed by having to spend his daylight hours as a polar bear until a faithful woman returns him to his superior and rightful human form. In the Celtic legend *The Selkie Girl* (Cooper, 1986), marriage between a human male and a seal-woman proves ultimately unsuccessful as the partners come from two completely different realms. In *The Crane Wife* (Yagawa, 1981), a Japanese folktale, it is the greed and selfishness of the human husband that destroys a wonderful union. Study of these stories can help to explain how different groups of human beings understand themselves in relation to the other creatures with whom they share their world.

SUMMARY

A story is understood, on at least one level, when readers are able to interpret the significance of its details and the patterns these form. When reading a story from a culture different from their own, readers must discover the meanings of the story's details to that culture before full understanding can be achieved. Careful study of cultural backgrounds of *Arrow to the Sun*, a Pueblo myth adapted by Gerald McDermott, and *Buffalo Woman*, a Northern Plains myth adapted by Paul Goble helps readers to appreciate more fully the stories themselves and the cultures that originally told them. Systematic study of each book will also provide upper elementary and junior high students a methodology for the study of similar myths from a variety of cultures.

REFERENCES

Alexander, L. (1967). *Taran wanderer.* New York: Holt, Rinehart, and Winston.

Black Elk. (1932). *Black Elk speaks,* as told to John G. Neihardt. New York: William Morrow.

Black Elk. (1953). *The sacred pipe,* edited by Joseph Epes Brown. Norman, Okla.: University of Oklahoma Press.

Campbell, J. (1949). *The hero with a thousand faces*. Princeton, NJ: Princeton University Press.

Campbell, J. (1988). *The power of myth*, with Bill Moyers. New York: Doubleday.

Cooper, S. (1986). *The selkie girl*, illustrated by Warwick Hutton. New York: McElderry Books.

Goble, P. & Goble, D. (1974). *The friendly wolf*. Scarsdale, NY: Bradbury Press.

Goble, P. (1978). *The girl who loved wild horses*. Scarsdale, NY: Bradbury Press.

Goble, P. (1984). *Buffalo woman*. Scarsdale, NY: Bradbury Press.

Goble, P. (1988). *Her seven brothers*. New York: Bradbury Press.

Green, R. L. (1953). *King Arthur and his knights of the round table*. Harmondsworth, England: Penguin Books.

McDermott, G. (1972). *Anansi the spider*. New York: Holt, Rinehart, and Winston.

McDermott, G. (1974). *Arrow to the sun*. New York: Viking Press.

McDermott, G. (1975) *The stonecutter*. New York: Viking Press.

Neihardt, J. G. (1951). *When the tree flowered*. Lincoln NE: University of Nebraska Press.

Shute, L. *Momotaro the peach boy*. New York: Lothrop, Lee & Shepard.

Stott, J. C. & Moss, A. (Eds.). *The Family of stories: An anthology of children's literature*. Toronto, Ontario: Holt, Rinehart, and Winston.

Underhill, R. M. (1965). *Red man's religion*. Chicago: University of Chicago Press.

Waters, F. (1963). *Book of the Hopi*. New York: Viking Press.

Yagawa, S. (1981). *The crane wife*, translated by Katherine Paterson. New York: William Morrow.

9

'Making' Drama With Literature

Anthony L. Manna and Arlene L. Lawson

INTRODUCTION

When children have access to various types of literature that address their immediate concerns, needs, and interests, they are more likely to be drawn into literature in personal ways. Literature that evokes personal connections encourages children to willingly give themselves over to the pleasurable work at hand — to infuse a poem, folk tale, or informational book with private and shared meanings, and, in the process, to make sense of it by drawing on what they know and feel and have experienced. As numerous studies have shown, children's personal involvement with the literature they hear and read provides them with a sturdy foundation for building a habit of reading and acquiring important reading and language skills. (Atwell, 1987; McNeil, 1982; McClure, 1985).

For teachers a primary task — and challenge — is to provide consistent opportunities for children to experience a wide variety of rich, meaningful literature that sparks a "live circuit" between reader and text (Rosenblatt, 1968). Teachers must also devise classroom strategies that not only make students attentive to the characteristics of literature they hear and read but also invite them to share with others the ideas and feelings that the literature evokes. When these things happen in an environment that supports collaborative meaning making, children gain confidence as readers, as they perceive and reflect on what they and other readers actually contribute to the reading process.

Of the many classroom approaches that can foster meaningful connections with literature, drama is particularly effective. In classroom dramas, students work together to "crack the code" of the literature — actually transforming the clues the literature contains for the real task of playing out and reflecting upon human issues and concerns. Drama opens up the text to children by directing them to explore the characteristics and elements of literature while they are also attending to the different aspects of human experience. Drama, in its most meaningful sense, encourages children to draw on the human situations contained in the literature and to relate these situations to their own lives. Because it provides a context where language can be shaped, shared, and acted upon for real reasons — a genuine need to communicate, explain, and express — drama has much potential for students and teachers of language.

PLAY, DRAMA, AND LITERACY

If literacy is "... the ability to inject one's own thoughts and intentions into messages received and sent; the ability to transform and to *act* upon aspects of the world via the written word...." (Boomer, 1985), then drama can be instrumental in enhancing the development of children's literacy skills. Through drama, children engage in social contexts where they use a variety of discourse styles, forms, and types. At the heart of every effective drama that unfolds in a classroom there is a dynamic literacy event where language is used to construct and sustain an authentic situation; to explore and reflect on significant issues and specific concepts and information; to exchange ideas, opinions, beliefs, and values; as well as to act, interact, and react. Drama also promotes greater language awareness by involving children in role play and dialogue where they alter and mediate their thought and ideas as well as process the speech and behaviors of others.

When drama is literature based, children delve into the spirit of the work to recreate the themes they discover there. This places them in an interactive mode with language, which is much like the stance readers must learn to assume to process the beliefs, ideas, and points of view that the writer lays before them. Through this transaction with the text, children make sense of what they read. They do this by playing along in the moment, improvising responses that are based upon their past and present experiences with concepts, ideas, and other literature.

Interaction through and with narration is not foreign to children. It is found primarily in the spontaneous dramatic play of childhood where fictional situations are routinely created and played out through narrative. Barbara Hardy (1977) believes that this urge to capture experiences through the medium of story is a basic human inclination. Hardy maintains that narrative is a fundamental medium that people of all ages use to organize their experiences. This inclination is a "primary act of mind:"

For we dream in narrative, daydream in narrative, remember, anticipate, hope, despair, believe, doubt, plan, rehearse, criticize, construct, gossip, learn, hate, and love by narrative. In order really to live, we make up stories about ourselves and others, about the personal as well as the social past and present. (pp. 12-13)

The human urge to dramatize already lived through as well as anticipated experience is just as natural (O'Neill, 1989). The dramatizing powers of the human mind are put to work whenever we reach into places, times, and people to sort them out. We shuttle back and forth between internal expectations about such encounters and the external reality of them — between what is and what is imagined. As O'Neill states:

The voices in our mind, . . . our skill in representing the actions and speech of others, our ability to see the other side of things, to create opposing opinions, to be able to anticipate answers to the questions we ask, are all built on our power to dramatize, to put ourselves in someone else's shoes. (p. 149)

In their play, children make stories collaboratively and individually. They fashion these out of many facets of their lives, including their memories, needs, tensions, and dreams, and they use stories to fantasize, explain, cope, imagine, heal, or understand what they are experiencing and have experienced. (Bettelheim, 1976; Smith, 1984)

An extended sequence from the spontaneous dramatic play of four-year-old Nate contains many of these characteristics. Over a period of several weeks, in a preschool environment, Nate created and maintained a tense outer space drama in which he was both the main character and director. Assuming the role of Captain Donatel, Nate was commander of a spaceship made out of multipurpose wooden blocks. His crew consisted of a number of his peers, in roles that ranged from computer operators and ground control experts to cooks and members of the military. Captain Donatel established strict boundaries and codes through which he advanced the plot ("Now we fight with lasers."), maintained order ("No boats here; it's a spaceship."), indicated acceptable and unacceptable behavior ("You can't be a ghostbuster in outer space!"), and relegated tasks (Said to the teacher in role as ground control: "You send troops from America."). Nate's drama revealed an intricate network of plots and subplots that carried the players from one intriguing, suspenseful incident to another, the central theme and focus deriving from Captain Donatel's mission to rid the universe of what he himself consistently described as "fear and danger." The incidents that Nate contrived to gather the players into this make-believe context and to sustain their commitment to it were dramatic in the sense that they contained a tension and a character in a conflict. True to the nature of drama, there was something constantly at stake. This not only gave the players a common ground and mutual cause but provided a base from which to improvise their sense of the tension between good and evil, and freedom and oppression in which many scenarios in the outer space drama seemed to involve the players.

Koste (1987) advises, it may be "dangerous to presume to know the specific reasons, motives, meanings of a child's play" (p. 60). However, certain aspects of Nate's drama revealed some personal issues that deeply concerned him at the time. Nate's father is a paleontologist who openly discusses his professional life with his son, particularly the fact that he spends a great deal of time on archaeological digs in wartorn countries. It seems, then, that Nate's determination to ward off the evil that lurked in outer space was somehow connected to the content of his life, and that he used drama as a vehicle to work through a personal concern. Perhaps his dramatic play also served as a catharsis: "to purge him of strong feelings — anxieties over loss and separation, over pride, identity, [and] relations . . . with other people. . . . (Koste, p. 92).

One thing we do know from a study of Nate's and other children's play is that the "as if" situations they create in their play cover a wide range of rhetorical techniques and narrative structures. These range from sequences acted out in chronological order with shifting points of view, asides, and anecdotes to loosely connected, impressionistic episodes that they maintain and return to over an extended period of time. Like seasoned storytellers, they imbue their play with logic, rules, and strict boundaries, all of which demonstrates how real their play can be for them (Piaget, 1962). "From a child's play," Bettelheim (1987) has written, "we can gain an understanding of how he sees and construes the world — what he would like to be, what his concerns and problems are" (pp. 35-36).

MOVING INTO LITERATURE WITH DRAMA

Classroom drama draws on the imaginative energies and curiosity that children bring to their social pretend play. When engaging students in improvised classroom drama, the teacher is actually trading on a convention and behavior in which most children have had abundant practice before entering school: the tendency to play out imaginatively all kinds of experiences, events, feelings, and concerns to identify and, in most cases, gain some control over them (Bettelheim, 1987). The drama leader's challenge is to tap into children's natural inclination to dramatize.

In the dramas they create outside of the classroom, children themselves usually take on the responsibilities of initiating and overseeing. In planned classroom dramas, where the intent is to enhance and enrich students' learning, the teacher provides the impetus and structure to enable the students to gain fresh insights and understandings. An important component of classroom drama, one usually lacking in children's spontaneous dramatic play, is conscious reflection. By encouraging students to step back from a dramatic event which they have been instrumental in developing, the teacher gives them an opportunity to examine such things as the issues that surfaced, the understandings and insights they gained, and the discoveries they made about the power of drama itself to reflect and distill human experience. Wagner (1976) believes that the key to unlocking learning through drama is to have students reflect on the dramas they create. "Such reflection," she maintains, "is the only thing that makes drama worth doing. If you cannot increase reflective power in people, you might as well not teach, because reflection is the only thing that in the long run changes anybody" (p. 77). For Bolton (1979), reflection is an agent that can cause "a change of insight [and] some shift in appraisal . . . that has involved a change of feelings" (p. 41).

When literature of any type enters the drama process, it serves as a force that focuses the drama on a specific phenomenon; its content, patterns, structure, concepts, and themes provide a foundation upon which action and character are set into motion and the issues and topics the writer reveals are discovered and considered through enactment. The teacher who builds a drama around literature has a number of essential roles and responsibilities to fulfill. He or she:

- Has a thorough command of the selection so that its elements can serve the drama by giving it substance, shape, and direction;

- Creates a supportive classroom environment that fosters risk-taking and openness to the thoughts and feelings students have as they interact with and through literature;

- Participates frequently in the drama in role as one of the characters found in or suggested by the literary selection in order to drive the drama forward and to fix and sustain student attention on a situation, dilemma, conflict, issue, or concept;

- Participates frequently out of role to suggest roles, to intervene, motivate, join the students in reflection on the drama, set a new course of action, assess the nature and caliber of student participation, and invite the students to notice the texture and shape of the drama and their involvement in it;

- Closely listens and observes for the sake of determining how the students' ideas and needs should direct the course of the drama so that the pressure and direction of the dramatic context can allow knowledge and understanding to emerge.

By its very nature drama is an interactive learning and teaching medium. As the original sense of the word suggests, drama involves "doing" — using language functionally and purposefully, acting on phenomena to get things done, expressing, communicating. Drama therefore requires the teacher to give up at least some of his or her control, to allow students the privilege of suggesting roles and situations, and to be tolerant of a certain amount of purposeful interaction, movement, and noise within the classroom. While involved in an improvised drama or presenting a drama they have formulated and rehearsed on their own, students will need to relate to one another in and out of role, to collaborate at times on small-group projects, to solve problems together, and, at other times, to rehearse and present scenes that evolve out of a consideration of such literary elements as character, setting, point of view, patterns of action, mood, and language style.

As with all good teaching, when clear objectives, well-defined and meaningful tasks, and a spirit of experimentation guide classroom projects and other activities, students willingly commit themselves to the work at hand, learning, as a result of the example and climate the teacher sets, that far from being a pleasant diversion from more serious classroom business, drama can be a compelling medium for exploring and expressing ideas and for learning new ones. given drama's potential for motivating readers to move into the very center of a work of literature and for relating the discoveries they make there to their own lives, drama can serve both teachers and students as much more than a mere follow-up activity that assesses student comprehension or involves students in retracing plot sequence. When the teacher invests drama with the kind of planning, structure, and pacing that characterize successful classroom processes, drama is more likely to enhance language development and learning and contribute to students' awareness of the many ways in which literature of all types and forms can open them to fresh insights and new or different understandings.

Teaching and learning of this kind takes relatively more time than prescriptive classroom methods. The benefits of such an investment of time and energy, however, are more often than not greater student involvement in the learning process and increased ownership of concepts, facts, and insights (Goodlad, 1984; Mandel, 1980; Wells, 1986). Drama, as the examples in this chapter will demonstrate, is not another subject to be tacked onto an already overcrowded curriculum; it is a learning medium, like writing, for example, through which students can explain, discuss, think through, and hopefully master any type of curricular content.

LITERATURE AS A CATALYST FOR DRAMA

Consider, for example, the ways in which a brief or extended drama sequence might draw teacher and students into *Lord of the Dance,* a picture book for all ages, written and illustrated by Tadjo (1988). In the manner of a folktale, *Lord of the Dance* uses the symbol of a personified mask to trace the history of the Senufo people of the Ivory Coast in northern Africa. The illustrator's stick-like figures and page decorations in vibrant colors reveal the different stages of the Senufo's development, from the simplicity of village life to the pressures and complications the Senufo face in a contemporary technological age. The book suggests a wide range of possibilities for dramatic explorations of culture, community, the effects of progress on a people, and the function of art. To align the book with the visual arts, for example, the students might make masks in the style represented in the illustrations, and incorporate them into their enactment of key scenes and passages, or they might study the illustrator's style and medium and use vegetable dyes to create decorated cloths that serve as integral props in their interpretations of Senufo life and living. Since music and dance are central aspects of Tadjo's interpretation of the Senufo, movement and music could be incorporated into art-related dramas that depict the culture described in the book as well as dramas that emphasize customs and other conventions in any type of culture that is different from the students'. A social studies connection can be made by examining the brief description of the geography and various cultures of the Ivory Coast that concludes *Lord of the Dance.*

With the help of the school librarian, students could research specific features of the Senufo such as family life, schooling, leisure activities, foods, the status of children, and occupations. This information could initiate or enrich dramatic events.

A drama based on *Lord of the Dance* might also give children an opportunity to consider one of the book's central themes, the encroachment of technology and other aspects of modernization on cultural traditions, particularly since these complications are pictured rather than described overtly. In this case, the drama would direct students to use visual clues as a means to infer examples of the changes modernization brings to a society and the positive and negative effects these changes can have on people's lives. A drama of this kind might well be put into motion with a lead provided by an honest speculation on the part of the teacher: "I wonder why. . . ," or "Isn't it interesting that . . . we have so many conveniences but not a lot of time to enjoy them?" (Wagner, 1976, p. 79).

Behind every effective drama there are a great deal of planning, an attention to sequence and design, and, at the same time, an ability to detect and follow previously unknown signs of a group's will and needs. In literature-based drama, the teacher must have command of the poem or tale or biography. Knowing its distinctive elements inside and out is necessary in order to be prepared for every twist and turn a drama may take. Often, a drama will emerge spontaneously when students take charge of the literature and indicate a drama's course. To be genuinely enthused about this literature is the teacher's first obligation.

INITIATING LITERATURE-BASED DRAMA

Children's ability and willingness to enter into the world an author or illustrator has created are measures, to some extent, of their success as readers. Similarly, the caliber of their belief in the "as if" situation a drama proposes determines the knowledge and awareness they gain from their participation in drama. To help build children's belief throughout the drama experience constitute two of the fundamental and formidable roles a drama leader must anticipate. In spirit and intent, the techniques a teacher uses to gather children into a drama are similar to the ones that summon up children's commitment to any type of classroom content. What needs to be at work here is the teacher's own commitment to literature and drama; student belief evolves out of this energy, for it is contagious.

How then does a teacher help students create a dramatic context they will believe in, within which they can stretch their minds and take risks safely? There are many techniques for initiating and sustaining belief.

Guiding the teacher's choice are such objectives and conditions as the temperament, needs, and concerns of the group; the nature and extent of both the students' and teacher's previous experience with drama; and the concepts and skills the students are expected to learn. At the heart of any choice the teacher makes is the need to motivate children to consent to what Heathcote (Wagner, 1976) calls the "big lie." By this Heathcote means the unspoken "rule" or convention by which all those joined in drama must abide: "'that we are at this moment living at life rate in an agreed-upon place, time, and circumstance and are together facing the same problem'" (p. 67).

One way to encourage the kind of belief that drama demands is to let the students themselves suggest a topic or a few details for dramatic exploration about a situation, dilemma, or conflict they have experienced within or outside of the literature they have heard or read. Although this approach charts an uncertain path for the teacher and students, it makes it possible for both to "own" the imagined world they will explore together.

Another way to establish belief is to provide an initial frame for the drama by asking a question or making a statement that places the students at the center of the issue or situation a particular selection of literature will later reveal to them. For example, in relation to *Tuck Everlasting* by Babbitt (1975): "How do you feel knowing that you have found the secret to staying alive forever?" Or, to identify with the characters they choose to play from *The Friendship* by Taylor (1987), the teacher might ask, "How will you deal with the hatred that certain members of your town feel for your family or friends?" In the primary grades, to anticipate a drama on *Too Much Noise* by McGovern (1967), the emphasis might be placed on old Peter's dilemma. "We are facing a real problem. What are we going to do about all the noise in this room?" In this way, students will be encouraged first to identify with the problems and conflicts literary characters face in order to devise solutions as they later play out literary situations. Thus, the involvement, feeling, and commitment essential for meaningful dramatic enactment are brought to the situation from within its characters and not artificially created from the outside by placing students into a contrived dramatic climate that forces them to take on predetermined roles to which they have nothing personal to bring.

On any grade level, the teacher also can build belief and set the stage for drama by:

- Introducing an object that is an important symbol or prop in a work of literature of one that can capture the attitude, spirit, or mood of the piece such as a pumpkin ("The Pumpkin" by Graves [de Regniers, et al., 1988, p. 44]", a photograph of a family member ("Lil' Bro" by Fufuka [Prelutsky, 1983, p. 136]), or a gourd or a map of the stars (*The Drinking Gourd* by Monjo [1970]);

- Using recorded, teacher-made, or student-made sounds to set the mood or tension for a piece such as *Mirandy and Brother Wind* (McKissack, 1988), *The Storm Book* (Zolotow, 1952), *Feel the Wind* (Dorros, 1989), *A Wrinkle in Time* (L'Engle, 1962), and *Hatchet* (Paulsen, 1987);

- Reading aloud a vivid passage from a long book to establish the context for a drama and inviting students to reveal and discuss, in role as one of the characters, what they feel, think, see, and need or desire as a lead to writing-in-role activities. The writings, in turn, suggest still-life tableaux in which several characters come to life in response to a cue from the leader and reveal things about themselves such as their thoughts and feelings, relationships with others, quandaries, goals, and concerns.

Another source for countless drama content is what Heathcote refers to as the "Brotherhood Code" (Wagner, 1976). A brotherhood code is a universal human condition that is found among people the world over and mirrored in literature of all types. Heathcote maintains that because we are all part of humanity, united by similar wishes, dreams, proclivities, and failings, we are therefore linked to each other in the drama that is life. Brotherhoods are connections we have with others through all time and circumstance, occupation, interest, need, or social and cultural condition. Creating a brotherhood among students involves choosing a situation or condition that unifies the group around a shared objective or feeling. Students will be expected to identify with and develop roles based on "... all those who have been in that same situation," (p. 49) those, for example, who have been fortunate, victimized, bored, fearful, or courageous as well as those who go on quests, journey into unknown territory, grow up, wage battles against injustice, or cope with loss, disappointment, or change.

Literature is a wellspring of many brotherhoods that have the potential to suggest dramatic contexts and to instill them with the essential elements of tension derived from conflict and dilemma that, in turn, is derived from character in conflict. The key to finding the universals inherent in brotherhoods is to look to the themes that resonate beyond the literal level of the words. *The Fortunate Isles,* by Townsend (1989), for example, deals on one level with three adolescents who escape from their homeland in ancient times in order to save their country from possible destruction. On the universal level, their heroic quest aligns them with all those who struggle against oppression, despotism, and injustice such as warriors in myths, contemporary freedom fighters, and advocates of human rights. These are conditions that suggest dramas that, depending on the age of the group, could be formed around literature with similar themes and structures such as *The Flame of Peace* by Lattimore (1987), *Nicholas, Where Have You Been?* by Lionni (1987), and several of the poems in *Street Talk* by Turner (1986). In the same manner, *Where's My Other Sock?,* a self-help book by Wirths and Bowman-Kruhm (1989), could initiate, sustain, or conclude a drama that evolves out of the need or desire to get control of one's life, to put one's life in order. In *The Snow Queen* by Andersen (1985) and the fantasy novels for older readers in LeGuin's Earthsea trilogy (1968; 1971; 1972), for example, this need entails a quest that culminates in personal awareness.

Students, too, may pose a brotherhood that will forge a bond among them. In one third grade, the students chose to explore different kinds of conditions inherent in friendship. Facilitated by roles and situations suggested by both the students and their teacher, the students drew on their own experiences as well as ones portrayed in various types of literature to consider the qualities that make good friends, the problems friendships cause, and ways to resolve arguments and cope with bad feelings. In addition to the situations found in the literature the children heard and read, brief scenarios placed the students in settings that ranged from a school cafeteria, a playground, and a classroom to a birthday party and a school bus. Examples of "all those who have been in the same situation" were gleaned from a number of books: *The Scott, Foresman Anthology of Children's Literature* (Sutherland & Livingston, 1984), *The Oxford Book of Children's Verse in America* (Hall, 1985), *Charlotte's Web* (White, 1952), *Friends Forever* (Chaikin, 1988), *But I'll Be Back Again* (Rylant, 1989), *Crow Boy* (Yashima, 1955), *Childtimes* (Greenfield and Little, 1979), *Frog and Toad Are Friends* (Lobel, 1970), and others.

In building dramas around brotherhoods, the teacher is encouraging students to fathom the large issues that literature reveals to them; namely, to act on, by playing out, the discoveries that the literature evokes, and to live with the consequences of their best guesses on how to deal with the conditions and situations they face in the safety of the dramatic context. Literature serves as a lens that fixes attention; it helps to fashion the group into a community of believers with a shared purpose.

SUSTAINING LITERATURE-BASED DRAMA SEQUENCES

Whenever the teacher integrated literature with classroom content in order to enhance and enrich students' experiences with topics, issues, and concepts, a drama can be set into motion to connect the content to life and living and to make it concrete and relevant. Like literature, drama has the capacity to slow the rate at which students encounter classroom topics and issues by providing a frame for inspection and reflection. The two literature-based drama sequences that follow lay out procedures for integrating drama and literature with various subject areas of a school curriculum. The first involves intermediate grade students in an exploration of historical phenomena that are introduced in social studies. In the second, titled "The Shadow World," children themselves led the way to several dramas about childhood fears, the characteristics of fantasy, and the differences between fantasy and reality.

The slavery issue gave the social studies drama its impetus and shape, and various types of literature helped to bring the phenomenon to life by demonstrating the effects that slavery had on people — both real and imaginary. The overall objective of the sequence was to have the students discover that history is an ongoing saga of the values, concerns, struggles, failures, and triumphs that characterize humanity's story. Inherent in the design and structure of the sequence were activities that could make students conscious of the value and power of historical records, the ways in which written documents preserve the spirit and facts of a given era, and the importance of heritage.

To initiate the drama, which extended over five classroom sessions reserved for social studies, the teacher created a dramatic context that placed the students into roles as members of a contemporary historical society in a small southern town that contains several historically significant buildings. Following a discussion of the nature and purpose of a historical society, the teacher assumed the role of one of the town's citizens who meets with the society to express her concern over the news that the section of town that some of the town officials plan to convert to a shopping mall contains a building that allegedly dates back to the Civil War era. During the meeting several members of the historical society agreed to examine the building to authenticate its historical value, a course of action that established the context for the second frame of the drama.

Before proceeding to the second frame, the teacher and students stepped out of role to plan and conduct some necessary research. Using illustrations and other print and nonprint sources of information, they examined the characteristics of Civil War-era buildings. In the process they built a vocabulary and acquired concepts that could be used in the second frame of the drama.

Returning to the roles developed in the initial scenario, the teacher and students played out a situation in which they inspect the building in question, and at the "concerned citizen's" promptings discover a secret passageway that was used to hide escaped slaves as they made their way to freedom in the northern states. At this point the teacher "froze" the drama so that the participants could once again step out of role to learn about the underground railroad and its link to the slavery issue. The students first listened to the teacher read *The Drinking Gourd* (Monjo, 1970), an illustrated book that tells of young Tommy Fuller's encounter with a family of runaway slaves that, at his father's bidding, takes refuge in his family's barn for several days. Meeting in several small groups, the students then read and discussed passages from literature on the subject of slavery and the underground railroad (List 9-1) in preparation for writing brief group reports and narratives which they shared when the class reconvened.

List 9-1
Literature About Slavery and the Underground Railroad

Blos, Joan. *A Gathering of Days: A New England Girl's Journal, 1830-32.* New York: Scribner, 1979. Grades 4-6.

de Angeli, Marguerite. *Thee, Hannah!* New York: Doubleday, 1949. Grades 3-6.

Merriam, Eve. "To Meet Mr. Lincoln." *In Sing a Song of Popcorn.* Selected by Beatrice Schenk de Regniers, et al. New York: Scholastic, 1988. Grades 2-6.

Fox, Paula. *The Slave Dancer.* Illustrated by Eros Keith. New York: Bradbury, 1973. Grades 4-up.

Hamilton, Virginia. *The House of Dies Drear.* New York: Macmillan, 1968. Grades 5-up.

Hamilton, Virginia. *The Mystery of Drear House.* New York: Greenwillow, 1987. Grades 5-up.

Embedded in the third frame was the need for official documentation that authenticated the role the building had played in the underground railroad. It was decided that unless there were some type of concrete evidence to prove the historical value of the building, it would not be possible to argue for its preservation. The need, then for documentation added the pressure that is necessary to sustain any drama with a genuine purpose and thus to maintain student belief. To pursue this course the teacher needed to devise an appropriate context for documentation, and therefore to create new roles — and new language registers — for both herself and her students. The focus she used to gather the students around the task was the town's bureau of records. In this context the participants could choose roles from among the bureau's personnel: archivist (the teacher, in role), historical architect, director, recorder, manager of deeds and other property documents, and so forth. In these roles, and with examples provided by the manager via the teacher, the participants examined and prepared a simplified version of a property title, a deed, and a plot (for property layout), each of which demonstrated that the building was indeed genuine and that its role in the underground railroad made it that much more valuable.

The fourth frame evolved naturally from the third, for, at the suggestion of the students, it was fashioned as a town meeting to provide the participants with an opportunity to debate the issue in various roles. Several represented the bureau of records, some the historical society; others were concerned citizens, while some assumed the stance that might be taken by the town officials who favored the construction of the shopping mall. The teacher served as moderator. Among other things, the debate that ensued took into consideration economics (The building would attract tourists. The mall would bring business.), aesthetics (The building was like a piece of the past. The mall would make the town look better.), and the issue of human rights and freedom (an argument for preserving them based on the significance of the secret passageway. It was not, after all, the need for a definitive resolution that guided the drama of the town meeting, but the opportunity that the debate afforded the students to persuade and justify as well as to listen considerately, to express motives, beliefs, and values as well as to process and respond to the arguments of others, and, equally important, to reveal what they knew about the condition of slavery and its mark on America's history.

The social studies drama could have pointed the way to many other learning possibilities. In subsequent scenarios on any grade level, the students might have assumed, for example, the roles of media personnel (television, radio, and newspaper reporters among them) who, during or after covering the town's ordeal, prepare and present written and oral reports in styles and forms appropriate to their respective media. The moral issues and themes inherent in slavery, social injustice, equality, freedom, civil liberties, and constitutionally sanctioned privileges and rights could have formed and supported numerous dramatic situations and many other roles. Along the way, the conflicts and characters depicted in a variety of literary genres could have suggested the type of content and structure that make events dramatic. For instance, students might have had access to plays (List 9-2) that center on the struggles and achievements of those who have attempted to preserve human dignity.

List 9-2
Selected Plays on Human Rights

Davis, Ossie. *Escape to Freedom: A Play about Young Frederick Douglass.* New York: Samuel French, 1976. Grades 5-up. The life of Douglass followed from plantation slavery to his escape to the North.

Falls, Gregory A. *The Pushcart War.* New Orleans, La.: Anchorage, 1986. Grades 4-up. A dramatization of a story by Jean Merrill which depicts the conflict between progress and tradition.

Harris, Aurand. *Steal Away Home.* New Orleans, La.: Anchorage Press, 1972. Grades 4-up. On a site of the underground railroad, two slaves tell of human indignities and injustice as they seek the freedom and promise of a better life up North.

Henderson, Nancy. *Walk Together.* New York: Julian Messner, 1972. Grades 7-up. Five one-act plays feature an Apache tribe's fight for freedom in the early 1900s, a Mexican family's determination to survive with integrity, and the problems faced by a group of children programmed by a computer.

Kraus, Joanna Halpert. *Mean to Be Free.* Bethel, Ct.: New Plays, Inc. 1980. Grades 4-up. Based on historical events, the play tells of two black children who traveled the dangerous underground railroad north to freedom, and the courageous actions of characters both black and white who helped them along the way.

Zeder, Suzan. *Mother Hicks.* New Orleans, La.: Anchorage, 1987. Grades 6-up. Set during the Great Depression, this play chronicles the personal journeys of three outsiders — an orphan, a deaf boy, and an eccentric recluse who is suspected of being a witch — to find themselves and each other in a troubled time.

THE SHADOW WORLD

The concerns expressed by kindergarten children over things that scare them provided the impetus for "The Shadow World," an extended drama sequence that filtered its way into a number of content areas over a three-week period. Prompted by the predicament that Williams (1986) depicts in *The Little Old Lady Who Was Not Afraid of Anything*, a picture book their teacher shared with them, many of the children had their own tales to tell of a wide array of things that frightened and disturbed them and provoked their imaginations: threatening sounds they invested with movement and shape; presences that lurked in the corners of rooms, outside of windows, in closets, and under beds; and strange neighbors with questionable intentions. Given the seriousness with which they described such things, and the vividness of their descriptions, it was obvious that these were real fears for the children, and they meant them to be taken seriously.

It seemed that dramas through which children could explore this vivid concern would hold particular promise for them. By examining such fears in the safety of the "no penalty zone" that dramatic contexts provide, the children would be given opportunities at least to identify their concerns and perhaps to be empowered to take charge of them through enactment and reflection (Verriour, 1989). Bettelheim's (1987) sentiments about the function and power of play in the child's life would be at the heart of this exploration. According to Bettelheim, "The most normal and competent child encounters what seem like insurmountable problems in living. But by playing them out, in the way he chooses, he may become able to cope with them in a step-by-step process . . . in symbolic ways . . ." (p. 36). In one important sense, then, the dramas that would give shape to childhood fears would serve children in the same way that literature often serves them. Like their encounters with literature, their experiences within the dramas they help to make can provide children with the type of objectivity or distance that can lead to fresh insight and understanding about specific emotions, problems, dilemmas, and pressures that both the literature and the drama uncover.

As "The Shadow World" unfolded, the scope of the sequence broadened. Movement, musical exploration, and the science of light, darkness, and shadows became integral components of the process, and fiction of various types as well as informational books and poetry held abundant possibilities for direction, focus, response, and participation. Over time, "The Shadow World" evolved into a more comprehensive sequence that leads children of all ages into what Sloan (1984) calls ". . . the symbols and images [the child] will use to express ideas, wishes, dreams, nightmares, and the like . . ." (p. 41). Eventually, the sequence included explorations of such topics as the difference between fantasy and reality and the characteristics of dreams.

The drama that centered on *The Little Old Lady Who Was Not Afraid of Anything* reflects the spirit and energy young children can bring to a dramatic experience that is shaped by the elements of literature that interests them. With its cumulative structure, zany predicament, repetitive, rhythmic phrasing, and satisfying resolution, the story has many of the characteristics that draw young children into a book and evoke immediate responses. On one level, and in a once-upon-a-time fashion, the story tells of a woman's encounter with a number of noisy objects (shoes, pants, a shirt, gloves, a hat, and a pumpkin) when she goes for a walk in the woods by her home. On a more subtle level (the illustrations contain many clues), the book demonstrates how the woman deals with her fear by hiding it from her mysterious guests. By keeping her wits about her she gains the upper hand; the objects utterly bewildered by their inability to frighten her form themselves into a scarecrow that watches over the woman's garden.

In primary grade classrooms where dramatic expression and oral interpretation of the literature are the norm rather than the exception, the call to "Let's act it out!" is a customary response to a story such as Williams'. It is the kind of book children like to have repeated, and they frequently memorize it after only a few oral readings on the teachers part. Often, the children who have memorized the text, even before they can read in the formal or standard sense of the word, choose the role of the narrator and, with book in hand, lead their peers through a page-by-page enactment of the tale.

With cumulative, uncomplicated stories like *The Little Old Lady Who Was Not Afraid of Anything,* an effective approach for the teacher to take when developing a drama is the linear method that children themselves use when they spontaneously enact a published story on their own. A linear approach begins with a quick review of the story's content and structure so that children have the basic details in mind when they launch into a dramatization of it. Although students should never be expected to dramatize the story exactly as it unfolds on the page, their understanding of the story's basic elements will allow them the freedom to improvise on it. This review can be guided by the answers to the fundamental questions that are at the foundation of any type of storymaking or dramatizing, namely, who, what, where, and why.

In a linear drama with Williams' tale, the teacher used a "voice-over" technique and directed the students to follow her instructions in the present tense (Morgan and Saxton, 1985, p. 214). For example, the teacher said to the children who were in role as many little old ladies: "It's getting late. We better start on our way back to our cottage. Let's start walking down the path. Better bundle up; there's a cold breeze out here." A voice-over could also assume a more direct approach with the story. In this case, the teacher-as-narrator would need to recast the tale in the present tense to sustain the illusion and the immediacy of dramatic tension.

In subsequent dramas, the teacher might approach the story's themes in a less direct manner. In one session, the woman's dilemma could be the focus. The children would choose their roles based on their favorite characters, with several children electing to be the woman, the shoes, the gloves, and so forth. Serving as arbiter or moderator, the teacher would direct the children to stay in role at their desks or on their story rugs and discuss the situation from their varying perspectives ("Shoes, why do you want to frighten the little old lady?" "Little old lady, what would you like to say to the pumpkin?"). At work here is a point of view; in role, children approach it, or any other literary element, from the inside out. Having children make drawings of the characters they portrayed is a worthwhile follow-up to dramas that attempt to put them in a character's shoes.

Often, young children's personal responses to the emotional content of the literature, such as their own tales of things that frighten them, can be the source of countless dramas. *Shadows,* written and illustrated by Canty (1987), evokes a wide range of personal responses from children because young Benjamin's experiences in the darkness of his bedroom often resemble their own. Benjamin deals with the imposing shadows that prevent him from falling asleep by confronting his fears head on through symbolic play (Piaget, 1926). As shadows form various shapes on the wall and floor of his room, Benjamin interacts with them by improvising movement and dialogue. This helps him to overpower and subdue them. Canty's eerie illustrations, rendered impressionistically in dark gray, black, and deep brown, extend the text by supplying details and emotional content. The illustrations also summon up children's memories of their own nighttime fears, ones that suggest material for various dramatic contexts.

In one second grade a brief drama, initiated by Shadows, began with the students sharing their nighttime fears. Following this, they moved into "self-space," a small area at a distance from others, where they used pantomime to build a room that they decorated according to the dictates of their imaginations. The teacher helped them to establish belief in the illusion by offering some basic directions and by building a room along with them. With basic narration in present tense supplied by the teacher, who continued to describe the events from a perspective of an involved participant ("I know there must be something in our closets. What should we do to find out?"), the teacher and children settled into the darkness of their rooms (a simple change in lighting helped to set the mood) and played out a frightened person's confrontation with threatening sounds and shadows. To close the drama, the students, maintaining their roles, attempted to fall asleep ("It's very late, and we're so tired.") For some of the children, sleep did not come easily. When Julie made a strange sound in her room, Brett, in his, bolted out of bed apparently to look out of a window. Sam then proceeded to pantomime turning on a radio or television set (humming supplied the sound) for some company.

In addition to pantomime, *Shadows* suggests movement. There is a moment in the book when Benjamin tries to alleviate his fear by forming a shadow with his hands which he casts on his bedroom wall. To have the students play with their own shadows, the teacher constructed a simple but large screen out of thin white acetate material that is used in the theater and is available in most theater supply shops. When a bright light is projected onto the screen from behind it, anyone who steps into the light casts a vivid shadow on the screen. Recordings of Debussy's "La Mer" and Dukas's "The Sorcerer's Apprentice" provided an impetus for movement, and poetry about shadows suggested a variety of images. From *Sing a Song of Popcorn* (de Regniers, et al., 1988), the teacher chose "8 A. M. Shadows" by Hubbell, and "Someone" by de la Mare, while *The Random House Book of Poetry for Children* (Prelutsky, 1983) supplied "Check" by Stephens, "The Snowflake" by de la Mare, and "Night Comes . . ." by de Regniers.

For older students, the sequence on childhood fears evolved into an exploration of literary symbols and archetypes and the interpretive value of art. Chris Van Allsburg's books are particularly effective vehicles for transporting older students from the familiar everyday world to worlds that exist in the imagination. He plays with dark, light, and perspective to give his illustrations a surrealistic quality and to add many possible layers of meaning to the aura of mystery and suspense that his books convey. Since he writes in cryptic style, he compels his readers to participate actively in "opening up" the text and filling in the gaps by using their imaginations.

The Mysteries of Harris Burdick (1984) is particularly intriguing for older students. The book contains fourteen haunting drawings, each of which is accompanied by a title and brief caption laden with innuendo. In his introduction, Van Allsburg notes that the drawings were passed on to a children's book editor by the elusive Burdick, who promised to return the following day with narratives to accompany them. Burdick never fulfilled his promise.

Each of the pictures Burdick left behind is a "mystery" in the sense that the accompanying title and caption hint at various themes and situations. In a compact, metaphoric way, the drawings and captions contain the basic ingredients of a dramatic event: tension, setting, and character-in-a-fix. The book also is well suited to classroom drama because it leaves much unsaid yet speaks to each reader or player in a very personal way, thus allowing various interpretations to emerge. The caption could well serve as the opening sentence to a dramatic event that the picture suggests.

In a "front door" approach to drama, the students first focus on one of the fourteen captioned drawings and use the clues it contains to develop a written narrative that is cast in the present tense. Next, they brainstorm for ideas that supply them with situations, characters, settings, and conflicts. After sharing some of the narratives for the sake of receiving feedback, they meet in small groups and prepare a presentation that can take the shape of an interpretive reading, a newscast, an interview, or a story theater format in which the characters pantomime the action while the narrative is being read.

The Mysteries of Harris Burdick also summons up several universal themes. In an indirect way, Van Allsburg fathoms the power both print and picture have for preserving meaning over time. He focuses, for example, on the multiple meanings that can be derived from a single work of art; the nature and function of art; and the artist's way of "seeing" — not necessarily in a linear, straightforward fashion, but in figurative, iconographic ways. Each of these has a potential for a "back door" approach to drama in which students are encouraged to consider broader questions; in this case, questions that lead to an awareness of the things art can tell us about a culture.

Approaching a drama on *The Mysteries of Harris Burdick* from the vantage of the books' latent themes, students could assume the role of archaeologists preparing to go on a dig in a foreign land. They would first need to research and discuss such things as the living conditions, social and family structure, politics, religion, climate, topography, and foods of the culture they are about to visit as well as the one they intend to learn about as archaeologists. At the site of the dig, they could be assisted by a trusted guide, the teacher in the role as an informed local citizen who is able to speak their language. While on the dig, the "archaeologists" will write letters home that detail their experiences, and they will keep diaries, journals, logs, or notebooks in which they record their successes, failures, and a host of insights. At an appropriate point in the drama, they can discover an artifact of their own invention and construction. Based on their knowledge of the culture's characteristics, the students would use the artifact to reconstruct the culture to which it belonged, perhaps in a manner similar to the one Lauber (1985) has used in *Tales Mummies Tell*. The students would culminate the drama by recording the details of their discovery for posterity and presenting the artifact and their findings to the officials at a museum (several students in a role). A book like *The Mysteries of Harris Burdick,* which suggests many more meanings than it reveals, encourages students to move beyond the surface features of literature and into a territory beneath the words and behind the pictures where possibilities surface, ones that conjure up images that tell of the drama inherent in life and living.

List 9-3
Selected Literature for "The Shadow World"

Adoff, A. *Flamboyan*. Illus. by Karen Barbour. San Diego: Harcourt Brace Jovanovich, 1988. Grades Pres-2. A young girl who wants to fly has her dream fulfilled.

Hamilton, V. *The People Could Fly*. Illus. Leo and Diane Dillon. New York: Knopf, 1985. All ages. American black folktales about familiar and unfamiliar characters and situations.

Hansen, R. *The Shadowmaker*. Illus. Margot Tomes. New York: Harper & Row, 1987. Grades K-4. The mysterious shadowmaker causes bedlam in Drizzle's town.

Jarrell, R. *Fly by Night*. Illus. Maurice Sendak. New York: Farrar, Straus & Giroux, 1976. Grades K-4. David has a dream that takes him far away from home and back again each night.

Langton, J. *The Fledgling*. New York: Harper & Row, 1980. Grades 3-6. Eight-year-old Georgie's desire to fly is fulfilled when she is visited by the Goose Prince.

MacDonald, G. *The Golden Key*. Illus. Maurice Sendak. New York: Farrar, Straus & Giroux, 1967. Grades K-4. Mossy and Tangle go on a journey that leads to personal identity.

Willard, N. *The Nightgown of the Sullen Moon*. Illus. David McPhail. San Diego: Harcourt Brace Jovanovich, 1983. Grades K-3. On her billionth birthday, the full moon travels to earth to fulfill a dream.

Zeder, S. *Wiley and the Hairy Man*. New Orleans: Anchorage Press, 1978. Grades 2-4. A one-act play in which a young boy confronts his fear of the night with his mother's help.

CONCLUSION

Drama's domain, like that of literature, is human experience, and drama's intent, like that of literature, is to awaken children to new or different ways of seeing themselves, the world, and others. If recent surveys of reading instruction in American schools have painted an accurate picture of the strategies teachers use to connect students with literature (Goodlad, 1984; Shannon, 1989), for a majority of American children this connection may be more akin to parsing a text or searching through it for intended and other ready-made meanings than to fathoming it for the awareness and understanding of human experience which literature can evoke.

Drama has the potential and power to alert children not only to the topics, issues, and themes literature invites them to consider but also to the ways their own ideas, impressions, and feelings contribute to and are shaped by their experiences with literature. When children fashion a drama out of the situations a particular literary text presents to them, they attend to specific characteristics of the text and recreate in role and in an imagined time and place the personal discoveries to which the literature has awakened them. By doing this with others, children use language to shape the social reality of a dramatic context and to bring it to life through enactment with others in an unfolding situation that engenders a rich variety of language.

Given the potential drama has for drawing children into literature in personal and meaningful ways and for encouraging reflection on the themes, issues, and situations literature provides them, a very significant role drama can play in classrooms is to keep the promises that, according to Shannon (1989), reading education was originally intended to fulfill:

> Reading as promised is supposed to enable us to read both the word and the world in ways that allow us to see through the mysteries, ambiguities, and deceit of modern living in order to make sense of our lives, to understand the connections among our lives and those of others, and to act on our new knowledge to construct a better, a more just, world. (p. viii)

REFERENCES

Atwell, N. (1987). *In the middle*. Upper Montclair, N.J.: Boynton/Cook

Bettelheim, B. (1976). *The uses of enchantment*. New York: Knopf

Bettelheim, B. (1987). The importance of play. Atlantic Monthly, 232, Feb. 1987, 32-41.

Bolton, G. (1979. *Towards a theory of drama in education*. London, Eng.: Longman.

Boomer, G. (1985). *Fair dinkum teaching and learning: Reflections on literacy and power*. Upper Montclair, NJ: Boynton/Cook

Fader, D. N. (1982). *The new hooked on books*. New York: Berkley.

Goodlad, J. (1984). *A place called school*. New York: McGraw-Hill.

Hardy, B. (1978). Towards a poetics of fiction: an approach through narrative. In M. Meek, A. Warlow, & G. Boynton (Eds.), *The cool web*. New York: Atheneum, 12-23.

Koste, V. G. (1987). *Dramatic play in childhood*. Lanham, MD: University Press of America.

Mandel, B. J. (Ed.). (1980). *Three language arts curriculum models: Prekindergarten through college*. Urbana, IL: National Council of Teachers of English.

McClure, A. (1985). *Children's responses to poetry in a supportive literary context*. unpublished doctoral dissertation, Ohio State University.

Morgan, N. & Saxton, J. *Working with drama: A different order of experience. Theory Into Practice*, 24, Su. 1985. pp. 211-218.

O'Neill, C. (1989). *Dialogue and drama: The transformation of events, ideas, and teachers. Language Arts*, 66, 147-159.

Piaget, J. (1962). *Play, dreams, and imitation in childhood*. New York: W. W. Norton and Co.

Piaget, J. (1926). *The language and thought of the child*. New York: Harcourt Brace.

Rosenblatt, L. (1968). *Literature as exploration*. New York: Noble and Noble.

Shannon, P. (1989). *Broken promises: Reading instruction in twentieth-century America*. Granby, MA: Bergin & Garvey Publishers, Inc.

Sloan, G. D. *The child as critic*. (2d Ed.). (1984). New York: Teachers College Press.

Smith, P. K. *(1984)*. *Play in animals and humans*. Oxford, Eng.: Basil Blackwell.

Wagner, B. J. (1976). *Dorothy Heathcote: Drama as a learning medium*. Washington, DC: National Education Association.

Wells, G. (1986). *The meaning makers*. Portsmouth, NH: Heineman.

CHILDREN'S BOOKS CITED

Andersen, H. C. (1985). *The snow queen*. Trans. by Eva LaGalienne. Illustrated by Arieh Zeldick. New York: Harper & Row.

Babbitt, N. (1975). *Tuck everlasting*. New York: Farrar, Straus & Giroux.

Canty, J. *Shadows.* (1987). New York: Harper & Row.

Chaikin, M. (1988). *Friends forever.* Illustrated by Richard Egielski. New York: Harper & Row.

de Regniers, B. S., et al. (Sel.). (1988). *Sing a song of popcorn.* Illustrated by many artists. New York: Scholastic.

Dorres, A. (1989). *Feel the wind.* New York: Crowell.

Fufuka, K. "Li'l Bro." in Jack Prelutsky (Sel.). *The Random House book of poetry for children.* (1983). Illustrated by Arnold Lobel. New York: Random House.

Greenfield, E. & Jones Little, L. (1979). *Childtimes.* New York: Crowell.

Hall, D. (1985). *Oxford book of children's verse.* New York: Oxford University Press.

L'Engle, M. (1962). *A wrinkle in time.* New York: Farrar, Straus & Giroux.

Lattimore, D. N. (1987). *The flame of peace.* New York: Harper & Row.

Lauber, P. (1985). *Tales mummies tell.* New York: Crowell.

LeGuin, U. K. (1972). *The farthest shore.* Illustrated by Gail Garraty. New York: Atheneum.

LeGuin, U. K. (1971). *The tombs of Atuan.* Illustrated by Gail Garraty. New York: Atheneum.

LeGuin, U. K. (1968). *A wizard of Earthsea.* Illustrated by Ruth Robbins. New York: Parnassus.

Lionni, L. (1987). *Nicholas, where have you been?* New York: Knopf.

Lobel, A. (1970). *Frog and toad are friends.* New York: Harper & Row.

McGovern, Ann. (1967). *Too much noise.* Illustrated by Simms Taback. Boston: Houghton Mifflin.

McKissack, P. C. (1988). *Mirandy and brother wind.* Illustrated by Jerry Pinkney. New York: Knopf.

Monjo, F. N. (1970). *The drinking gourd.* Illustrated by Fred Brenner. New York: Harper & Row.

Paulsen, G. (1987). *Hatchet.* New York: Bradbury Press.

Rylant, C. (1989). *But I'll be back again.* New York: Orchard Books.

Sutherland, Z. & Livingston, M. C. (1984). *The Scott Foresman anthology of children's literature.* Glenview, IL: Scott, Foresman.

Tadjo, V. (1988). *Lord of the dance.* New York: J. B. Lippincott.

Taylor, M. (1987). *The friendship.* Illustrated by Max Ginsburg. New York: Dial.

Townsend, J. R. (1989). *The fortunate isles.* New York: Lippincott.

Turner, A. (1987). *Street talk.* Illustrated by Catherine Stock. Boston: Houghton Mifflin.

White, E. B. (1952). *Charlotte's web.* Illustrated by Garth Williams. New York: Harper & Row.

Williams, Linda. (1986). *The little old lady who was not afraid of anything.* Illustrated by Megan Lloyd. New York: Crowell.

Wirths, C. G. & Bowman-Kruhn, M. (1989). *Where's my other sock?* Illustrated by Molly Coxe. New York: Thomas Y. Crowell.

Yashima, T. (1955). *Crow boy.* New York: Viking.

Zolotow, C. (1952). *The storm book.* Illustrated by Margaret Bloz Graham. New York: Harper & Row.

10

A Writer's Path to Literacy

Natalie Babbitt

It all begins, of course, with words. Single words, and then groups of words, and then groups of groups, until all at once there are stories, fact and fiction, and the stories are everywhere. Outside, coming into your head, and then inside your head and going out. You don't know this when you are little, but that doesn't mean it isn't happening. Everyone of every age has stories to tell and everyone tells stories, formally or informally. And everyone uses words to tell their stories.

Of all the things humankind has invented, from the hammer to the video camera, language is the most useful and the most astonishing. We take it for granted, and indeed it does seem as if words are cheap and easy to acquire. After all, they belong to everyone. All we have to do is, first, listen and then, second, learn to read and write. But it turns out that it is not to simple, for there are other things involved in the process — things that are not as widespread and universally available as a perfect world would have them be.

I was lucky enough to be born into a house full of words and music, but not at all the words and music of the classics, not Tolstoy and Bach. We didn't discuss literature at dinner or go to the symphony. Mostly, at dinner, we laughed, and in the evenings my mother read aloud to my sister and me, we played games, we listened to the radio. Part of this climate was deliberately designed for the benefit of us children and part of it wasn't. My mother was responsible for the deliberate part. The part that wasn't deliberate was my father's contribution. Still, though both of them had college educations and both began as teachers, neither was self-conscious about words and music. I don't know what my mother read when she read to herself, but I remember my father reading swashbuckling, romantic novels such as those by Raphael Sabatini and Sir Walter Scott — reading them over and over — and also murder mysteries by the dozens. Nothing self-conscious about that.

My mother contributed reading aloud and piano music — music for singing; she could play any song in any key by ear. I have realized only recently that I have no idea where she learned to do that. My father contributed the word music.

Word music is rare and getting rarer. I think I am lucky to have been born to parents of a generation that had to memorize and declaim poetry when they were children. Nobody makes children do that anymore. My father could, and frequently did, recite reams of poetry no longer considered much worthy of attention: Scott and Tennyson, for instance, long works strongly rhymed and metered that could be lilted out with extravagant gestures and dramatic intonations. He recited doggerel, too. "Round and round the rugged rock the ragged rascal ran" was a particular favorite. Although he loved the romance of the poems, he didn't recite with any special seriousness; mainly, he recited to make us laugh. We always did laugh, over and over at the same things, because they were always funny.

There is a subtler side to word music, however, and this my father understood completely, though I don't know where he learned it. Perhaps one is born with it. Oddly, he was tone deaf; he loved the songs my mother played on the piano, but he couldn't carry the simplest tune. Nevertheless, he understood the music of words and used it to wonderful effect. This kind of music is hard to explain except by example, so here is an example.

My father had a collection of imaginary inventions among which was "a pep tonic for the elderly" that he planned to call Cavort. He could just as easily have described it as "an invigorating medicine for old people," but that phrase, though it means the same thing, has no music. "Pep tonic" has music and so does "elderly." Put them together and you have a small symphony of sound. "Pep tonic" and "elderly" are also funny together, and when you add "cavort" you have a gem of rare design. A very funny gem. The word "cavort" is almost never used. I cannot image why not; it is a fine, sharp word that always makes me think of goats. Goats are funny, and the notion of the elderly cavorting like goats is funny. But most of all, the phrase "a pep tonic for the elderly, called Cavort" is music. It pleases the ear before it tickles the fancy. Word music by no means has to be funny; it just happened that my father's mostly was.

Some of us are tone deaf. Many of us can carry a tune perfectly well, but the sound of our voices when we sing is not pleasing, not to ourselves or to anyone else. All of us, however, understand music at some level having nothing to do with ear drums and vocal chords. Music is rhythm first and foremost, and we learn rhythm from our mothers' heartbeats long before we are born. Then, we listen to words, and words have rhythm, too. We can be taught to be conscious of hearing it, in speech and in writing. Nursery rhymes and then perhaps Dr. Seuss, who has taught several generations of children to listen to the sound of words and their rhythms. This may not have been his primary intention, but it has been an effect, widespread, I like to think, and beneficial, even when unconscious.

So, first we listen. The words and music my house provided — I should say "houses," for we moved often — were informal at first. They became more formal when my mother began to read aloud.

Somewhere along about 1937 and '38, when I was five or six, my mother acquired a long list of what were at the time judged to be children's classics and proceeded to read every one of them aloud to us. It took a long time, for there must have been between twenty-five and thirty titles: *Alice in Wonderland* and *Through the Looking-Glass; Penrod; The Water Babies; Heidi; Peter Pan; Pinocchio; The Yearling; Bambi;* Kipling's *Just-So Stories* and *The Jungle Book; Robinson Crusoe; Treasure Island; Robin Hood* and the King Arthur stories; and others I've now forgotten. *The Wizard of Oz* was not on her list. Neither were the works of A. A. Milne, *The Wind in the Willows,* or *Little Woman.* Who can say why? List-makers have their crotchets, just like everyone else. However that may be, I, with an ear sensitized by my father's "ragged rascal" and Cavort, preferred the books with words that made music. Funny music. This meant that I preferred Lewis Carroll, Rudyard Kipling, and Booth Tarkington. The others wrote perfectly good stories, but their words didn't make good music; not for me, anyway, not when someone was reading them aloud.

My sister, who is two years older than I, came sooner to the appreciation of a good story, a thing quite separate from good sound, and came to it in a more scholarly way; that is to say, thoughtfully, from the head down. We were, of course, reading to ourselves as the years went along, as well as being read to — our mother wisely did not try to monitor what we brought home from the library — and my sister's tastes were developing along different lines from mine. She preferred, for her own reading, long novels like *Little Women;* I preferred fantasy.

My mother had a series of books that had been hers when she was a child. We always called them "the blue books" because their boards were bound in dark blue cloth. They are long since gone, so I don't know their official collective title. Each book in the series was devoted to one kind of writing for children. One consisted of Mother Goose, poems by people like Eugene Field, and longer works like *Hiawatha.* Another contained all the best-loved nursery tales from *The Three Little Pigs* through Aesop's fables. There was also biography, and history, and volumes of that sort, which held no interest for me. One was full of fairy tales, including *The Arabian Nights*, and one held all the best-known Greek and Roman myths, told by someone — not Hawthorne — with a flair for the dramatic. There were color-plate illustrations, each protected by a page of thin tissue.

Why is one child drawn to *Little Women* and another to *Jason and the Golden Fleece?* Why does one like to weep over the death of Beth March while the other revels in the wicked deeds of Medea? There has to be a rational reason. My husband has said that he prefers his fiction clear and direct; he says that fantasy puts life at one remove, layering the rational with the irrational so that life is given a protective, distancing glaze. My sister would say the same. Perhaps they're right, but for me, fantasy was — and is, or should be — drawn from something far more fundamental than Louisa May Alcott ever thought of. Louisa May Alcott was writing, as many fine writers do , about herself, coming to the general from the particular. But myths are about everybody; they come to the particular from the general.

When I read *Little Women ,* I identified with Amy — no doubt because I was a youngest child with a sister a lot like Jo and appreciated the Lauries of this world. When I read *Jason and the Golden Fleece,* I identified with everyone in the story. I was enlarged. It didn't remind me of my own life; it took me out of the confinement of that life and showed me I was part of something wider and deeper and, in a strange way, simpler and more reassuring.

I learned to appreciate a good story not from the head down, thoughtfully, like my sister, but from the heart up, passionately. Nothing reasoned and critical about it — all feelings — and if the words in the stories made good music at the same time, then they stuck to my brain until at last they became one with it.

As for the blue book fairy tales, some I liked and some I did not. The same applied to my copy of Andrew Lang's *The Red Fairy Book.* I think I understand why, now. The fairy tales I liked had interesting heroines who were active, like Medea, not passive. Cinderella was passive; so were Snow White and Rapunzel. But the princess in *The Frog Prince* went after her man through thick and thin and didn't balk at chopping off her little fingers to add the last rungs to a ladder. And Graciosa — well, Graciosa was a bungler; she couldn't do anything right, but Percinet loved her anyway.

I don't think, looking back, that fairy tales did anything for my soul. What they did do was teach me the rules that govern the construction of a fantasy story. These rules are difficult to write down in any sensible way — at least, I find them so — but when someone else, a scholar, Joseph Campbell, for instance, writes them down, it's rather like an introductory course in psychology. You find you already knew it all; you just hadn't known you knew it.

Occasional students of mine over the years have assumed that you can throw anything into a fantasy, make anything happen at any time. After all , it's a fantasy, isn't it? Actually, the opposite is true. You can throw anything into realistic fiction because real life is random and things happen all the time that make no sense. Fantasy fiction, however, is in its way rather rigid. It was invented not to make sense of worldly life but to make sense of the life of the soul. The body may reel and totter, and change direction and speed, or lie down altogether in the dark; the soul's path should be straight and sure, cutting cleanly through pain and adversity toward light.

Nobody told me these things. They might have, if I'd taken the appropriate courses in college. But I was a studio art major, scrounging for yet another kind of music. I didn't even know I knew anything about fantasy until I picked up Joseph Campbell's *Hero With a Thousand Faces* more than two decades after college graduation and several years after I'd begun to write fantasy fiction. Hey, I said to myself as he explained the rules, I knew that — that's what I've been trying to do — how extraordinary! I had learned it all from *The Red Fairy Book* and the blue book of myths. Because of this discovery, I always tell children, if they ask about it when I visit them in their classrooms: the best way to learn how to write stories is to read stories.

In spite of the differences between my sister's reading tastes and my own, we both loved P. L. Travers' *Mary Poppins*. *Mary Poppins* was the first book I loved that was written — I knew for a fact — by someone still alive. Everybody else was dead, or probably dead, so far as I knew. Actually, Booth Tarkington didn't die until 1946, but since *Penrod* was published in 1914, it was logical to assume, by the time I discovered it, that its author would be dead. Certainly Lewis Carroll was long gone, and Kipling, though he survived until 1936, was gone, too. Not that any of it mattered, particularly. We didn't , thank goodness, ever have to write to authors in school — a pernicious practice and entirely irrelevant to reading, in my opinion. But P. L. Travers was still alive and was writing more books about Mary Poppins even as we read the first one. This was tantalizing. I hoped she would hurry up; I hoped her stories would keep on being good, and, mostly, they did. But I had no curiousity about her as a person. There had always been books and always would be, so obviously somebody was writing them. It didn't matter who that somebody was; what mattered was that whoever it was should keep at it, especially P. L. Travers.

It may seem from all of this that I did nothing but read books and listen to books when I was a child, but that was by no means the case. I spent a great deal of time drawing, and playing with my friends and listening to the radio. There was time for everything. There is the same number of hours in a day when you're a child as there is when you're an adult; they're just longer hours. Time is different for children, and I wish someone who knows about such things would write a book that explains why. No, I was not a bookish child. My sister was bookish, but not I. Perhaps this was so because she was serious, or at least was so labelled in the family and at school. I was not so labelled. A report about me from a high school teacher says, severely, "Her attitude somewhat lacks seriousness."

I don't know, really, whether I was less serious than my sister or she less frivolous than I. Certainly she was always a better student, but I have since known brilliant students who were not in the least serious. However that may be, I admired my sister extravagantly. She was funny and strong and told wonderful stories. When we were allowed to sleep together now and then, we played a game we called "Children," but it wasn't a game at all. "Children" consisted of my cozily listening in the dark while my sister told new stories about the adventures of a family she had created. I don't remember any of the stories now, only the delicious ambiance. But my sister was going to be a writer when she grew up, like Jo March. That had been decided. I was only going to be an artist.

It was my sister who led me, finally, away from fairy tales. She began, in junior high, to read long, hard books that were two inches thick, or seemed to be. Books like *The Cloister and the Hearth* and *Kristen Lavransdatter*. So I read them, too. The habit of reading, after all, had been long since established. But I wasn't very selective; I read my sister's books but also anything else that came to hand. I had learned to read for story, and most stories seemed interesting. I no longer read for music but for content. I was not in the least analytical. I could tell the difference between a well-written book and a poorly written one, but if the story appealed to me, I didn't care if it wasn't well told. By the same token, if a story didn't appeal to me, I didn't care if it *was* well told. This is still true and I don't apologize for it. In fact, I think it's very common. My husband can't stand Henry James, and I can't stand William Faulkner — both wonderful writers, but everyone can't like everything.

There are people who are fond of saying that in the good old days, before television, all children were readers. This is a wishful rewriting of history, I'm afraid. Not all of my friends were readers. Economic levels seem to have had nothing to do with it; not intelligence levels, either. Some read, some didn't, and that was the beginning and the end of it. I think my sister and I were readers because we were comfortable with words and because our mother deliberately planned that we should be and made it attractive and possible. A third reason is probably the fact that we saw our father reading and could tell how much he enjoyed it. He would put down *Scaramouche* with a happy sigh and say, "That Sabatini! What a storyteller." My father had four passions: my mother, fishing, the Republican Party, and reading. A strange combination; no two had anything in common, particularly not my mother and the Republican Party.

So, first we listen, and observe, too, perhaps. At least, I seem to have observed my family's pleasure in books. Learning to read on my own was easy, but writing stories was something else entirely.

I don't remember ever being asked in school to write a story. It's possible that my memory has failed me here — possible, but unlikely, because my school years are more vivid to me than many years that have come along since. I was often asked to write an essay, but never a story. I wrote one or two on my own — one, still extant, is about a dog named Rags, circa perhaps 1940, written in pencil in a small blue spiral notebook — and I wrote verse sometimes. Writing was my sister's turf; nevertheless, I have always had a head that makes stories. My daughter Lucy, has the same kind of head. It is not necessarily a blessing.

A head that makes stories can and continually does create an entire plot out of one passing thought. This is the ways it works: You look at the clock and see that your husband should have been home from his office fifteen minutes ago. At once the story unreels. He has been mugged. He is bleeding in a gutter. The police find him dead and come to tell you. You gather your children from their far-flung points. The funeral is planned, accomplished, the children disappear. You are alone. You pack up and move out. With nowhere to go, you become a derelict. No, scratch that. You become a . . . Then, the door opens, your husband walks in, the story is over. It has taken maybe 30 seconds to compose itself before it vanishes.

This type of story-making is common, of course; we are all storytellers where our own fears are concerned. There is an advanced kind of story-making head that also imagines entire novels starring strangers passing on the street, the unseen dog barking somewhere in the distance, the orphaned children of the raccoon flattened on the highway, the sweet-faced old lady in line at the grocery check-out with seven boxes of steel wool. This kind of head spins out and forgets story after story every day. It makes the stories unbidden, automatically, almost compulsively. In the wink of an eye a scene sets itself, including weather, props, subsidiary characters and problems to solve. Of these visions, if you can call them that, there are perhaps ten thousand a year. For me, one in twenty thousand may linger, take hold, and become a real path to a real idea that might or might not make a real story.

Heads that make stories do not all turn to the writing of fiction, and thank goodness for that. Certainly it was never my intention to turn to the writing of fiction. I wanted to be an illustrator. But you can't make pictures for stories unless there are stories to make pictures for; the story must be there first.

The old Chinese proverb notwithstanding, a single picture is not worth a thousand words. Not if the painter of the picture wants to make a single, particular point. Heads that make stories can make at least a dozen, all different, out of one picture of a sweet-faced old lady buying seven boxes of steel wool. Pictures are open to interpretation, which is why psychologists sometimes use them to probe our subconscious minds. Fiction is open to interpretation, too, of course, but only up to a point. The storyteller can insist, and the reader must give way. The storyteller can insist and the illustrator — any responsible illustrator — must give way. It all begins with words.

So, years later, in order to have something to illustrate, I began to write stories, and as I did, the old lessons in word music surfaced. My father's voice, reciting poetry or inventing some new product, stylishly described. My mother's voice, reading *Alice in Wonderland* aloud. "State your evidence," says the King of Hearts. "Shant," says the cook. *Shant?* Of course, *shant. Won't* and *I refuse* don't make good music.

Somebody in a *New York Times Book Review* essay recently described an eager writing student asking a visiting author if he thought she could ever be a good writer. "I don't know," he responded. "Do you like words?" It all begins with words.

The old lessons in construction of a fantasy came back, too — those lessons that are so difficult, if you are not a scholar, to explain. If you've always been a reader, you simply know them, and, unless you get involved with teaching, you don't ever have to explain them. I have gotten involved with teaching — of college students — and have been greatly frustrated trying to explain. How do you know when a story is on the right path? How? You just know. But that is not sufficient in a classroom situation. I have about concluded that creative writing can't be taught at all. Perhaps it's like mental health: Either the circumstances of your life have been conducive to it or they haven't. Mental health is more important than storytelling, needless to say, but perhaps the two are analogous on this one point. No one can teach you how to be happy, and no one can teach you how to make a beautiful sentence. That is only an opinion, of course. I should say that *I* have no idea how to teach it. It has to have been done early and at home, by osmosis, and the lack of it, for someone who deeply wishes to be a writer, can be a serious problem.

Then there is that business of liking words, as the visiting author suggested. For a writer, not liking words is equivalent to a painter not liking paint or a swimmer not liking water. The English language seems to me sumptuously rich: I get the same feeling from a thesaurus as I used to get from the super-size box of crayons with its 48 different colors. The notion of teaching English as a second language here in the United States is a sad thing to me. Other languages have music, too, I know, but English is our language and it has its own particular sounds that make up its own particular music, even if it is a mixture of Latin and French and German seasoned with other, stranger, tongues.

I lift up my little grandson to look at the high shelf of animal statuettes that are my prized, though meager, collection. I point them out, naming them one by one, and I wonder if he is hearing the exotic music of their names. Rhinoceros. Giraffe. Polar bear. Elephant. Kangaroo. Chimpanzee. Later, looking with him at a picture book full of farm animals, I wonder if he is hearing the flat clump of *their* names. Pig. Horse. Cow. Goat. Sheep. One stubby syllable will suffice for domestic life, evidently. Life in the wild requires something more melodic. I wonder if my grandson hears this. He seems to. My statuettes make him smile and babble, while the picture book animals get only sober, silent study. Of course, the wild animals are three-dimensional, while the farm animals are drawn on flat pages. Never mind. He will hear it all eventually. He is growing up in houses full of words and music.

We hear a lot these days about the dangers of television and the fear that reading is slowly disappearing. I don't know. It seems to me that children now are not so very different from my grammar school friends. Teenagers, like the world they are testing, are different, but children don't seem to be. The grammar schools I visit seem full of eagerness and openness to new ideas, new words, new music. Heads are full of stories going in and coming out. Then adolescence swamps them, like night for Coleridge's ancient mariner: ". . . at one stride comes the dark." However, and fortunately, the dark is temporary. My grandson, too, will be swamped in his turn, but only for a while. Poetry, songs, and stories, administered early, do not wear off so easily.

Like everybody else, I am getting older. There are days when I wish I had a bottle of Cavort in the medicine chest, but just imagining a bottle of Cavort will turn my mood around. The music of the word is a pep tonic all by itself and does its work as well as the medicine itself might have done. The bottle would be dark brown, I think, disguising the color of the stuff inside. Its label would be dignified, its ingredients obscure and listed in very small print. It would probably giggle as you poured it out into a spoon. Mary Poppins would approve of that. I am endlessly grateful to my father for his word music and to my mother for her long list of classics. For being literate means more than simply knowing how to read and write: Being literate means listening — and learning to love the language.

Index

Contributors

Karen D. Wood is an Associate Professor at the University of North Carolina at Charlotte. Prior to receiving her Ph.D. in Reading Education from the University of Georgia, she taught middle school and was a K-12 instructional coordinator. She is author of numerous articles and chapters and is currently co-editor of *Reading Research and Instruction*. She has recently joined the authorship team for the 1993 Macmillan-McGraw Hill basal reading program.

Phyllis Allen received her Masters Degree from the University of North Carolina at Charlotte. She is a third grade teacher at Shamrock Gardens Elementary School.

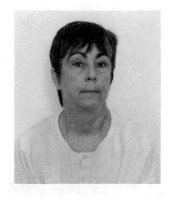

Natalie Babbitt received her B.A. in Studio Art from Smith College. Her first venture into children's publishing was as illustrator for a book written by her husband. She published her first book on her own in 1967 and has to date over a dozen books to her credit and has illustrated another half dozen, all written by Valerie Worth. Among her best known works are *Tuck Everlasting* (1975), *The Eyes of the Amaryllis* (1977), and *The Devil's Storybook* (1974), all ALA Notable books.

William Blanton received his Ph.D. in reading education from the University of Georgia. Currently he is co-editor of *Reading, Research, and Instruction* and coordinator of the center on Excellence in Teaching and Learning at Appalachian State University.

Karen D'Angelo Bromley is an Associate Professor of Education at the State University of New York at Binghamton. She is the author of *Language Arts: Exploring Connections*, published by Allyn & Bacon.

James Flood is a professor of Reading and Language Development at San Diego State University. He has taught in preschool, elementary, and secondary schools and has served as a Language Arts/Reading supervisor. He is currently involved in teacher preparation and research in the language arts/reading. Among his numerous publications include *Teaching Students to Read, Teaching Reading to Every Child,* and *Language and the Language Arts,* coauthored with Diane Lapp.

Violet J. Harris received her Ph.D. from the University of Georgia. She is currently an Assistant Professor at the University of Illinois at Urbana-Champaign in the Bureau of Educational Research, where she currently conducts research in children's literature, multiethnic children's literature, and literacy materials created for African American children prior to 1950. Her articles have appeared in publications such as the *Langston Hughes Review, Children's Literature Association Quarterly, Journal of Negro Education. The Lion and the Unicorn,* and *Young Children.*

William A. Henk is an Associate Professor of Education at Pennsylvania State University — Harrisburg where he teaches courses in elementary and diagnostic reading instruction as well as in tests and measurements and reading psychology. He received his Ph.D. in Reading and Educational Psychology from West Virginia University. He has published numerous articles and is co-editor of the "Reading Technology" column in *The Reading Teacher.* He is also a Chief Consultant for the Pennsylvania Statewide Reading Assessment Project.

Jay Jacoby is an Associate Professor of English at the University of North Carolina at Charlotte, where he has directed the Writing Center, Composition Program, and is currently serving as Interim Department Chair. His work has appeared in *The Advocate, CEA Critic, College Composition and Communication, English Journal,* and *The Writing Center Journal.*

Diane Lapp is a Professor of Reading and Language Development at San Diego State University. She has taught in elementary and middle schools, has conducted field-based teacher preparation programs, and has served as a consultant, supervisor, and evaluator for public school reading programs throughout the United States. In addition to the books she has coauthored with James Flood, she has coauthored a number of other titles, including *Language Skills in Elementary Education,* and is one of the editors of *The Handbook of Research in the Teaching of Language Arts.*

Arlene L. Lawson received her Masters of Liberal Studies from Kent State University. She is particularly interested in youth in crisis and conflict management.

Anthony L. Manna is an Associate Professor at Kent State University. He received his Ph.D. in English Education/Educational Drama/Children's Literature from the University of Iowa. He is Publications Director of the Children's Literature Association and is visual arts column editor of *Children's Literature Association Quarterly*.

Timothy V. Rasinski received his Ph.D. at the University of Georgia. He is currently an Associate Professor at Kent State University.

Robert J. Rickelman is an Associate Professor at the University of North Carolina at Charlotte. He received his Ph.D. in Reading Education from the University of Georgia. He is co-editor of the "Reading Technology" column in *The Reading Teacher* and is on the editorial advisory board of *Reading Research and Instruction*.

Jon C. Stott is Professor of English at the University of Alberta. He received his Ph.D. in English from the University of Toronto. He is author of several books, including *Children's Literature from A to Z: A Guide for Parents, and Teachers, Canadian Books for Children: A Guide to Authors and Illustrators* (with Raymond E. Jones), and numerous chapters and articles. He was a founding member of the Children's Literature Association and has also served as its President.

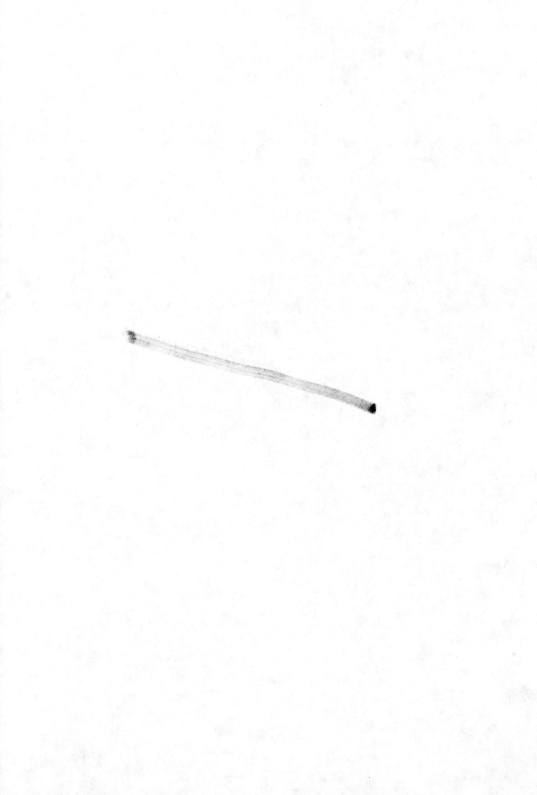